GOD'S HEALING GRACE

TAKING JESUS AT HIS WORD

Wayne R. Edwards

Foreword by Dr. Charles E. Van Engen

"This is a truly astonishing book—an experience by experience account of what happens when we take the promises of Scripture and the words of Jesus at face value—and then live out the reality of the instructions Jesus gave to all disciples. It is an extraordinary record of faith in action, dynamically illustrating how healing and evangelism are inseparable companions at the heart of the great commission to go into all the world and make disciples. I pray it will inspire many to take Jesus at His word and walk forward in faith, bringing hope and healing to many as Jesus heals the broken-hearted and sets the captives free."

Peter Horrobin
Founder of Ellel Ministries International (1986)
and Gates of Hope International (2023)
United Kingdom

"Wayne's personal search for scriptural truth, as it relates to the sometimes contentious subject of healing, is shared in this book in a captivating and compelling fashion. The book strikes a wonderful balance between inspiration and a call to humility before an awesome God whose judgements are unsearchable, and whose ways are past finding out (Rom. 11:33). The personal encounters that he shares in the book are powerful testimonies that will challenge and encourage every reader not to waver at the promise of God through unbelief, but to be strengthened in faith, giving glory to God, and being fully convinced that what He has promised, He is also able to perform (Rom. 4:20-21)."

Pete Ondeng, Author
Africa's Moment
Kenya

"This book has the potential to develop disciples of Jesus who follow Him in His healing ministry, and become more than conquerors as they align themselves with the authority of the Messiah."

Tim Vink, Director of Spiritual Leadership and Outreach
Alliance of Reformed Churches

"*God's Healing Grace* challenged me to reconsider the importance of confession, repentance and forgiveness in the healing of the sick and injured. Reading it was a great blessing."

KB, Church Planter, Mission Leader,
Mission Trainer, Business as Mission Coach

"Wayne Edwards describes a unique, decades-long healing and deliverance ministry, meticulously documented. Knowing the author as I do, I can vouch for the authenticity of the events as presented. I echo the importance of deep and meaningful repentance, and rejoice in the dozens of lives that have been changed by this faithful Gospel witness. Prepare to be challenged and inspired!"

Rev. Tony Swanson, Eastern Region Executive Officer
Africa Inland Mission

"*God's Healing Grace* fanned the flames of my faith and stirred my soul to worship. The writing is refreshingly honest and reminds us that Jesus Christ is very much alive and as powerful and loving as He has ever been."

Jen C., Marriage and Family Therapist
Barnabas International

"The healing miracles as narrated in *God's Healing Grace* remind us that Jesus Christ is the same yesterday, today and forever, and encourage us to take Him at His word. This book will touch the heart of anyone who reads with an open mind. I recommend it to pastors as well as those in missions. When Jesus sent His disciples out, He told them to expect miraculous signs. Let us take Jesus at His word."

Rev. John Kitala, Administrative Secretary
Africa Inland Church
Kenya

"The author gives us inspiring examples of God's healing hand in present-day life. As a missionary surgeon I am challenged to continue to look to the Great Physician for ultimate healing."

Russell E. White, MD, MPH, FACS, FCS(ECSA)
Director of Cardiothoracic Surgery, Tenwek Hospital
Bomet, Kenya

"This book is an inspiring firsthand account of two mission co-workers' journey of submission to the word, will and way of Christ. Having known them for 19 years, I witnessed their journey into this ministry of healing and deliverance. You will grow and be challenged as you witness the power of the Holy Spirit to transform lives."

Rev. Derrick Jones, Supervisor
Reformed Church in America Mission Programs in Africa

"Wayne and June Edwards are disciples of Jesus Christ who have fully lived what John Mark Comer has written about in *Practicing the Way: Be with Jesus. Become like him. Do as he did.* The Edwards have lived with Jesus among a people group He loves eternally, taking Jesus at His word and doing what He did—healing miracles and all—providing contemporary evidence of God's desire to bring *sozo*—salvation/healing—to all."

Bruce Dahlman, MD MSHPE
Jesus follower and founding member
Christian Academy of African Physicians

"In February of 2013, Wayne prayed for my shoulder, which had been very weak and painful and was significantly impairing my mobility. God graciously healed me! I've witnessed Wayne and June's love for the Amaro people for the past thirty years, so it was a joy to read *God's Healing Grace*. The years of personal wrestling as well as the stories of miraculous healing demonstrate that Jesus gives the power and authority of God's kingdom to ordinary people doing God's extraordinary work."

Rev. John Becker, CEO
3P Ministries
Strategy Coordinator, Africa Inland Mission International

GOD'S HEALING GRACE

Taking Jesus at His Word

Wayne R. Edwards

Foreword by
Dr. Charles E. Van Engen

MILL STREET PRESS

San Luis Obispo, CA

God's Healing Grace
Taking Jesus at His Word

God's Healing Grace, Taking Jesus at His Word may be purchased in bulk for educational, ministry, small groups, business, fund-raising, or sales promotional use. For information, please e-mail: *Godshealinggrace@gmail.com.*

Softcover ISBN 978-0-9990722-6-4

ePub ISBN 978-0-9990722-8-8

Contents

Acknowledgements

I have received considerable help during the journey of writing this book. First, I want to thank my brother Richard and his wife, Sharon, for encouraging me to write it. Sharon volunteered to take my notes and help form them into these finished stories. Richard was also a great help with the editing. They stuck with me throughout the whole project and I'm deeply grateful for the roles they played.

I also want to thank my daughter Jane, who took time out of her busy life as an executive and mother to help with the editing, and made this a better book. My cousin Steve also offered helpful suggestions. I'm grateful to Shel Arensen, a longtime friend, for the improvements he made as copy editor.

Henry Miersma gave advice and encouragement to keep the project moving early on, and graciously offered to do the formatting, get the necessary licenses and copyrights, and publish the book.

Thanks to Jason, my son-in-law, for the book's beautiful cover design.

I especially want to thank all the people in these stories who took the risk of allowing June and me to pray for them. You had the courage and humility to open your hearts to the Holy Spirit, and you persevered in faith until you received God's healing grace.

I can't express how grateful I am for my wife June, who has been a partner in every way, as we've shared this journey of learning and ministry together. We wouldn't be who we are without God's transforming work in each of us. Our children Jane, John, Ann and Edwin, and their families have also taught us so much. Their childhood years, their continued maturation in relationship, their deepening understanding and their growth as followers of Jesus have been some of God's greatest gifts to us.

Most importantly, I want to thank and praise our Lord and Savior Jesus Christ who, through his death and resurrection, conquered death and released his healing power into the world. "By his wounds we have been healed." Without Christ and the entire triune God none of the stories in this book would have taken place. All glory and honor to God the Father and the Lord Jesus Christ!

Foreword

A central aspect of the word-and-deed ministry of Jesus involved physical healing. One cannot read the Gospel narratives about Jesus without being immersed in stories of the many people who were healed physically, liberated from evil spirits, and/or resurrected in the power of the Holy Spirit, through the ministry of Jesus as he "went throughout all Galilee, teaching in their synagogues and proclaiming the gospel of the kingdom and healing every disease and every affliction among the people" (Mt 4:23; see, for example, Mt 8:16; 12:22; 15:28; 17:18; Lk 9:11; Ps 103:3). In the Gospels, there are more than 50 references to physical healing in the ministry of Jesus. After Christ's resurrection and ascension, the New Testament highlights the importance of this aspect of the Gospel witness by giving us detailed and specific stories of how the disciples, as followers of Jesus, went about the towns and villages proclaiming the Gospel of the Kingdom and healing. (See, for example, Acts 5:16; 8:7; 9:34; 10:38; 28:8). In that sense, the story of the Book of Acts continues through the Church's life and witness today.

During the past twenty centuries the power of the Holy Spirit to physically heal the sick has been confirmed over and over again. The New Testament emphasis on physical healing is consistent with stories of healing sprinkled throughout the Old Testament. Healing is presented in the Bible as a loving act of a gracious and merciful God. Wayne and June share that biblical perspective. Consistently in their ministries and in the stories narrated in this book is a conscious concern and care that physical healing is not to be a kind of "hook" that would seek to convince people to become followers of Jesus merely because of the physical healing. Wayne and June have discovered what Jesus, Peter, James, Paul, and others in the early church also experienced – that merely because someone is physically healed or because someone sees a person being healed does not necessarily lead to their conversion. In fact, down through the history of the church, such phenomena have at times led to severe persecution and even death of the one who was healed.

The narratives gathered in this book are also not stories of seemingly magical power emanating from the spiritual prowess of a healer, shaman, or guru. Here the reader will not read about large crowds gathered to hear a wonder-working healer and receive healing at the hands of the preacher. That kind of ministry has its place in the annals of the Church's life and mission, but this book is different. It tells the story of a humble, simple, surprised, amazed cross-cultural missionary family who discovered that the Holy Spirit had graced them with the gift of healing.

Well-trained in modern scientific medicine, well versed in the biblical theology of God's work of physical healing in God's mission, linguistically and culturally careful and sensitive, this couple were surprised by God's grace. This book is not a counter against the importance and effectiveness of modern medicine. The reader will notice that Wayne and June do all they can through modern medicine, given the economic, cultural, religious, and political realities of the people among whom they live and work. Additionally, over their long cross-cultural missionary endeavors, they have learned that the Holy Spirit's grace in healing is integral, even foundational, to their "scientific" healing procedures.

This book is a personal journal. Following the pattern of Luke's writing in Acts, this book simply tells the stories of the Holy Spirit's physical healing of many people. The fact that Wayne and June have kept such a detailed record of people being physically healed is remarkable. The reader will recognize that because of issues of personal safety, these are not their real names. But, having known them for many years, I vouch for the authenticity of their identity and of the manuscript. This book is not fiction.

Healing in the Bible includes physical healing but is only a part of the wholistic healing that involves a transformation of spiritual health, mental health, personal relationships, and way of life wherein folks experience reconciliation with God, themselves, others, and creation. Throughout Scripture, all God's people are called to pray for healing.

Additionally, following the exhortation of James, the elders of the church are to pray for the healing of the sick (James 5:13-15). But there is more. In addition to general prayers for healing, the New Testament teaches us that the Holy Spirit gives the church a special gift – a charism – of healing. In Paul's understanding, this gift is on a par with other gifts like wisdom, knowledge, faith, working of miracles, prophecy, discernment of spirits, tongues, and the interpretation of tongues (I Cor 12:8-10). These gifts are part of an extensive illustrative (not exhaustive) long list of more than twenty gifts of the Holy Spirit found in Romans 12, I Corinthians 12, Ephesians 4, and I Peter 4. Beginning in Acts 2, Luke describes how the early church lived out these gifts in their life together in Jerusalem, even under severe persecution.

A delightful part of the story of Wayne and June's ministry has been the way the Holy Spirit surprised them, worked on teaching them, and almost had to push them into finding out that they had been given the gift of healing. During the first twenty years of their missionary service, they did not know what the Holy Spirit had in mind. During the second half of their ministry the Holy Spirit's work of healing has been important and transformational both for them and for the new believers with whom they work.

Dear reader, take your time reading each chapter of this book. As you read, remember that the stories are not about Wayne and June. They are about the work of the Holy Spirit in the lives of people. I encourage you to take a moment to praise God for God's grace and love for all humans, everywhere. And pray for Christians around the world, many of whom experience the Holy Spirit's grace of healing as they live in situations of severe personal, social, and religious persecution.

Rev. Charles (Chuck) Van Engen, Ph.D.
Arthur F. Glasser Senior Professor Emeritus of Biblical
Theology of Mission, School of Intercultural Studies,
Fuller Theological Seminary (SIS/FTS)
Founding President and CEO of Latin American Christian
Ministries/Programa Doctoral en Teologia PRODOLA

Introduction

For nearly 40 years, my wife June and I have been Christian missionaries to an unreached people group in East Africa. For the first 20 years, we regularly incorporated prayer while treating the sick at our little bush medical dispensary and during home visits. By God's grace many people recovered following medical treatment and prayer in Jesus' name. When it came to difficult cases in which medical treatment was not adequate or available, we prayed for God's intervention, asking Jesus to do the miraculous. But those prayers did not often yield the results we hoped for. Rarely did we see miraculous healings occur.

We love the Lord Jesus Christ and are grateful for the privilege of following him as his disciples and carrying out his commission to make more disciples. We had always believed that Jesus *could* miraculously heal the sick today, yet wondered whether it was *his will* to heal in each particular situation. Did God have a higher purpose that the sickness might serve? Was the timing perhaps not right? Did we, the ones praying or seeking healing, lack sufficient faith? So we always ended our prayers with "we pray this all according to your will," while wondering what his will was. These questions, and our desire to give God an out, actually expressed our hidden and unrealized doubts.

Our primary work as missionaries was to share about Jesus Christ, along with the hope and freedom he offers to all people through his death and resurrection. We did this through our medical work, our development projects like digging wells, and through lots of conversations over steaming cups of *chai* in our home and our neighbors' homes in our village. We prayed for individuals, for families, and for the whole community to take Jesus' hope and freedom for themselves. But, year after year, this did not happen. During a time of discouragement and frustration from the lack of positive response to the Gospel, I cried out to

Jesus, asking what we were missing. What needed to change? How could we be more effective in sharing the Gospel and drawing people into his kingdom? In reply, I sensed Jesus saying, "Do what I was doing."

I thought we *were* doing what Jesus did. We were loving our neighbors. We were treating the sick and helping the poor. We were doing community development to help make people's lives better and, of course, we were sharing the Gospel of Jesus Christ and making disciples whenever the Lord opened the way. But the depth of the spiritual darkness that oppressed many of the people in our community compelled us to keep seeking and studying.

I began to reread Matthew, Mark, Luke, John and Acts. I was looking at Jesus with fresh eyes. I wanted to watch what he was doing and hear what he was teaching. As I read, I asked myself four questions and jotted down my answers:

1. Who did Jesus heal?
2. When did he heal them?
3. Who did Jesus not heal?
4. Why did he not heal them?

At the same time I reviewed both the Old and New Testaments to identify potential obstacles or 'blocks' to receiving healing from Jesus. What I discovered changed my understanding and practice. Though Jesus didn't heal all the sick in Jerusalem, Judea and Galilee, he healed everyone who came to him seeking healing. Everyone! The man born blind, the woman who had bled for 12 years, Peter's mother-in-law in bed with fever, the paralytic lowered through the roof, the boy suffering with an evil spirit, Jairus's dead daughter, the deaf and mute, and so many more among the multitudes. He healed them all! Jesus never turned anyone away!

But that was back then, right? That was *Jesus*. I kept reading.

As I read on, I saw the progression and made an important connection. Jesus first gave his authority and power to heal the sick and drive out demons to his 12 original disciples (Matthew 10 and Luke 9). Then he gave that same authority and power to 72 disciples (Luke 10). Finally, in the great commission (Matthew 28:18–20) Jesus commanded *all* his disciples to teach *all their* disciples to obey *everything* he had commanded them. I realized that every one of these accounts was pointing me to one conclusion: Jesus' authority and power have also been entrusted to his disciples today, including me!

Hebrews 13:8 assures us, "Jesus Christ is the same yesterday, today and forever" (NIV). Jesus has not changed, nor have his commands or the Gospel. So can we take Jesus at his word? Can we believe that his authority and power are also ours and can we act upon that belief? Are we today still called to believe and obey what he commanded? Yes!

"Do what I was doing" kept going through my mind. June and I decided to believe and obey, even though it felt risky, even when we didn't see immediate results or the results we were expecting. The more we learned—from books, from others, from our own experience and, most importantly, from the Scriptures—the more healing we saw. We also noticed that more of the new converts remained firmly in the Christian faith (which is always a challenge in a Muslim context).

In the early years of our ministry, we saw very few healing miracles. Today about half of the sick and injured we pray for are miraculously healed. Sometimes there is partial healing; sometimes additional healing comes as we persevere in prayer. At this point, whatever a person's situation, we come with the working assumption that Jesus is willing to heal everyone who comes to him.

Aware that our knowledge will always be partial, June and I have chosen to be lifelong learners on this journey, always asking and seeking and knocking. This has sometimes been uncomfortable; not only are some people not healed when we pray, some of the things we've learned do not fit easily into tidy theological boxes. However, the core elements of what we do—confession, repentance, receiving forgiveness, forgiving others—are basic Christian practices.

One key foundational building block that we personally have found of prime importance is abiding in Jesus in our daily walk. Fruitful healing prayer comes when we abide in Christ and he in us as the Lord himself taught us in John 15.

Jesus said,

**"Abide in me, and I in you…
for apart from me you can do nothing."**
John 15:4–5 ESV

Each ministry context is different and God gives a variety of gifts to his people. We are not attempting to teach a particular methodology by recording these stories. Nor are we licensed therapists, although we have often found ourselves involved in pastoral counseling while praying for the sick. What we have been led to do is share our experiences as missionaries to an unreached people group and our encounters with others the Lord has brought into our lives. Each of the stories in this book is a firsthand account of events we ourselves witnessed and each is based on field notes we kept over the last 20 years. Most happened in or around our village in Kenya, but some occurred in our travels in the US and beyond. Because some of the stories contain sensitive personal details and in some cases information that could have serious repercussions for the people involved, most of the names and places have been changed.

The reader will notice that the sequence of stories doesn't follow any particular order. I chose this more random arrangement to keep the reader's interest and to allow each story to be used by the Holy Spirit to speak in its own unique way.

Perhaps the very fact that the experiences described here are those of two missionaries firmly rooted in Reformed theology will make it more possible for our fellow disciples to consider their implications. We hope these accounts will encourage, inspire and further equip the body of Christ to pray for the injured and sick, and to boldly proclaim the kingdom of God, trusting that they will grow in understanding and practice along the way.

INTRODUCTION

"*I am sending you to open their eyes, so that they may turn from darkness to light and from the power of Satan to God, that they may receive forgiveness of sins and a place among those who are sanctified by faith in me.*"

ACTS 26:17-18 ESV

1

....

A Place to Build

April 1996

Amaro Region, Kenya

Our call from God was clear: we were to bring the Good News of Jesus the Messiah to an unreached people group, the semi-nomadic Amaro tribe living in the vast arid region of eastern Kenya. We spent our first year in eastern Kenya living with older seasoned missionaries and mentors, Rob and Florence, while we learned the unwritten Amaro language. Then, over the course of several months and many trips to various locations, we and Rob and Florence worked to discern more specifically where God intended us to invest our lives. When it became clear that we were being led to live among and love the people in Duma, a village about two hours away, the next step was to ask that community if they would welcome us to live among them.

Their welcome would have to include a place where we could erect a sheet metal prefab hut to live in. Because of the hot arid climate, we were looking for a place with large trees for shade from the equatorial sun. We wanted to be near the seasonal riverbed so that a good water source would be available, but we also needed the right soil for our home so that when the rains came we would not be living in a mucky mess. We hiked through the bush, interacted with community members, and hiked through the bush some more, but we could not find the right place.

A big meeting had been planned with the area chief and village elders. But in the weeks prior to this meeting, after many more bush hikes scouting for that right location, we felt discouraged. We simply couldn't find a place that met all of the requirements.

The week before the scheduled village meeting, scouting around one last time, several of us split up to cover more ground. Jack, Rob and Florence's son, who was visiting briefly and had come along for the day, joined in the search. About noon when the sun was the most intense, June and I made our way back to the parked truck some distance away to wait for the others to return. We were both very thirsty and discouraged.

Jack was the last of our group to emerge from the bush. He surprised us all by announcing, "I think I found the place!" We followed him into very dense bush, but not too far away from the riverbed. The area was tangled and full of thorns; a warthog and gazelle startled and ran as we made our way forward. Our hopes rose as we counted five large acacia trees and then realized that the soil was right as well. The peace in our hearts was an additional witness: this was the right place.

On the day of the big meeting we were ready. However, several village elders came not only with a general wariness, but with a particularly strong objection: the local people were Muslims and we were Christians. On the other hand, they knew we would bring services their community badly needed: medical care, treatments for the village's livestock, and resources for water development as well as community development. The elders deliberated for a long time, wrestling with the pros and cons of welcoming us in. Finally, access to "injections" and other medical care won out. They extended an invitation for us to move into their village.

Then Rob surprised us. He stood up and began to speak to the group gathered under the acacia tree: "Wayne and June will move here on three conditions." Having no idea what these conditions were, we listened attentively!

Rob continued, "First, you must give them a piece of land where they can put up their house and other buildings. Second, you must share your water resources with them. Finally, you must give them the freedom to share what the Bible says."

That third condition created quite a stir! The village leaders did not like it. A group of the older elders moved to the shade of another tree to more freely discuss what had been proposed. About 45 minutes later they rejoined the larger group and, to our delight, extended their invitation. We were welcomed to move into their village.

After the meeting, about 80 men from the larger group walked with us and the chief to the parcel of land the Lord had led us to ask for. We circled the whole area and said, "This is the place that we would like to have!" We expected some opposition, but no one voiced even one objection. "You want this place?" the men confirmed. "Okay, you can have it."

In the course of that next week we packed up all our earthly possessions and left the security of living within 100 yards of experienced, wise, encouraging Rob and Florence, to move to our new home and community.

The first task was using our machetes to cut enough of the thick bush to clear a space for a tent. Almost instantly about 40 men showed up to watch. We greeted them and attempted chatting a bit, but soon realized that we were the entertainment of the day. So we set up our tent and cleared a simple cooking area to make meals on our *jiko*, a clay charcoal one-burner cooker. Then we worked to clear more bush so that our Toyota Land Cruiser could be parked near our tent and supplies.

In the Amaro culture, one doesn't eat in the presence of others without offering to share the food together. We didn't have enough to share with the 40 onlookers so we couldn't eat. Even more disconcerting, we had no *choo* (latrine). Our only recourse was to grab the shovel and head off into the bush—aware that everyone knew where we were headed and why.

At nightfall the men simply turned and went home. I asked several of them to come back the next day with their machetes to help us clear more of the underlying bush so it would be easier to see any snakes that came near our tent and supply area.

Very early the next morning Boro, one of the older elders, came up the trail to greet us. Amaro greetings are extensive and thoroughly oriented to relationship. We respectfully greeted this elder as "Abba" and he became our father figure in the village. After completing the raft of expected and routine greetings, Boro asked an additional question: "Aren't you afraid to sleep here?"

"No," we answered. "God is with us."

Additional elders and the other men weren't far behind Boro, so we all greeted each other.

On each of the next three mornings Boro was first up the trail, and he always asked that same question, "Aren't you afraid to sleep here?" By the fourth morning we had become suspicious. This question wasn't part of the normal greetings.

"Why do you keep asking us if we are afraid to stay here?" we asked Boro.

He did not want to respond, but we kept encouraging him to tell us. Finally he asked, "Do you know anything about evil spirits?"

At this stage in our lives we knew very little about evil spirits, but I responded, "In God's word we learn that Jesus drove demons out from people." Then I shared a short Bible story of a time when Jesus had done just that.

This was enough to prompt Boro to say more. Sheepishly he went on to tell us, "This place where you placed your tent and campsite under these large acacia trees is the home where all our village evil spirits live."

After thinking for a moment, I asked, "Are the evil spirits still here?"

Boro said, "No, they have moved."

When I asked where they had moved to, he pointed and named a place at some distance from the plot of land we'd been given.

We learned later that many of the men who had approached through the thick brush the morning after our first night, expected to find us dead. No one ever purposely ventured into this particular thick bushy place unless to look for a lost sheep or goat, and then only during daylight hours. They would never enter at night because they feared for their lives.

After a week had gone by, a rumor began circulating that since the evil spirits had not harmed us, we must be in an alliance with them. "No," we told the people, "this is not the case. The reason the spirits left is because God has moved here with us."

Without our being aware of it, God had arranged for our arrival to include a power encounter between the powers of darkness and himself, knowing that the local people would regard such an event as very significant. It was significant for us too, but we could not then imagine all God would teach us in the years ahead about his authority over those powers, authority he has also given to us, his present-day disciples and followers of his Son Jesus Christ.

A PLACE TO BUILD

But he was pierced for our transgressions; he was crushed for our iniquities; upon him was the chastisement that brought us peace, and with his wounds we are healed.

ISAIAH 53:5 ESV

And when Jesus entered Peter's house, he saw his mother-in-law lying sick with a fever. He touched her hand, and the fever left her, and she rose and began to serve him.

That evening they brought to him many who were oppressed by demons, and he cast out the spirits with a word and healed all who were sick. This was to fulfill what was spoken by the prophet Isaiah: "He took our illnesses and bore our diseases."

MATTHEW 8:14–17 ESV

2

....

What a Day!

In a letter to our children, all adults now and living in the United States, I recounted the adventures and opportunities of just one particular exhausting day in the life June and I share in Kenya. Join the extended Edwards family and read edited excerpts from that letter.

April 19, 2016
Duma, Kenya
Hi kids,

I wrote up some details for you about the events that happened yesterday.

After waking up at 4:30 am, Mom and I began the day by spending our abiding time, coffee in hand, with the Lord. At 6:30 I went outside to have Bible study with the KPR (Kenya Police Reserve security men). We are reading through the book of Acts. It vividly illustrates God's immediate presence and involvement in the lives of Jesus' disciples. My hope is that it will help the men grasp that simply following a religion is quite lifeless compared to a relationship with the living God.

At 7:30, while we were finishing breakfast, Musa came to receive the retirement package we had put together for him. He's been a good and faithful daily wage worker off and on for the last 29 years—a faithful friend, really. He was happy with the package. It was a bittersweet moment. I really appreciated working with Musa through the years. He still lives close by, but I'll miss the daily interaction.

I spent the morning in the office, catching up on administrative work and periodically going out to talk to people and praying with some. Mom was very busy in the dispensary. It was a huge 'Clinic Monday' with lots of people coming from quite a distance. Mom got home about 4 pm and was pretty wiped out.

I took off on my *piki* (motorcycle) to a distant village to visit a paralyzed man who recently returned home from the hospital. Mom had referred him to the Kola Hospital a couple weeks ago to rule out tuberculosis of the spine, since his wife recently finished TB treatments. The doctors couldn't figure out what was wrong with him. I had transported him home last Friday after he got as far as Duma by the *soko* truck.† He had asked me to come and see him in a few days.

We had a wonderful visit. Three of the man's married sons and a visiting village elder, as well as the paralyzed man himself, listened intently as I spent about two hours explaining the Gospel. The men asked great questions.

I told them that Jesus not only saves us from our sin, makes us right before God and gives us eternal life, but he also heals *today*. I told three or four stories of miraculous healings I had witnessed firsthand—some involving people the paralyzed man knew personally. I was going to pray for his healing, but then sensed that he wasn't ready. The Good News was completely unfamiliar to him; he would need some time to absorb what he'd heard.

Since it was already 6:30 and beginning to get dark, I told my host that I would come back another day and share more stories with him. The men said they were grateful for the time together.

In the next home, down the path a bit, a family was waiting for me. Three weeks ago, during the Easter weekend, Jesus had healed this elder's back. Since then, he and his family have been meeting with me every week; we've been going through the biblical accounts of creation, the fall of Adam and Eve, and Cain murdering Abel. That night I told the story of Noah.

While I was sitting on the mat under the stars and half-moon waiting

---

†   *soko* truck: the market truck that comes through the area once a week to transport people and goods to and from the market, which is two to five hours away depending where one boards the truck.

for the elder and other family members to return from evening Islamic prayers, I visited with one of the elder's sons, a young man of maybe 16–18 years. I asked him how his shepherding work had gone that day. He told me that he hadn't gone out because he was injured.

He explained that he had fallen four days ago while chasing some wayward sheep and goats. Tripping over a stump caused him to collide with a tree, wrenching his arm and shoulder backward. He was in a great deal of pain, and I noticed that he was holding his shoulder at an odd angle. I asked him to raise his arm; it trembled as he attempted it, and he had very little range of motion. Just then his father and older brothers returned.

As I was about to begin the review of what we'd covered over the past weeks, the elder and his sons told me that they would try to listen, but many other things were going through their minds at present. I asked what those were.

The day before, many of the family's flock of sheep and goats had become lost. Hyenas had killed and eaten four of them. Some of the animals had been found, but the men had spent most of the day looking for the three that were still missing.

We prayed together in Jesus' name that if the remaining lost sheep and goats were still alive, the Lord would bring them back home safely.

We began reading the story of Noah and the flood, but soon after we started, the son who had been herding the milking cows all day arrived home without them. He said the cows were lost. We live in a very flat region with only bushes and short trees, so the men feared that hyenas would find the missing cows if the family didn't find them first. The father, who has 18 children, told three of his sons who were sitting with us to get up and go search for the lost cows right away.

After the young men headed out with their flashlights and spears, I suggested that it would be good if we asked Jesus to bring all the cows home safely. The men there agreed, so I prayed in Jesus' name that the lost cows would be found and brought home.

About 20 minutes into our Bible reading and discussion, we began to hear the sweet chorus of the returning cows and their penned up hungry bawling calves. The cows had come home on their own from the southeast. Only one milking cow was still missing—the weakest of the herd. Another son was immediately sent to look for the lost cow by following the tracks. (The three sons who had been sent out to search for the lost cows returned several hours later; they had headed toward the southwest, the wrong direction.)

I said, "Let's give thanks to Jesus for bringing home seven of the eight lost cows, and let's pray that if the last lost cow is still alive, she will be protected from the hyenas, and Jesus will bring her safely home."

After we prayed, we continued with the story of Noah and the flood. We wondered out loud what the story tells us about God, what it teaches us about human beings, and what it tells us about how we are to trust God and obey. Because the family had already been introduced to Jesus the Messiah, I asked them to consider how Jesus is the ark God has provided for our salvation.

The elder asked, "Who created Jesus?"

I launched into a careful explanation of the mystery of the Trinity, beginning with creation and moving to the climax of the Word made flesh in Mary's womb: Jesus, the Word of God and the Son of God.

One son seemed to grasp what I had said and explained it to the others. Wanting to avoid potential misunderstandings, I went on to say that the Jesus spoken of in the Qur'an is described very differently and that we learn from the Bible that Jesus is one with the Father and the Spirit. Three persons, one God.

Just then the son who'd been sent out to look for that last and weakest of the cows came home; the lost cow was with him!

Following the cattle tracks, he'd finally caught a glimpse of the lost cow a long way out by the dam. The very next moment he saw a hyena grab the cow and sink its teeth deep into her leg. The boy managed to scare the hyena off and then walked the cow home.

We sat there together, mentally calculating the timing of the rescue; we'd prayed that Jesus would protect that cow from hyenas and bring it safely home, and Jesus did! The whole family rejoiced in the safe return of that weak and wounded cow, grateful for God's gracious provision.

It was now 9:10 pm and I had a 30-minute *piki* ride in the dark ahead of me. I closed our gathering in prayer, giving thanks to Jesus for all he had done that night, then got to my feet and headed out to the *piki* and put on my helmet.

But the Holy Spirit stopped me. He reminded me about the son who had been injured a few days earlier—Ismail, who had listened attentively all evening. For a moment I considered ignoring the Spirit and heading for home. In my mind I argued that it was late; I was tired.

I removed my helmet, turned around and walked back to Ismail who was still sitting on the big mat with the others. I knelt down beside him and asked how he was doing. Ismail said he still had a lot of pain; he prodded the painful place in his shoulder.

I asked Ismail if he would like to be well and if he would be willing to come to Jesus. "Jesus will heal you," I told him. Ismail said yes, he would like that. Then I asked Ismail's father (who Jesus miraculously healed of a bad back three weeks prior) for permission, which he gave.

I reviewed with everyone that the one who is about to heal Ismail is Jesus the Messiah as explained in the Bible—the One who came from heaven, died on the cross and rose from the dead three days later. *This* is the Jesus who will heal Ismail. They all acknowledged that they understood.

I bent down on one knee, placed my hand on Ismail's shoulder and prayed. Then, in Jesus' name and authority, I commanded all the pain to leave and the shoulder to be healed. A few minutes later I said, "Amen."

When I asked Ismail how he was feeling, he said he still had pain, and I could see that his injured shoulder was still drooping. Then others in the family told me that Ismail had hurt his knee as well as his shoulder, and that he had been limping the last four days.

So I placed one hand on Ismail's shoulder and the other hand on his knee and prayed again. This time, after about a minute or so, there was a slight pop in the shoulder, though I felt nothing in the knee. After a few minutes I asked Ismail again how he felt. This time he exclaimed that the pain was gone! The shoulder wasn't drooping any longer; it was level with the other. I asked him to raise his arm. Ismail raised both arms exuberantly to the sky.

I asked him to stand and test his knee. He marched around in circles announcing that his knee had no pain at all. We all laughed with joy watching Ismail walking and pumping his arms up and down with a big smile on his face. We prayed again, thanking Jesus for his healing grace. Finally, I headed for home rejoicing. (It wasn't until later that I realized the full extent of the miracle: the ball had been out of its socket for four days before we prayed and God answered by healing Ismail's dislocated shoulder—even more cause for rejoicing.)

Unbeknownst to me, while all this was going on, a large group of men from Duma were bringing a 25-year-old man to our house—where Mom had been anticipating a nice quiet evening of answering the emails clogging her inbox. The young man had just been bitten by a snake at the *dukas* (small shops) at about dusk. The snake had gotten away, but it was reported to have looked like a big red cobra.

Mom spent two hours at the clinic with the patient and his family, treating the young man with prayer, injections and the high DC voltage low amperage electric shock treatment for snake bites. The dispensary was out of anti-venom, but last month Mom had heard that the Weema Health Center, 60 kilometers away, still had some doses. The family decided to send a relative on a *piki* right away to get a couple of vials.

I returned home about 30 minutes after everyone had gone home. I got a quick bite to eat and showered. We headed for bed and quickly fell asleep.

We were in a deep sleep when, sometime after 10:30 pm, one of the KPR volunteers came up to our bedroom window to tell Mom that the husband of a woman who had just given birth at her home was calling her to come, because his wife was in trouble. *"Taka gad hinteene!"*‡ The trained birth assistants could not extract the placenta. Mom jumped out of bed and headed to the clinic to grab her maternity bag. Then she was transported by *piki* to the home.

I'll let Mom take over the story here.

Mom: The only detail I want to add is that after a couple of deliveries in our new maternity room, the hut deliveries are suddenly seeming so *dirty!* I guess it's not surprising since the mom and baby are literally in the dirt all throughout. This home had only a few goatskins and old gunny sacks to keep people out of the dirt. I tried squatting to stay above it for a while, but finally gave up and just sank down onto the dirt floor with them. Sometimes at least the dirt is hard, but this floor was all loose, dusty dirt, not even sand. Even Musalima (the trained birth assistant who has been with me in the last two maternity room deliveries) complained about the dirt and conditions for birth, and advised them to come use our maternity room in the future.

Thankfully, our prayers and oxytocin—intramuscular and then intravenous—worked well. There was only minimal additional blood loss when the placenta finally came out about half an hour after I got there. The new mom had already lost a lot of blood though, and was pretty weak and very anemic (IV fluids only help to a point). Also, when I examined the baby boy, I saw that he had clubfeet. I'm sending pictures to the doctors in Kijabe and asking for advice about what we should do to help. The little boy may need surgery.

Dad again: Mom returned home about midnight, filthy from all the blood and from sitting on the dirt floor. She was tired, but thankful that Jesus had answered the prayers for a safe delivery. And she was grateful that the new mom was now *"akum dansa gad tai!"*‡ Mom took a shower and once again headed for bed.

An hour later, while Mom was sleeping hard, the same volunteer KPR came to our bedroom window to tell us that the anti-venom had just arrived from Weema and the patient was waiting for her. Mom shot out of bed again, perhaps a bit slower, and spent an hour or so administering the two injections that have to be given very slowly while watching for any ill effects.

When she got home Mom was all sweaty, so she took a third shower, and finally fell into bed again at about 2:30 am. I got up at 4:30 to begin the day. Thankfully Mom slept in a bit.

What a day!

---

‡   *"Akum dansa gad tai!"* expresses the satisfactory physical condition of a woman who has just given birth. Literally translated, this phrase means that the woman is "sitting down well." In other words, the placenta came out in its entirety. So *"Taka gad hinteene"* means that she is not yet sitting well, or the placenta has not yet come out.

For if you forgive others their trespasses, your heavenly Father will also forgive you, but if you do not forgive others their trespasses, neither will your Father forgive your trespasses.

MATTHEW 6:14–15 ESV

Then his master summoned him and said to him, "You wicked servant! I forgave you all that debt because you pleaded with me. And should not you have had mercy on your fellow servant, as I had mercy on you?" And in anger his master delivered him to the jailers, until he should pay all his debt. So also my heavenly Father will do to every one of you, if you do not forgive your brother from your heart.

MATTHEW 18:32–35 ESV

3

....

Miia

October 21, 2017

Duma, Kenya

Today, at one of the prayer days for our Amaro Team, we sat under the shade of our tin roof, open-sided carport. We began the day by reading Acts 3, the account of Peter and John healing the lame man in the name of Jesus of Nazareth. Miia, a Kenyan nurse on our team, had a pounding headache, but hadn't told anyone. She could hardly turn her head from side to side.

The team split up into small prayer groups; Miia, Gloria, Sadie and I found ourselves together. Miia shared with us about her headache. I asked her if she would like to come to Jesus and have him heal her headache. She said yes, so I reviewed the Gospel with her and the group. This included reminding everyone that Jesus came from heaven, healed the multitudes, died on the cross and rose from the dead. I said, "Jesus healed all who came to him. He never turned anyone away!" We spoke out what Hebrews 13:8 says: "Jesus is the same yesterday, today and forever." In doing all this, we were helping dispel any doubts and increasing everyone's faith, helping Miia to become ready to receive.

One of the questions I usually ask people seeking Jesus' healing is whether there is anyone they have not forgiven, as I have seen many times how unforgiveness can act as a 'block' for healing. I asked Miia if there was anyone who had wronged her that she had not forgiven. She paused for a moment and answered, "Yes, my uncle." We read Matthew 6:14–15 together, which says, "For if you forgive men when they sin against you, your heavenly Father will also forgive you. But if you do not forgive men their sins, your heavenly Father will not forgive your sins" (NIV).

Hearing Jesus' assertion that our Father in heaven won't forgive our sins unless we have forgiven others, Miia prayed out loud and, by an act of her will, forgave her uncle who had wronged her. We discussed Ephesians 4:26–27 about giving the devil a foothold if we keep our anger or unforgiveness beyond sunset. She was quick to state she did not realize that before, and she didn't want to give the devil any right into her life. So she confessed holding on to the grudge as sin, and also asked Jesus to forgive her for hanging on to her anger. As a demonstration of her repentance, she stated out loud in prayer her choice to live in a forgiving way in the future.

Afterwards, Gloria, Sadie, and I laid hands on Miia and prayed with Jesus' authority: "Jesus, thank you for your grace and the work you did at the cross to redeem us back to yourself. Together we ask that you pour out your healing power on Miia now and remove the headache from her, in Jesus' name. Amen." I continued, "In the name and authority of Jesus Christ of Nazareth, I command the spirit of pain to leave. In Jesus' name I tell Miia's head to be well, be healed."

Jesus immediately took most of her headache away. She could once again move her head from side to side, although some pain still remained. We prayed again; and then again, using Jesus' name and authority, we commanded the remaining pain to leave her head. She was released from the headache more completely.

Later, after the group had spent time praying for other needs, I asked Miia how her head felt. She said, "Only a slight ache still exists deep inside, but it's much better." In my early years of ministry, I would have stopped here, or actually, after that very first prayer. We had prayed, Miia had experienced significant healing, so that amount must be God's will for healing for Miia that day, right? But now, here, I asked Miia if she would like to pray again for more healing and for it to be complete. She agreed, so again Gloria, Sadie, and I put our hands on her head and led in prayer. This time the headache left entirely and gave her no more trouble the rest of the week.

Later, Miia shared with us that she had come to understand how crucial it is to forgive when wronged; Jesus himself commands it. She prayed throughout the week and was quick to forgive each person God's Spirit brought to her mind. She also took the step of calling the uncle who had wronged her family. She told him she had forgiven him and asked for his forgiveness for having held a grudge against him.

At Iconium they entered together into the Jewish synagogue and spoke in such a way that a great number of both Jews and Greeks believed. But the unbelieving Jews stirred up the Gentiles and poisoned their minds against the brothers. So they remained for a long time, speaking boldly for the Lord, who bore witness to the word of his grace, granting signs and wonders to be done by their hands.

ACTS 14:1-3 ESV

4

....

Amina

June 2013

Amaro Region, Kenya

Elders from a village some distance away had invited me to share the word of God with them, so they made arrangements for me to travel there near the end of June to meet with several men from the village. We all sat together in Sego's traditional round grass hut on cow skins on the dirt floor. Sego's wife, Amina, sat unseen behind a thin stick divider in the back.

I read Genesis 1–3 to the group and then used other passages as a bridge to explain how the salvation God had promised is fulfilled in Jesus. Finally, to help everyone understand that Jesus is alive and still working miracles, I shared about the many miracles Jesus had done very recently, including the story of my own father's healing from liver disease.

After three hours of teaching and discussion, Sego asked me to pray in Jesus' name for his wife who had been suffering from a toothache for two weeks. Part of one of Amina's molars had broken and was showing decay. She had been in such severe pain for two weeks that she had been unable to sleep, and this tooth was so sensitive to heat that she could not drink hot *chai*, a favorite staple typically enjoyed multiple times a day in Amaro life.

I invited Amina to come out from behind the stick divider and have a seat facing me on the cow skin among the elders. Since we had been sharing about the Gospel for the last three hours, I simply checked in with Amina to be sure that she also understood. With permission, I placed my hand on her cheek where the bad tooth was located. I praised Jesus the healer and thanked Jesus for all the people he has healed to confirm the Gospel. I went on to ask Jesus to heal Amina's tooth to confirm the Gospel and show his love and grace to her.

After saying "Amen," I commanded Amina's tooth to be well and commanded the pain to cease in the name and authority of Jesus Christ. We waited for about a minute, then I removed my hand.

We concluded our meeting and I returned home.

A week later I returned and asked Amina how her tooth was feeling. She said, "It is all well. It does not hurt anymore."

I asked, "When did it get better?"

"That very day that you prayed and asked Jesus to heal it," Amina answered.

AMINA

If any of you lacks wisdom, let him ask God, who gives generously to all without reproach, and it will be given him. But let him ask in faith, with no doubting, for the one who doubts is like a wave of the sea that is driven and tossed by the wind. For that person must not suppose that he will receive anything from the Lord; he is a double-minded man, unstable in all his ways.

JAMES 1:5–8 ESV

And Jesus answered them, "Have faith in God. Truly, I say to you, whoever says to this mountain, 'Be taken up and thrown into the sea,' and does not doubt in his heart, but believes that what he says will come to pass, it will be done for him. Therefore I tell you, whatever you ask in prayer, believe that you have received it, and it will be yours."

MARK 11:22–24 ESV

5

....

Kathy

November 6, 2013

Nairobi, Kenya

June and I traveled to Nairobi and had the delight of seeing our good friends, Jered and Kathy, at a mission guest house in town. They had arrived from the United States just the night before.

It had been a year and a half since we had last seen each other, but just like many other times through the years, our reconnection was immediate and deep. We picked up just where we left off, as if we had seen each other only yesterday.

We noticed that Kathy was wearing a hand brace and kept her arm close to her stomach. We asked her about it.

Kathy explained that for the last 11 months, since last December, she had been struggling with a bad disk in her neck. In January the pain became severe and began to shoot down her right arm. It was extremely painful and felt like fire, she told us. She went to multiple doctors searching for relief. After an MRI and CT scans, her surgeon said she needed surgery; yet her regular doctor said she could try physical therapy first. Wanting to avoid surgery if possible, she chose physical therapy.

Jered and Kathy's insurance paid for the physical therapy sessions for six months, right until the week before they left for Kenya, but now would not cover any further sessions. While the therapy had helped reduce and manage the pain, the pain still came and went with varying degrees of intensity. Kathy used the brace to keep her hand immobile, but the pain was constant. For months she was not able to take walks because the extra movement was too painful.

Because of all June and I had been learning and experiencing, a lot of our conversation with Jered and Kathy that evening revolved around the topic of healing. We also talked quite extensively about doubt after I asked Jered directly at dinner, "What is doubt?" Working through doubt had been one of the things June and I were processing and we had seen many instances where doubt had been one of the blockers or barriers to someone receiving healing, especially for mature Christians.

Jered and Kathy had a lot of questions. We talked through Scripture together and June and I shared stories about the healing miracles Jesus had been doing among our friends and the people in our village. Kathy told us later that as she listened to account after account, she found her own doubts fading and her faith growing.

After our meal we moved into the living room to continue our discussion. It was about 8 pm when Jered pushed back a bit and said, "But Wayne, we just can't know *for sure* what God's will is when it comes to healing."

We understood Jered's concern. It was ours as well when we first began our journey of learning how to pray for healing.

We shared more about what we had been learning and we looked together at Scripture. In John 4:34, Jesus said, "My food is to do the will of him who sent me and to finish his work." In the next chapter, in John 5:19, he says, "I tell you the truth, the Son can do nothing by himself; he can do only what he sees his Father doing, because whatever the Father does the Son also does." In John 6:38 he says, "For I have come down from heaven not to do my will but to do the will of him who sent me." In each of these instances, Jesus said he did what he saw the Father doing and that he came to do his Father's will.

And what was it he was doing? He was teaching. He was calling people to repentance. He was healing people. While Jesus did not heal all the sick people in Jerusalem, Judea and Galilee, he healed *everyone* who came to him. Everyone. He never turned anyone away. We shared with Jered and Kathy how we had come to believe that Jesus' words and actions revealed that it was the Father's will to heal everyone who came to Jesus.

At 9 pm, often jokingly called "missionary midnight" by many bush missionaries, we said good night. Both June and I were eager to pray with

Kathy for healing for her arm, but since they had not asked, we did not suggest it. It was clear they needed time to process all they had heard.

In the morning we noticed that Kathy was not wearing her hand brace. She told us that before going to sleep, she had looked again for herself at the Scriptures we'd referred to. Then, in the middle of the night, she woke up with severe pain in her shoulder and arm. "Why didn't I ask Wayne and June to pray for healing for me?" she sighed. Then Kathy sensed the Holy Spirit speaking to her, "Why do you need Wayne and June? I am right here."

I can come to Jesus myself, she realized. So she did. She asked for a miracle of healing for her arm and neck. She asked and believed. "Yes," she reminded herself, "this healing belongs to me because of what Jesus has done at the cross."

The pain instantly disappeared.

Later that day the four of us went on a long walk together. Kathy had no pain. The next morning, still no pain. And on the third day, still no pain. We praised God for his grace.

We have noticed that often it simply doesn't occur to a believer to ask Jesus for healing. Like Kathy, going to doctors and praying for God's help in managing pain comes quite naturally to us. But when we hear accounts of the healing miracles Jesus works today, we begin to wonder and then to hope. Once we realize that it's the Father's will to heal all who come to Jesus, we can, like Kathy, believe we are qualified to receive healing from Jesus; we can respond to the call of the Holy Spirit to come to Jesus as Healer just as we come to him as our Savior.

Follow-up: When Kathy and Jered left Kenya for the United States, Kathy was still free of pain. On November 19, 2023, ten years later, Kathy said she continues to enjoy full pain free mobility in her entire arm and shoulder. Thanks be to God!

Jesus said: "Truly, truly, I say to you, whoever believes in me will also do the works that I do; and greater works than these will he do, because I am going to the Father. Whatever you ask in my name, this I will do, that the Father may be glorified in the Son. If you ask me anything in my name, I will do it."

JOHN 14:12–14 ESV

6

....

Walter

*A note before you read: This story includes details about using Jesus'
authority to cast out demons as part of the counseling and healing process.
Because the devil is very legalistic and claims rights he has been given, we
have found the need to address the footholds demons can claim. Fear and
unforgiveness, for example, are common footholds or rights the demonic
can claim in a person's life. In some cases, unclean spirits can have a role to
play in an illness or injury. When ministering to a person in need of healing,
Jesus wants the whole person well—the spirit, soul and body.*

November 16, 2014
New York, USA

Every two to four years, most missionaries return to their home
country to connect with the churches and people who support them,
speaking at church services and similar events, and raising support. This
is often called "home assignment" in the mission community. While
back in the United States on a home assignment in 2014, June and I were
invited to preach during the morning service at a Reformed Church in
New York, where my older brother pastored at the time. The topic of
our message was *Making Disciples: Jesus the Savior, Healer and Deliverer.*
After the service there was a luncheon which most of the congregation
attended. June and I shared again, going through what we have come to
call a "Scripture/Miracle medley," which is a mix of Scripture passages
and stories of Jesus' miracles, similar to the format of this book.

Several church members talked with us afterwards, processing what they had heard and asking questions. One man, Walter, who was 55 years old and a city building inspector, asked to meet with us for prayer.

Walter had been in an automobile accident a week and a half before; he had been rear-ended and was experiencing a lot of pain in his back, neck and legs. He walked very stiffly and was unable to move his head from side to side with ease. Walter explained that he also had arthritis in his upper neck and spine. He had been homebound since the accident and was taking a lot of pain medication.

Because Walter was determined to attend worship, he hadn't taken any pain meds that morning; he wanted a clear head so that he could drive safely and pay attention during the service. As a result he was now in a lot of pain.

Sitting together in the church sanctuary with Pastor Rich (my brother) and his wife Sharon, June and an elder named Eric, we began with prayer. We didn't know where this time would take us, but we knew that as always we are totally dependent on the Holy Spirit to guide the process. So we asked for his wisdom and clear leading for Walter and each of us seated together. Then we asked Walter to share his story. Walter said he experienced the same symptoms when he hurt his back 20 years ago. He had been doing particularly heavy construction work at that time and one day when he was getting dressed, he suddenly felt as if his back had just snapped.

We found it interesting that Walter's current symptoms were similar to those he experienced 20 years ago, so we asked Walter to say more about what had been happening at the time.

Walter remembered that he had finished a long day at work and was getting dressed after his shower, when he fell to the ground and could not feel or move his legs for at least 30 minutes. After a few hours the feeling in his legs gradually came back. Walter had undergone back surgery following this incident.

When we asked who he felt was responsible for his injured back, Walter replied, "My supervisor at work." He and other construction workers had been pressured to lift and carry heavy loads that were more appropriate for machinery to handle.

Now, 20 years later, Walter was suffering from the same sort of back pain after his recent accident. Walter also told us that he had been rear-ended in a previous auto accident four years earlier.

We discussed forgiveness, and reminded each other of Jesus' words and the importance of it. We asked Walter if he had forgiven the drivers of the other cars. He said that he had not specifically thought about it before. We also asked him if he would be willing to forgive his construction supervisor from 20 years ago. Walter was willing to forgive each person, and stated his forgiveness verbally in prayer to God.

When we asked him if there was anyone else he had not forgiven, he thought of his father.

Walter's father had left his mom when he was young. This was in the 1960s when most other families were intact. Walter related that he had experienced a lot of pain and trauma in his relationship with his dad.

When he was 11 years old, Walter had walked into the room while his dad and brother were talking about a father and son basketball game. When Walter asked his dad, "Who were the dads and sons playing against?" his father laughed at him for not knowing what father and son games were.

This shaming was typical throughout Walter's childhood. The painful question still echoing in his mind was, "How *could* I know these things when my dad wouldn't teach me?"

We asked Walter, "In light of what Jesus has done for each of us, his grace of forgiveness even when we didn't deserve it, would you be willing to forgive your father?" He was. Walter prayed and then forgave his dad. Then we spent some time working to instill in Walter's heart and mind the truth of *God's* father-love for him. Truth like the fact that God the Father sent his Son to rescue Walter from his sin, so he could receive forgiveness and gain eternal life. That is amazing love.

We asked Walter if he had any reason to doubt that Jesus would heal him. "No," he said, "except I don't feel worthy to receive healing from Jesus."

We asked what he meant.

Walter said that feeling unworthy had defined his whole life. It was an especially apt description of his childhood, which had been very tough. His mother regularly told Walter and his brother what a sacrifice it had been to raise them. "I could have had a better life without you," she would say to the two boys. "The reason I have to work so hard to make ends meet is because of you."

He remembered one day in particular when his mother had walked in on their horseplay and said, "I wish you'd never been born."

"She was very tired," Walter explained. "She was working two jobs to make ends meet."

We dealt first with the trauma of his dad leaving his family. We asked Jesus to bring up the time and memory of that early trauma and bring healing to Walter's soul and spirit. We asked Walter, as the child he was at that time, to forgive his dad for leaving and for all the rejection he'd experienced. We asked Jesus to heal all the pain, and in Jesus' authority commanded any demons that might have taken advantage of the trauma to leave.

We did the same with the verbal wounds his mother had inflicted.

Next, we moved to the injury to his back 20 years before. Praying out loud, Walter chose to forgive the supervisor of his construction crew. He also asked Jesus to forgive him for holding on to his anger and failing to forgive as the Lord told us to do (Matthew 6:14–15, 18:21–35). We asked Jesus to heal Walter's soul and spirit and then to bring all the healing forward into the present so that Walter, now in 2014, could be made whole.

From there, we continued on to the time Walter's car had been rear-ended. We asked Jesus to bring to his memory the car accident of four years ago. Walter didn't blame the driver, and in fact, recalled how the driver came up to his car and apologized. Yet, while praying out loud, Walter forgave the driver, and again we asked Jesus to heal all the pain in his soul and spirit as well as in his body. In Jesus' name, we commanded any demons that might have gained a foothold to leave.

Finally, we addressed the most recent car accident. We asked Jesus to heal any and all soul and spirit wounds. We again commanded any demons to leave in Jesus' name. Then we asked Jesus to heal the physical pain in Walter's body. We prayed for complete restoration and health.

Then we asked Walter to stand up. Everyone present laid hands on him and prayed for the various parts of his body that had been injured and were in pain.

After a few minutes, we asked Walter what he was feeling. At first he was quiet. Then he began to test his neck by turning his head side to side very slowly and cautiously. He had been unable to do that a few minutes before. We asked him to walk a bit and test things out.

He said, "My neck feels good; the pain is gone and it's loose."

Although his lower back was a bit better, he still had pain. We laid hands on Walter's lower back. We thanked Jesus for the healing we'd received and asked Jesus to continue and complete it.

After a few minutes we stood back and again asked Walter how he felt. He tried walking again. He began to lift his knees high while he walked, testing and twisting his back from side to side.

"The pain is gone!"

I asked him to see how far he could bend over, to try touching his toes. Walter was hesitant, remembering how much pain and stiffness he had experienced before we prayed. I said, "Just go as far as you are able; stop if you feel any pain."

Walter cautiously bent over more and more until he touched his feet. He straightened up and said, "It's a miracle! The pain is all gone."

We thanked Jesus for his grace.

November 19, 2014 (Three Days Later)

We received this news about Walter in an email from Pastor Rich and his wife Sharon:

"Walter is doing well. He spoke about the time of healing during our consistory meeting last evening. He said he left the sanctuary that afternoon 'feeling like a million dollars.' He called it a miracle. He did some stretches under the hot water in the shower the next morning, which also felt good. Then when he went out into the cold, his neck area tightened up. He's had some minor back pain since, but says he's been reading Scripture even more avidly than before, and staying very close to Jesus, his Healer, and knows that he's continuing to heal."

December 6–7, 2014 (Two Weeks Later)

During a brief visit we made to Rich and Sharon's home, Rich told us that Walter was working again. At one point he'd had some physical therapy and became worse, but he'd bounced back. Rich said Walter was feeling great—about 90% better. Walter has been in God's word daily and is growing in the Lord.

October 3, 2020 (Six Years Later, During Covid)

Pastor Rich and Sharon received an email from Walter (who had moved to Washington state):

"I am doing well. I've been furloughed from my school bus driving job with schools closed.... I have however been quite busy with projects at home. We purchased a camping trailer and needed a space to park it at our house, so I poured a concrete parking pad. Our concrete driveway was broken up so I rented a jackhammer and took out the old driveway and formed and poured a new driveway. I'm currently in the process of building a retaining wall. I guess that's the best way to convey the healing power of God I experienced following the praying over my severe neck and back pain. I am so grateful to Wayne and June for bringing God's healing power to me."

WALTER

57

If you abide in me, and my words abide in you,
ask whatever you wish, and it will be done for you.
By this my Father is glorified, that you bear much
fruit and so prove to be my disciples.

JOHN 15:7–8 ESV

7

....

David

June 2013

Midwest, USA

Whenever we've been on home assignment in the United States, our home base has been a small town in the Midwest. Our son John became best friends with David who lived just a couple blocks away, and who was in the same grade as John in the little Christian school our kids attended there. John and David's friendship deepened when David came to Duma to visit us for a month when both boys were in eighth grade.

The year David and John graduated from college, David brought his wife Connie to Duma for a visit with John. While in Duma they witnessed some healing miracles Jesus was doing in the village and at our home.

At the Wednesday night prayer meeting in the home of our coworker, David told the group that he had followed Jesus for years. Many times he had asked God to guide his doctors and bless the treatments or surgeries, but he had never thought to ask Jesus to heal his knees. After witnessing two healing miracles during the past week, he wanted to come to Jesus and ask for the miraculous healing he needed.

David had injured his knees several times over eight years of playing sports. Five surgeries later, he still suffered from chronic pain, stiffness and weakness. At the end of his junior year in college he injured one of his knees again while playing for his college soccer team. Doctors told David that this latest injury would require another surgery. He decided to delay surgery and spent his senior year sitting on the bench.

I had flown to Nairobi for a board meeting, but June, another nurse on our team, our son John, and David's wife Connie laid hands on David's knees and prayed for healing. In Jesus' name and authority they ordered his knees to be healed. David's legs started to shake. The shaking continued for 10–15 seconds.

The group moved into praying for other people and situations, forgetting to go back and ask David how his knees were doing. Over the next two days, his knees continued to improve.

Two days later I flew back home to our village and greeted David and Connie. David told me about the prayer meeting a few nights before, how the group had prayed for his knees to be healed, and what had happened over the next couple of days. The first morning after the prayer time David woke up feeling less pain and stiffness in his knees. He and Connie prayed throughout the day. Using a phrase sometimes spoken by those in healing ministry, they reminded themselves, "This healing belongs to us because of what Jesus did at the cross."

David told me, "For seven years I had to force myself to get out of bed because my knees hurt so much and were always stiff. After I would get up each morning, my knees would loosen up and become less painful. But this morning when I woke up, my knees had no pain or stiffness whatsoever. And not only that, my knees feel strong."

I said, "Praise God! That's wonderful. Hey, let's play some basketball this afternoon and try those knees out." That afternoon he played basketball without pain and with knees that felt strong.

A few weeks later David and Connie returned to the United States, but they promised to keep in touch. Five weeks after leaving Duma, Connie wrote to tell us that David's knees were still doing well.

May 2014 (One Year Later)

A year after his knees were healed, I asked David if I could share his story when I spoke at churches during our next home assignment in the US. "Praise the Lord, my knees have been great!" David emailed me back. "I praise the Lord every day for that. I would love it for you to share my story."

I included David's story in my speaking plan and, a year after that, shared it with an adult Sunday school class where David's mother was one of the participants. She chimed in after we had finished and told the class that when David came home and shared his story of being healed, she had not initially believed him. She had gone to all the doctor appointments and was with him when he had the various surgeries. Then they went on a family hike. "When I saw David jumping from one boulder to the next, I *knew* his knees were healed."

May 2023 (Nine Years Later)

David and Connie now have four children and are missionaries themselves in Asia. David reports that his knees continue to be strong and well.

*You shall not covet your neighbor's house; you shall
not covet your neighbor's wife, or his male servant,
or his female servant, or his ox, or his donkey, or
anything that is your neighbor's.*

EXODUS 20:17 ESV

*For while we were living in the flesh, our sinful
passions, aroused by the law, were at work in our
members to bear fruit for death. But now we are
released from the law, having died to that which held
us captive, so that we serve in the new way of the
Spirit and not in the old way of the written code.*

*What then shall we say? That the law is sin? By no
means! Yet if it had not been for the law, I would
not have known sin. For I would not have known
what it is to covet if the law had not said, "You
shall not covet." But sin, seizing an opportunity
through the commandment, produced in me all
kinds of covetousness.… So the law is holy, and the
commandment is holy and righteous and good.*

ROMANS 7:5–12 ESV

*There is therefore now no condemnation for those
who are in Christ Jesus. For the law of the Spirit of life
has set you free in Christ Jesus from the law of sin and
death. For God has done what the law, weakened by
the flesh, could not do. By sending his own Son in the
likeness of sinful flesh and for sin, he condemned sin
in the flesh, in order that the righteous requirement
of the law might be fulfilled in us, who walk not
according to the flesh but according to the Spirit.*

ROMANS 8:1–4 ESV

8

....

Samantha

June 2013

Duma, Kenya

After spending several days listening to our stories of people who had been healed through deliverance, Samantha asked for help one evening while we were sitting together in our living room. She told us that she had been struggling with bitterness and covetousness for a long time. When others did well or received nice things, she felt sad, angry, and bitter and often became moody and critical of others. Envy even spoiled the joy of being engaged. When her sister received a larger, more expensive engagement ring than her own, Samantha was consumed with jealousy.

These kinds of situations had put a strain on her relationship with her husband. She also realized that this chronic stronghold in her life affected her relationship with Jesus; it was not as strong and healthy as she wanted it to be.

Along with reading various Scriptures together, we asked the Holy Spirit to reveal the root causes of these problems. Samantha felt convicted both from the Scriptures and from her own heart. She began confessing her sin of not forgiving others and of coveting what other people had.

At first, Samantha struggled with how to pray. She kept saying, "Help me, Lord, to repent for...." We gently paused the prayer and explained that Jesus can always be counted on to help. We saw that Samantha needed to be taught about her own will, as well as how repentance was distinct from confession and forgiveness. Once Samantha understood that she could make a *decision* with her will, she was able to *choose* to turn away from coveting, and to forgive where necessary.

Samantha, her husband Jack, June, our son John and I prayed together. After Samantha led in prayer by forgiving others, she confessed her own sin of having hung onto past hurts, rather than forgiving at the time of the hurt, or as Ephesians 4:26 says, "before the sun went down on her anger." She repented and thanked Jesus for his forgiveness. I introduced the possibility that some unclean spirit or spirits may have gained entry into her life due to her previously unrepented sin. Now that Samantha had broken those past footholds, I asked her for permission to explore the possibility of driving any such spirits out with Jesus' authority, and she agreed.

I looked straight at Samantha and said, "In the name and authority of Jesus Christ of Nazareth, I command the spirit of covetousness to leave and not come back. Your rights have been removed by Samantha's confession, repentance and Jesus' forgiveness. Go now to the place Jesus Christ sends you. You must go now!" I repeated this same process for the other unclean spirits of greed, unforgiveness and anger.

Samantha described the sensations she felt as the spirits began to move. One by one the spirits left through her arms, fingertips, legs and toes, and from her head.

After we were done, Samantha said she felt light and free.

Follow Up

Below are excerpts from an email we received from Samantha some weeks later, after her return to the United States.

"Hello! It was great to hear from you guys…! Sorry it took a couple days for this reply.... We have been hanging out with family all weekend. We have had a blast explaining our trip to everyone here! They all can see how much the trip has influenced us and how much the people of Duma have made a way into our hearts! We want you to know that we have been very intentional about sharing with our families what God has taught us in Duma."

Samantha went on to recount their experiences of praying for healing for others and driving out demons since returning to the United States. Then she continued, "It was also very awesome to talk to my siblings about my deliverance from the devil's footholds. I could tell that they were all in agreement that I had been held captive by the sins we had discussed.... Jack and I also talked to them about how they can't just follow a religion, but they need to follow Jesus. We encouraged them to walk passionately with Jesus and choose to live for him daily! I also asked my parents for forgiveness.... My dad said he was proud of me and is rejoicing that my walk with Jesus has grown so much.... My parents were very supportive! We have a renewed relationship as a family, and I am so thankful for the healing power of Jesus! I have so much freedom and excitement for God's word and what he wants to teach me. God has really been so good!"

Samantha then described her own continued efforts to resist Satan's attacks and his efforts to tempt her to covet again. She wrote: "I repeat, 'I have learned to be content whatever the circumstance' over and over again. God is on my side and I have been fighting with my sword and belt of truth as best as I can.... Praise God!"

In another email, dated July 7, 2013, Samantha wrote: "I want to add that Jesus has renewed and healed my heart...! I truly believe Jesus has freed me! Praise God for his love and grace! Also, I have been having a lot of amazing conversations with friends about the need for forgiveness. The Live Dead Journal (a collection of articles by people who have lived and worked in challenging places) talks about forgiveness and how, in order to forgive, we have to surrender our right to feel hurt/oppressed/rejected and hand it over to God. We have discussed how forgiveness is a lifelong process of handing over the hurt and letting God heal us. YAY JESUS for being so real and alive in our daily lives :)"

Now there was in Joppa a disciple named Tabitha, which, translated, means Dorcas. She was full of good works and acts of charity. In those days she became ill and died, and when they had washed her, they laid her in an upper room. Since Lydda was near Joppa, the disciples, hearing that Peter was there, sent two men to him, urging him, "Please come to us without delay."

So Peter rose and went with them. And when he arrived, they took him to the upper room. All the widows stood beside him weeping and showing tunics and other garments that Dorcas made while she was with them. But Peter put them all outside and knelt down and prayed; and turning to the body he said, "Tabitha, arise."

And she opened her eyes, and when she saw Peter she sat up. And he gave her his hand and raised her up. Then, calling the saints and widows, he presented her alive. And it became known throughout all Joppa, and many believed in the Lord.

ACTS 9:36–42 ESV

9

....

Baati

December 7, 2018

Duma, Kenya

December is one of our rainy seasons in Eastern Kenya and there had been a heavy rain that afternoon. We were winding down and taking showers toward the end of the afternoon when we began to hear sounds of wailing coming from the village; they sounded like mourning cries, like someone had died. More and more voices kept joining in, adding their own anguished cries.

Eventually, through the wailing, we heard the noise of several motorcycle engines coming down our driveway. Just finished with her shower and dressed in a clean dress, June grabbed her *hagodo* scarf, the traditional head covering all women wear in public, and began to tie it back on. I reversed course from entering the shower and quickly redressed into my dirty clothes and walked out into our living room without shoes. Through our screened open windows, I saw our good friend Gana pulling up on one of the motorbikes holding a toddler in his arms, limp. *"Nu karkarā!"* he cried out, "Help us!" As they pulled up, the men on the other motorcycles called out that the little girl had drowned.

Still tying on her *hagodo*, June ran out the door and met Gana in the driveway as he climbed off the motorbike. *"Armā çisisā!"* "Lay her here," June said, directing him to lay the girl's body in the wet sand right there. The child was Baati, the only daughter of Moti and Obo, a young couple who lived near the village center.

Later more details emerged as people pieced together what had happened. That afternoon, after the rain and while her mother was away collecting firewood, the girl had been playing in an ankle-deep muddy water puddle with a four-year-old neighbor boy. No one had noticed when the two children wandered away from the first puddle. Nearby, surrounded by some short thorn bushes hindering visibility, was a deeper muddy water hole that had been dug out a few months before when a neighbor was building a new mud house. It had also filled with water in the rain and when Baati stepped in she went right under.

Not realizing she was in trouble, the little boy she was with sat down next to the pool of muddy water and waited. Several minutes passed, and eventually an older neighbor child walked by and saw a small part of a body visible just above the water. She ran home to tell her mother, who rushed to the muddy water hole and pulled Baati out. Seeing that the little girl was not breathing, she left the body, and ran back to the nearby homes wailing, "The girl is dead, the little girl is dead!" Hearing the outcry, women from all the nearby homes rushed out of their huts and gathered around the body, all wailing; these were the cries we had heard. How many minutes had it been since Baati had first fallen into the hole and been submerged in the water? Perhaps 15 minutes by then?

Hagarso, a neighbor and the father of the four-year-old, heard the commotion. He and other village men ran to the scene. Hagarso found his little son sitting next to the water hole, the little girl's body lying beside him. He put his hand on her chest to check for signs of life but could find no sign of breathing or heartbeat. More men arrived and more women began wailing. After several minutes, Gana, one of the neighbors, lifted the little girl upside down by the ankles and some water came out of her nose. Moti, Baati's father, arrived just then; he saw his daughter and became, as his neighbors described him later, entirely *mudamti*, which means shocked and unable to function.

Another neighbor, Abdul, arrived and suggested they bring Baati to our home. "Why? It's too late! She's dead," some replied. This discussion took several more minutes. Everyone at the scene believed the little girl was dead and nothing could be done for her.

Someone suggested they begin organizing to dig a fresh grave. Burials there often happen the same day a person dies. The group spent another several minutes debating this.

After listening to perhaps 15 additional minutes of community deliberation, Gana abruptly took action. Partly just to get away from the wailing chaos and indecision, he scooped Baati up in his arms. Along with Abdul and several other men, he got on one of the newly arrived *pikis* (motorcycles) and traveled the three minutes to our home as fast as they could. As they rode on the rough path, Gana thought he possibly noticed one gasping breath.

Now, June knelt next to Baati and instinctively prayed while also checking her airway; June compressed her chest about five times, hoping to bring the water out. Only a small amount of brown dirty water dribbled out of her nose. Praying softly but out loud for Jesus to protect her and restore her to us, June paused quickly to evaluate the little girl and noticed she had begun taking slow, irregular, loud, gurgling and gasping breaths. She felt for her pulse; her heart was beating. She vomited a small amount of water and June moved her onto her side.

People all around were talking and shouting; many were praying out loud to Allah, asking that he help Baati, and that his will be done. I stayed back on the veranda to give June space to work since she was already surrounded by a crowd of men with many more adding to their number. Baati was breathing a little more regularly now, but she still sounded very gurgly. Her stomach continued to be distended.

Minutes were ticking by. June shouted for me to get the flashlight and her stethoscope from the house. Baati vomited a little more, but she was otherwise totally limp, though she held her jaw rigid. I gave June the flashlight and stethoscope and knelt down beside them. June checked Baati's pupils; they were about 2mm and did not react to the light (very concerning!). Her respiratory rate was now 28 and heart rate 120: these were not bad numbers, considering the trauma she was experiencing. She vomited a small amount a third time.

"She's barely breathing with a lot of gurgling in her lungs," June told me. "Her pupils aren't responding to the flashlight."

With her clothes still wet, I put my hand lightly on little Baati's chest and prayed silently. I struggled at first with what to pray for. Everything was pointing to brain damage if she lived. "Yet, Jesus, you are the God of miracles," I prayed in my heart. "We need a miracle now." Several minutes later, looking directly at Baati, I spoke out loud: "In the name and authority of Jesus Christ, I command all the rest of the water still inside Baati to come out of her." Beside me, June prayed silently along, then asked out loud for God to also protect her brain and heal her of any internal injury. Just seconds later, with my hand still on her, Baati suddenly vomited out a large volume of muddy water. It reminded me of a pressure hose. She opened her eyes for about five seconds, then closed them again. The crowd exclaimed and bustled around us.

Now Baati's breathing eased significantly, but she did not wake up. June checked her eyes again with the flashlight and her pupils still did not react. She began grinding her teeth, a behavior often indicative of brain damage after oxygen deprivation.

Minutes were ticking by. Finally, being allowed by the men, a large group of women, probably around 40, arrived on foot from the village. The men reported that the girl was now breathing on her own, but they warned them not to wail and cause a commotion.

Realizing how wet Baati's clothes were, we peeled them off and wrapped another dry cloth around her that her grandmother, who had just arrived, had brought with her. Baati was still grinding her teeth and her pupils were still not responding when June shined the light into her eyes.

"Let's move her to the picnic table and wrap her even more warmly. She feels cold," June said. Baati's grandmother was kneeling next to us, and she and I lifted Baati's body and carried her to the picnic table. June ran inside to get her iPad to do some research. Baati continued to grind her teeth and was still totally limp. How much time had passed? Too much!

Her breathing was now very quiet and clear. Twice I asked June to double check with the stethoscope to make sure she was still breathing because her chest was hardly moving. Now that she was wrapped up it was also harder to see her breathing. June was reading about how blood sugar can be affected with severe brain damage and sent Abdul to the clinic for her glucometer and a few other supplies.

I continued rubbing Baati's little back and patting her gently, praying silently for a miracle. When Abdul returned from the clinic, June rechecked Baati's pupils and they reacted a bit to the light! When she pricked her finger for a blood specimen, she jerked slightly. Her blood sugar was 9.6—not too abnormally high.

About 15 more minutes had passed since we moved Baati to the picnic table. The crowd of women sat on the concrete veranda floor around the picnic table. Her grandmother sat anxiously on the wooden bench beside her. With my hand still on Baati's back, I spoke out loud and commanded, "In the name and authority of Jesus Christ of Nazareth, Baati, get up." I then reached out to pick Baati up, thinking that I would hold her upright and have her head rest on my shoulder, but as I lifted her, she stood on her own two feet on the table, opened her eyes and looked around at everyone. The crowd collectively gasped. We all knew we were witnessing a miracle. June examined her. Within five minutes Baati seemed totally fine. It was as if she had never drowned or had any trauma.

Baati's grandmother was holding her now, exclaiming her relief over and over again. I asked everyone to be quiet to thank God together. We held out our hands and thanked Jesus for his mercy and this miracle.

As a precaution, June injected Baati with an antibiotic to prevent pneumonia from all the dirty water that had been in her lungs, and we said our goodbyes. Baati's grandmother carried her home. Her parents told us the next day that she got home and went outside to play.

Later I asked Moti, her father, why he had not come to our house when the other men brought Baati's body. Moti said that he had been in shock and thought his only daughter was dead.

June went to the home the next day, to see for herself how Baati was doing. She found her out playing with the neighbor kids. Her grandmother's house was like Grand Central Station, loaded with friends and relatives who had come to see Baati for themselves. June had a great opportunity to recount Jesus' miraculous work, and invited the houseful of women to reconsider and receive the grace of the Gospel of love and power of Jesus for themselves. Everyone listened attentively, but no decisions were reached.

A few days later I interviewed both Abdul and Shoptu (the grandmother) separately. Their accounts follow.

Abdul, the neighbor: "I saw that Baati had drowned, and since she was not breathing, concluded she was dead. They decided to bring the body to Wayne and June's house mainly to get away from all the chaos of the women wailing and crying.

"For about 15 minutes after arriving at Wayne and June's home, Baati was not responding well. Though she vomited a little water three times." Abdul concluded, "I thought that there was not much chance that she would live.

"Then I saw Wayne place his hand on Baati's chest and heard him say, 'In the name of Jesus Christ of Nazareth, I command Baati to vomit all the water from her lungs.' Within seconds Baati suddenly vomited a very large amount of water, which we eventually realized was all the water left in her lungs and stomach.

"I was surprised to see the power of Jesus do that," Abdul said.

Shoptu, the grandmother: "I was sitting a few inches from Baati while she was lying on the picnic table. Baati was just lying there limp, not waking up, and regularly grinding her teeth. After about 15 minutes Wayne, with his hand on Baati, said, 'In the name and authority of Jesus Christ of Nazareth, rise.' Then Wayne picked Baati up and instantly she stood on her own feet, opened her eyes and looked around. We were all in great shock and rejoicing. Jesus saved my granddaughter!"

Three Years Later

Little Baati has grown since the drowning and is a normal, healthy little girl. She now has two other siblings. Recently, while visiting in their home, her father and I reflected on God's grace and we thanked Jesus again, all these years later, for her miracle.

March 3, 2024

I had an opportunity to talk with Baati's father a few days ago. Baati is now in school and at the top of her class. "She is very smart," her father said, with appropriate affection and pride.

There shall not be found among you anyone who burns his son or his daughter as an offering, anyone who practices divination or tells fortunes or interprets omens, or a sorcerer or a charmer or a medium or a necromancer or one who inquires of the dead, for whoever does these things is an abomination to the LORD.

DEUTERONOMY 18:10-12A ESV

For at one time you were darkness, but now you are light in the Lord. Walk as children of light (for the fruit of light is found in all that is good and right and true), and try to discern what is pleasing to the Lord. Take no part in the unfruitful works of darkness, but instead expose them.

EPHESIANS 5:8-11 ESV

10

....

Alia

November 1, 2006

Duma, Kenya

Alia was the eldest daughter of a large family in our community and we hired her to help with housework while June worked in the clinic. We shared *chai* and ate meals together each day. Over the years as she worked in our home, Alia became like family.

We often talked about Jesus with Alia at lunch or in conversation with other guests who visited our home. We talked about Jesus' life on earth, his teaching, miracles and death, and how through dying and coming back to life, he conquered death and now offers new life to anyone who believes and follows him. At the time, Alia's father often listened to Bible tapes on his hand-cranked cassette player and Alia often listened with him.

About eight months into our relationship, June and I both noticed a marked change in Alia's demeanor. Before, she had been quiet and often seemed sad, but recently she seemed much happier, sometimes even exuding joy! We asked her about it and Alia told us that she had run to Jesus as her Savior and asked him to forgive her sin.

We were thrilled with this news. We spent considerable time discipling her over the coming weeks and months. Due to the enormous pressure and persecution a new believer from a Muslim background often faces from family and community, it is very important to teach them the word of God and help them grow in their relationship with Jesus. This all takes time and is, in fact, a lifelong journey. Experience has taught us that many new believers turn back to Islam—some estimate up to 80%.

Because we have been learning that unrepented personal sin, generational sin and severe trauma—before and after conversion—can sometimes result in demonization, June and I met with Alia privately. Over time I have come to understand that demons can have a significant impact in a person's life even when that person believes in Christ. Demons cannot legitimately claim ownership of individuals who belong to Christ, but these people can acquire an unclean spirit when footholds have been established. A believer in Christ who has an unclean spirit, evil spirit or demon, is a person who is *demonized*. The unclean spirit(s) in this case would then be considered an intruder(s). On the other hand, the term *demon possession* refers to those situations when a demon or demons have control over a person and claim to have full rights to a person.

As we read 1 John 4 and 5 together, Alia realized that to have followed Islam was contrary to the word of God. It was sin and rebellion against God. We explained that it was possible that this had created an entry point for an evil spirit or spirits.

Alia understood and confessed to Jesus her sin of following Islam in the past; she repented and promised she would not return to the practices of Islam. Alia claimed Jesus' cleansing blood shed on the cross for her forgiveness. Now having broken any ground unclean spirits could claim, June and I ordered the spirit of Islam to leave Alia.

Alia was surprised to sense a demon beginning to manifest with pain and tingling in the back of her shoulder. As we commanded it to leave, Alia felt it move down her arm and out through her fingers. She kept glancing at her arm as if shocked and trying to figure out what was happening. Once Alia realized the demon had left, she felt better. June and I, however, were quite sure there was more work to be done.

We had become aware of a local custom that often results in demonization. When there is a bright moon during the nights prior to a wedding, unmarried young men and teenage girls from neighboring villages gather to sing and dance far into the night. This seems to begin harmlessly, but during this dance, called *Hinesse,* evil spirits take control of the dancers. In the darkness both the young men and young women allow themselves to become channels for demons and begin exerting extraordinary strength and endurance.

June asked Alia if she had ever participated in *Hinesse*. She had done so only once, she said; then her father prohibited her from doing it again. When we asked her where she thought this kind of dance comes from, she exclaimed that it definitely is not from God, but from the evil one.

Based on Scripture shared with her, Alia confessed her sin of participating in the *Hinesse* dance and repented. We ordered the demons of *Hinesse* to leave. Both of Alia's arms started trembling, one more than the other. With sensations beginning in her shoulder blades, one demon left through her left hand and the other through her right hand; then she felt fine.

We praised God for his deliverance and asked him to anoint Alia afresh with his Holy Spirit.

Alia's joy only increased day by day. Her hunger for God's word and for knowing Jesus also grew.

April 2007 (Six Months Later)

Alia's father and grandfather had arranged a marriage for her with a young Muslim man from a very authoritarian Islamic family. She herself had no say in the matter. The day after her wedding, Alia was given a *hirsi* (a charm made by a witch doctor or religious leader) to wear around her neck. Although the charms are an attempt to protect a person or place from evil influence and harm, the charms can create an opening for demons. Alia's new husband told her that it was a good thing and that she should put it on. Thinking it was simply a gift from her husband, rather like jewelry, she put it on.

We noticed the *hirsi* later while visiting her in her new home. With her husband present we did not have the liberty to address the issue.

On April 19, 2007, Alia had permission from her husband to first come to the clinic and later spend the day at our home. That morning at the clinic June found an unexplained mass in Alia's abdomen. After the clinic work was completed for the day, June and Alia came to the house. Sharing lunch together gave us an opportunity to encourage Alia and continue teaching her from the word of God.

Once I was made aware of the mass found in Alia's abdomen, we joined together in prayer. A manifestation began to be felt in her abdomen and traveled through her leg and then exited out her toes. Then we spent some time praying for Alia's healing. When June checked again, there was no sign of the mass.

While we continued talking together in our living room, we asked Alia if, as was common, she'd been told that her husband has the power to deny heaven to her if she does not please him. Yes, her new husband had told her that.

We explained that her husband has no authority to do such a thing. Jesus is her Savior and what he accomplished by his death on the cross and his resurrection from the dead is all she needs. She is saved by grace.

When we asked if she had shared her faith in Jesus with her husband, we were sad but not surprised to learn that Alia's husband wants nothing to do with Jesus.

We noticed that she wasn't wearing the *hirsi* that we had seen earlier at her home, and asked her about it. She said it was in her house, but she wasn't wearing it anymore because her neck had been achy ever since she first put it on. We discussed the possibility that even having the *hirsi* in her possession could provide a continued opening for evil spirits. We explained what the Bible says about sorcery and helped Alia understand why it's detestable to God. Since the *hirsi* had been a gift from her husband, she didn't want to displease him though she thought he would understand, since it seemed to be causing her neck pain. Alia decided she would burn the *hirsi* privately as soon as she could after she returned home. She prayed out loud, breaking any rights an unclean spirit might claim, by confessing her sin, expressing her repentance, and receiving forgiveness through Jesus' work on the cross.

I commanded any unclean spirit that had claimed a foothold in Alia's life to leave her in Jesus' name. Alia described a manifestation that traveled from her neck, down her left arm and slowly left through her fingers. She also experienced a tingling sensation moving from her stomach and slowly down her left leg. The tingling remained in the ankle until I again ordered the demon to leave. After a minute or so she felt the tingling move through her foot to her toes, lifting away from the tips of her toes.

Alia felt better! The ache in her neck immediately disappeared.

April 27, 2007

I visited Alia a few days later at her home. She told me that the very evening she returned home from visiting us she burned the *hirsi*. I asked her if she sensed any other changes. Alia said that the pain in her neck and her headache were gone from the moment the two demons left. She also told me that prior to the deliverance, her heart always pounded hard. Since that time her heart rate has slowed down and she has peace. We praise God for his goodness and deliverance.

March 6, 2008 (A Year Later)

It is the custom for newlyweds to often live in their own hut on the same home compound of the bride's father's family. This way the daughter's father can keep an eye on his new son-in-law to make sure he treats his daughter well. When the bride is about to deliver her first child or a year has passed, the couple will often move to the husband's father's home compound.

Nomadic lifestyles require families to move from place to place out in the Africa bushlands to find enough grass and water for their animals to survive and reproduce. When water or grass become scarce, families will pack up their simple hut dwellings, load everything on donkeys and head out in search of better water and grazing.

When we returned to Duma after a six-month home assignment, we learned that Alia and her husband had moved away with her husband's nomadic family to look for better grazing land and water for their livestock.

One day I had to pick up a sick woman from a nomadic village way out in the bush that happened to be near Alia's nomadic home. Alia's father traveled with me that day to help me clear any overgrown bush along the way. (We always carry machetes in the truck for this purpose.)

We decided to take advantage of the proximity to visit Alia and her newborn baby boy. After having welcomed us to sit on cow skins on the hard packed dirt floor, Alia immediately went to work stoking her cooking fire back to life. Next, she poured water into her aluminum teapot and grabbed one of the carved wooden milk jugs hanging high in the hut. After adding some fresh milk and tea leaves, she placed the teapot on the fire so that she could serve *chai,* the customary way to make guests feel welcome.

Alia's husband was out herding the cows for the day, but one of her brothers-in-law who lived a few feet away in another hut came in to join us.

While sipping on *chai,* I noticed a charm around the baby's neck and a string tied with a stick around his wrist, and another around Alia's wrist. I asked about these items. Alia knew only that the baby's name was written in the pouch around his little neck. The brother-in-law piped in and said that the purpose of the sticks was to help keep evil spirits away.

I wanted to ask about the *hirsi* but, with all the extended family and neighbors moving in and out of the house, it wasn't the right time for that question.

When a brief opportunity presented itself to speak with Alia alone, I explained that the charm could exert a harmful spiritual influence on the baby and on her family, but then we had to begin our return journey and couldn't delay any longer.

Some weeks later, after returning to Duma from a funeral in another village, we met Alia at her parents' home where she was visiting for a few weeks while her husband went on a journey to sell cattle. We gained permission from her father to have Alia stay with us in our home for three or four days. It was a good time to catch up on each other's lives and find out how Alia was doing.

Alia still seemed unaware of the significance of the items she and the baby wore, but she said her husband had made the charm and tied it on the baby with the small stick that had a tiny hole cut in the center. She continued to wear something similar on her own wrist.

We talked with Alia about our concern that these charms create openings unclean spirits can exploit. Wearing such items could enable the enemy to get a foothold. They are power objects; wearing them is trusting in magic. When Alia seemed unconcerned, we explained that anyone who becomes a child of God through faith in Jesus Christ trusts *Jesus* to be their protector. The use of charms says in essence that we don't trust Jesus to protect us.

Since Alia had experienced several deliverances in the past, we built on her experiences to explain again how evil spirits can gain an entrance, and how a person can become demonized. We read about practices the Lord detests from Deuteronomy 18, and asked Alia what *she* thought about the small stick tied around her wrist.

"It is not of God," she said.

Alia made a decision to repent of this sin. She cut off the object around her wrist and we brought it outside together and threw it into the charcoal cooking fire. She asked Jesus to forgive her and decided she would never put on another charm again. She thanked Jesus for his forgiveness and all he did for us at the cross.

June and I asked Alia for permission to explore whether any demons had taken advantage of the opportunity the charm had presented for them to establish a foothold in her life.

We ordered any evil spirits that were present to leave Alia, stating that her confession, repentance and Jesus' forgiveness had removed any right they had to afflict her. In the name of Jesus Christ of Nazareth, we commanded any demons present to leave and never come back; in Jesus' name we also forbade the demons from entering or influencing her child.

Both Alia's arms tingled like scorpion stings, and she felt the manifestations exiting through her fingertips.

We repeated the command in case there were more demons. Her legs also began to tingle like scorpion stings and the demons moved down her legs and out her toes.

We repeated the command a third time and Alia experienced another demonic manifestation leave through her toes. Then she had a great sense of peace.

Alia said her heart had been heavy, but now it had become very light. Heaviness was replaced by joy. We thanked God for her deliverance.

And now, Lord, look upon their threats and grant to your servants to continue to speak your word with all boldness, while you stretch out your hand to heal, and signs and wonders are performed through the name of your holy servant Jesus.

ACTS 4:29–30 ESV

11

....

Musa

2007

Duma, Kenya

At 12 years of age, Elema and Haroba's son Musa was the primary shepherd for his family's goats and sheep. Every day he took the sheep to find good pasture and water. He protected them from wild animals; he kept them from getting lost. Musa never had time to go to the village school, but he was well-schooled in keeping livestock safe and he knew each sheep and goat by name.

When Musa fell sick with a mysterious disease, shepherding became impossible. In the early stages of his illness his parents brought him to our dispensary. The nurse in charge at the time treated him for Brucellosis and sent him back home to recover. As the illness became more severe, pain prevented him from walking at all, leaving him lying all day in his mother's small grass hut.

About four weeks later, on a busy clinic day when June was treating adults and children with a variety of health issues, she was surprised to see Elema bringing his son Musa to the dispensary in a wheelbarrow. Since Musa had not returned, the clinic staff had assumed he had recovered and was again out with his sheep and goats. After listening to their story and trying to treat Musa again for this mysterious disease, June asked Elema to bring me a note in which she described the situation and suggested that I pray with them.

Elema, a close friend of mine, sat down with me by the workshop. His wife had taken their son back home in the wheelbarrow. We talked together about his son's inability to walk. I listened carefully as he explained all the different ways they had sought help for Musa. This included treatments at the clinic, traditional natural methods, and Islamic leaders "doing religion" on him. Nothing seemed to help; his son was still in pain and unable to walk.

I asked if he and his wife would like to bring their son to Jesus the Messiah for healing. Elema said he would talk it over with Haroba.

The following day Elema told me that he and Haroba had decided to give us permission to pray for their son in Jesus' name. I said that I wanted him to bring his son and his son's mother to our home and we would ask Jesus to heal him. He agreed.

The following day Elema again placed his son in a wheelbarrow and pushed him to our home. I called June to take a break from her clinic work to come and join us. The five of us, with Musa still in the wheelbarrow, found a quiet place in a room of a newly constructed fuel storage building. I explained to Elema and Haroba that the one who was about to heal Musa is Jesus Christ of Nazareth. The one who would heal was not the Jesus taught in Islam, but the Jesus of the Bible who came from heaven, who died on the cross and rose three days later and went back to heaven—the one we are expecting to return someday soon.

I asked, "Do you understand this? I want it to be very clear who is going to do the healing today for your son Musa."

The parents said they understood.

June and I placed our hands on Musa's hip and legs and began to pray. Then, using Jesus' authority, we commanded Musa's legs to be healed and to become well and strong.

We didn't see any immediate change in his condition. We talked for a few more minutes standing around Musa and said our goodbyes. Then Elema pushed his son back home in the wheelbarrow.

The following day, after greeting Elema at our home, I asked how his son was. He said that Musa was back out shepherding the sheep and goats! He had awakened that morning without any pain or weakness and went out to take care of the animals as before.

I said, "Praise God!" and thanked Jesus for his grace. Elema, being a Muslim, found it hard to give credit to Jesus or to acknowledge him as the

Son of God. Islam teaches that Jesus was only a prophet and just a man. Elema couldn't accept or understand that Jesus is one with the Father and the Holy Spirit—the Triune God. At this point Elema was only able to acknowledge that God had healed his son.

Today

Sixteen years have passed. Musa is married now and has started a family. When I visited their home recently, Musa told me that he remembers what Jesus did for him when he was 12 years old and that he wants to learn more about who Jesus is. His father still struggles to understand how within one God there can be three divine Persons, but he has come to acknowledge that it was Jesus who healed his son that day so many years ago.

Come to me, all who labor and are heavy laden, and I will give you rest. Take my yoke upon you, and learn from me, for I am gentle and lowly in heart, and you will find rest for your souls. For my yoke is easy, and my burden is light.

MATTHEW 11:28–30 ESV

12

....

Jered

October 2016

Duma, Kenya

Our friend Jered (who was introduced in chapter five), an 83-year-old longtime supporter of our work, was visiting us along with his wife for three weeks. On Saturday morning, October 24, Jered spent some time with me in the workshop getting ready for the deep well solar pump installation we were going to do the following week in Tula. I had stepped away to help someone when Jered, who was still at the shop, began to have pain in his chest and down his arm. He sat down, sweating and feeling nauseous. Finally, he got up and walked slowly to the house to look for the nitroglycerin pills he always traveled with due to his heart issues. (Jered's first heart attack happened in his late 40s. At that time Jered opted for medication over surgery. Stents and pacemaker came later.)

Jered slipped a pill under his tongue, but it didn't seem to help. He continued to feel miserable. He went to his room to lie down without telling anyone what was going on. Later, still feeling very sick, he got up and went to sit on the couch in the living room.

When I walked into the house sometime later, I saw Jered sitting there. His skin was ashen and he was sweating. He told me what had been happening. We were 260 miles from the nearest hospital emergency room. After a few minutes, I asked, "Jered, would you like to go together to Jesus and pray for your heart?"

With no hesitation Jered agreed.

Since our house is full of women and children from the village most of the day, June and Jered's wife Kathy went with us to our bedroom in the back of our house where it's quieter. I recounted the Good News of Jesus Christ—the Gospel message Jered loves and is so familiar with. I reminded us all that Jesus healed everyone who came to him, and that he accomplished tremendous things through the cross and the resurrection. We remembered together that neither Jesus nor the Gospel message has changed. As Hebrews 13:8 says: "Jesus Christ is the same yesterday and today and forever."

I asked Jered, "If you were in that crowd 2,000 years ago when Jesus was healing everyone, would he heal you too?"

"Yes!" Jered responded.

"Jesus loves you so very much, Jered, and he calls each of us to come with the faith of a child. In Matthew 7:7-11, Jesus said, 'Ask and it will be given to you; seek and you will find, knock and the door will be opened to you. For everyone who asks receives; he who seeks finds; and to him who knocks, the door will be opened. Which of you, if his son asks for bread, will give him a stone? Or if he asks for a fish, will give him a snake? If you, then, though you are evil, know how to give good gifts to your children, how much more will your Father in heaven give good gifts to those who ask him!'"

Then I asked another question. "Jered, is there anyone in your life who has wronged you that you've not forgiven?"

He thought for a moment, and then said that he needed to forgive one of his sons.

Jered and Kathy's firstborn had often been very harsh, and he said that he didn't like his family. He'd made a habit of speaking contemptuously about his whole family. Jered has always loved his son deeply and now realized that he needed to choose to forgive him for the hurtful things he had said about them over the years.

We went to prayer together. Jered painstakingly called to mind each hurtful event and forgave his son for every insult and wound. Jered also asked Jesus to forgive him for holding onto his anger and for withholding forgiveness from his son for so long.

I asked Jered if there was anyone else he needed to forgive. No one came to mind, so June, Kathy and I placed our hands on Jered's chest and shoulders. We thanked Jesus for his grace and salvation. We thanked him for inviting us to come to him all the time. I refreshed and built up our faith by praying several memorized Scripture passages, saying before each, "Jesus, you said…."

"I tell you the truth, anyone who has faith in me will do what I have been doing. He will do even greater things than these, because I am going to the Father. And I will do whatever you ask in my name, so that the Son may bring glory to the Father. You may ask me for anything in my name, and I will do it" (John 14:12–14 NIV).

"He called his twelve disciples to him and gave them authority to drive out evil spirits and to heal every disease and sickness….' As you go, preach this message: "The kingdom of heaven is near." Heal the sick, raise the dead, cleanse those who have leprosy, drive out demons. Freely you have received, freely give'" (Matthew 10:1, 7–8 NIV).

Having been strengthened and encouraged by God's word, with Jesus' name and authority we commanded any spirit of infirmity to leave. We commanded Jered's heart to be well, the pain to be gone and all damage healed.

After waiting several minutes, we said, "Amen," and asked Jered how he felt and if he sensed anything.

He told us he felt much better. He was no longer sweating. His skin color had returned to normal. Though still a bit weak, he said definitively, "I am healed."

After lunch he took a nap. Once he got up, he went to the workshop feeling good.

The next day was Sunday, and all of us rested. On Monday Jered and I traveled to Tula (an hour's drive away) to work on the pump installation for a deep well. We continued that work, going back and forth throughout the week. I regularly checked in with Jered as we worked together to ask how he was feeling.

During the remaining two weeks he spent in Duma, Jered continued to feel fine. June and I traveled back to Nairobi with Jered and Kathy, and some days later they flew back to the United States as originally planned.

What Happened Later:

After Jered and Kathy returned home, we received emails from Kathy over several months telling us about Jered's various visits to his longtime cardiologist. The emails were received according to the dates below:

December 5, 2016

After Jered's first visit to his cardiologist, Kathy wrote: "Doctor's words: 'It sounds like you had a heart attack. What did you do?' Jered: 'We prayed and I was healed.' Dr Davis: 'I can't believe it! Your heart is looking better than I ever saw it. I'm going to order an echocardiogram to see what's going on.' Jered: 'I have been healed, but if you want to, that's fine.' Dr Davis: 'Amazing. In the bush of Africa! Prayer!' The doctor is shaking his head. Jered is feeling better than he has in years. God is good."

January 9, 2017

Kathy sent another update: "We will never forget 2016 with you folks. Just last week the cardiologist affirmed again that Jered did have a heart attack and then he went on to say that we have to prevent another one by getting Jered's blood pressure in the normal range. So twice a day he has to take his blood pressure and record it. It is perfect now that we cut out taco chips and cheese and all the Christmas candy is gone."

January 11, 2017

I emailed back with specific questions and Kathy replied right away.

"Hi Wayne, A few quick answers to your questions. The nuclear stress test has shown Jered's heart to be stronger and in better condition than any past test has. No heart damage from a recent heart attack but no doubt in the cardiologist's mind or in those he consulted that Jered had a heart attack in Duma. Even Jered's experience of feeling it was the last minutes of his life and his concern for me were signs of a person having a heart attack.

"The doctor asked again for the details of how the healing took place. He finally concluded that it was prayer that healed Jered. Not sure the doctor is a believer, but he certainly is giving God the honor for healing Jered's heart; plus the doctor is sharing this with other doctors."

Nine months later another email from Jered and Kathy offered more details. Before their visit to Duma, Jered's heart had been using the pacemaker about 85 percent of the time. Now the pacemaker wasn't being used at all. Dr. Davis had confirmed that Jered's heart was completely healed. Without calling it a miracle, Dr. Davis said only, "It is unexplainable," and that he wishes all of his patients were in Jered's condition. He didn't suggest any restrictions and told Jered, "You not only look like you are in great shape, you are in great shape." Jered and Kathy replied, "To God be the glory."

And God was doing extraordinary miracles by the hands of Paul, so that even handkerchiefs or aprons that had touched his skin were carried away to the sick, and their diseases left them and the evil spirits came out of them.

ACTS 19:11-12 ESV

I write these things to you who believe in the name of the Son of God, that you may know that you have eternal life. And this is the confidence that we have toward him, that if we ask anything according to his will he hears us. And if we know that he hears us in whatever we ask, we know that we have the requests that we have asked of him.

If anyone sees his brother committing a sin not leading to death, he shall ask, and God will give him life—to those who commit sins that do not lead to death. There is sin that leads to death; I do not say that one should pray for that. All wrongdoing is sin, but there is sin that does not lead to death.

We know that everyone who has been born of God does not keep on sinning, but he who was born of God protects him, and the evil one does not touch him.

We know that we are from God, and the whole world lies in the power of the evil one. And we know that the Son of God has come and has given us understanding, so that we may know him who is true; and we are in him who is true, in his Son Jesus Christ. He is the true God and eternal life. Little children, keep yourselves from idols.

1 JOHN 5:13-21 ESV

13

....

Henry
(My Father)

2011

Southern California, USA

Our home assignment in the United States was planned for 2011 and our firstborn daughter, Jane, was getting married in Northern California in early July. My parents planned to drive up for the wedding from their home in Southern California, but a few weeks before the wedding, Dad became ill. Henry is a first-generation immigrant to the US, moving from the Netherlands when he was 15 years old. He married my mom and together they raised a family of six kids. He owned and ran a small auction business. He was 79 years old that summer and had just been persuaded by all of us kids to retire. Just a month before, Dad had sold his trucks and moved into a smaller place with Mom.

It was so rare for Dad to be sick that everyone in the family assumed this was the flu and that he would bounce back as quickly as he always had.

But when it came time to plan for the eight-hour road trip to the wedding, Dad asked to stay home. He was having episodes of diarrhea that made traveling that distance simply too daunting, and he still wasn't feeling well.

After the wedding, June and I went back to the Midwest—our home base while we were on home assignment. From there we traveled around the country to visit the various churches that support us.

The first week of September my sister Lisa called to tell us that Dad was not doing well and that he might have only a few days left to live. We flew into action, rearranging and canceling most of our remaining speaking engagements. We got a flight out the next morning to Southern California, arriving at Dad and Mom's house about 1 pm. Dad was lying in bed, so weak he couldn't lift his head from the pillow.

June and I strongly advocated for bringing Dad to the hospital, but he was adamant: he didn't want to go. He said, "I already tried that; it didn't help."

We continued to press him, reminding him that June, as a medical professional, would know what questions to ask and would understand the doctors' answers. Finally, Dad agreed to go.

We called the ambulance and they arrived in eight minutes. The EMTs lifted Dad from his bed and transported him to the hospital. June and I followed. In the ER Dad was listless and his heart rate fluctuated from very high to concerningly low. Dad was immediately admitted.

After five days, the doctors and staff were able to get most of Dad's organs functioning again (they had been shutting down before he arrived at the hospital). But the doctor told the family that Dad's major issue was cirrhosis of the liver, with the primary symptom of ascites.

The doctors transfused Dad with albumin to help compensate for his diseased liver and performed paracentesis to drain over seven liters of fluid from his abdomen. The doctor warned us that once Dad left the hospital, his health would decline quickly. He would need to be brought to the hospital's outpatient clinic to have his abdomen drained periodically because his liver was no longer able to process the buildup of fluids.

The hospital helped get Dad into a palliative care program and arranged for a hospital bed and oxygen to be delivered. The day after Dad returned home, the hospice/palliative care doctor arrived to make sure Dad had everything he needed. Once she had examined him, she told us he required hospice services. She filled out the necessary paperwork to make this change.

June and I moved in with Dad and Mom so June could take care of Dad. At that time, we were thinking he had only a few days to live before making the transition to heaven and being with his Lord.

Dad had no appetite and slept about 20 hours a day. When he was awake, I would sit beside his bed and read aloud Bible passages about heaven and the promises of God.

After a few days, all 11 of us siblings and spouses gathered at a friend's home to talk about Dad's condition and what each of us could do to contribute to his care in the days that remained. Wanting to say our goodbyes well, we all agreed to visit Dad one-on-one to explore any unfinished business and make sure forgiveness, if needed, was fully and freely given and received.

Dad held his own for about a week, although his increasingly swollen abdomen was making him very uncomfortable. Thankfully, God had already provided the very people who could help get us to the next step.

Our longtime dear friend, Jennifer, who is a head nurse at a local hospital, and her brother, Dr. Mike, had a suggestion: we could ask the hospice doctor to order the insertion of an external drain so that June could drain the abdominal fluids for Dad every day at home. Dad was so weak that he couldn't lift his arms, much less get out of bed; it simply wasn't feasible to try to bring him to the hospital every week for the procedure. The doctor and surgeon would understandably be resistant to our request because of the possibility of being sued should an infection develop, so Jennifer and Dr. Mike suggested we use the phrase "for comfort measures."

Forewarned, we made it clear right away that we wouldn't hold the doctors or hospital liable for any unwelcome outcome and that we were prepared to sign papers to that effect. The next day the hospital gave permission for the procedure.

That hurdle behind us, we faced the next: how would we get Dad out of the house and into our sister Linda's car to bring him to the hospital? Dad himself couldn't help at all; we wanted to be careful not to injure him in any way.

We're not sure who came up with the idea, but we called the fire department. Could they help us? They were happy to help and came right over with sirens and lights blaring—both a fire engine and a smaller fire department vehicle. The paramedics scooped Dad out of bed and into

Linda's car and offered to come back later to do it again in reverse. We were so grateful for their cheerful and spirited assistance.

At the hospital a full seven liters of fluid were drawn from Dad's abdomen and the external drain was inserted. The technicians trained June and sent us home with two cases of the one-liter glass vacuum bottles.

Once again Dad was holding his own. Every day after breakfast, like clockwork, June would drain at least 1100 cc's (1.16 US quarts) from Dad's abdomen through the external drain. The regular draining of the fluid clearly made Dad more comfortable.

Dr. Mike wanted us to be prepared for some of the more difficult things we could expect as Dad neared the end. He explained that liver patients often vomit blood just before death. This is especially common in patients experiencing ascites. He suggested we keep some dark colored towels at hand.

Whenever Dad was awake, I sat beside his bed reading to him from the Bible, highlighting passages about heaven. Dad had no appetite, but we continued to encourage him to eat and drink.

About ten days after going on hospice, we woke in the middle of the night to the sound of Dad vomiting. We hurried in and saw that he was covered in blood. We both grabbed towels and tried to catch what we could. I remember thinking, "This is it; Dad is passing away."

But he survived the ordeal. We cleaned him up the best we could and we all went back to sleep.

Dad continued to hold his own. All the while I was aware of the Holy Spirit moving in my heart, encouraging me to talk to my dad. Earlier on, like the rest of my siblings, I had talked to Dad privately asking about the possibility of any lingering issues needing forgiveness between the two of us. Neither of us had been aware of any. But there was one subject God had been prompting me to talk with him about—a subject I found hard to broach. Dad was dying, I reasoned; was it necessary to bring up something that would almost certainly make him feel ashamed and sad?

Sunday evening about 6 pm I stood in the doorway to Dad's room. I saw that he was lying awake in his hospital bed. I asked if I could come in to talk to him.

I said, "Dad, I love you very much and I am so very grateful that God placed me in our family. You've raised us to love God. You and Mom led us to faith in Jesus Christ so that I came to know Jesus as my Savior and Lord when I was only eight. You taught me to work hard and live my life with integrity. I am very grateful that you are my dad."

"There is something the Lord has placed on my heart to talk to you about, Dad," I continued. "It's not easy for me to bring this up. But if you're willing, I would like to talk to you about it."

Dad told me to go ahead, so I continued, "There are three things I want to talk to you about. The first thing I want to do is read a short passage of Scripture and have you listen to it. Then I would like you to share what the Holy Spirit is saying to you."

Dad agreed, so I read the passage and waited.

After a couple of minutes, Dad spoke. He told me that he had sinned.

I responded, "Yes, you have, Dad."

When Dad was in the hospital the first time, the doctor explained to us that Dad's liver had been damaged by his drinking. Dad had become a quiet alcoholic. This news blindsided us; it seemed so unlike Dad. While we were growing up, we'd see Dad have a glass of wine now and then, or an occasional beer, but we had never seen him overindulge.

At this point though, June and I had been living in Africa for 25 years. No wonder we hadn't realized Dad had fallen into this trap.

But there was a way out. I reminded Dad that God's word says that if we confess our sin, the Lord will forgive our sin and cleanse us from all unrighteousness (1 John 1:9). I went on to explain the difference between confession and repentance.

Dad said he was ready to pray.

Dad led in prayer and it was an honor to pray with him. Dad confessed that he had misused alcohol and had dishonored his Lord. He asked Jesus to forgive him. He told Jesus he wouldn't touch another drop of alcohol again as long as he lived.

"Jesus is very pleased that you've come to him," I told Dad. "And he's pleased with your decision."

Then I pressed on to say, "Dad, the second thing I want to talk to you about tonight might be hard for you to understand, but I want to try to explain. The doctors tell us that your liver is so damaged that nothing more can be done for you medically. Given your age and condition there aren't medications or surgeries that can cure your liver. But I wonder if there's been a spiritual component contributing to the damage of your liver."

I was wondering if Dad's hiding his sin had given the devil a foothold in his life and the opportunity to damage his liver. I wondered if an evil spirit might be involved. June and I had seen even believers in Christ need and receive deliverance from demons, so I shared several of these stories with Dad, and then offered to pray for any deliverance Dad might need.

Dad said he didn't understand everything, but he gave me permission to go ahead.

I got up and moved to Dad's side and placed my hand on his abdomen over the liver area. I repeated in prayer Dad's confession of his misuse of alcohol and stated that he had chosen to repent of his sin. I proclaimed that any right or foothold that our enemy the devil had taken because of Dad's hidden sin had been broken by his confession and repentance. I confirmed that Dad had been completely forgiven because of what Jesus accomplished at the cross. Then I commanded all unclean spirits of addiction, alcoholism and infirmity to leave Dad in the name of Jesus Christ and never to return.

After several minutes I said, "Amen," and sat back down.

I asked Dad if he sensed anything going on while we were praying. He said, "I feel so different."

Then I moved on to the third thing I wanted to talk to him about.

I reminded Dad that there was nothing more doctors or medicine could do for his liver and that it looked like he was about to enter heaven. "Heaven's a wonderful place and we are not trying to keep you from going there, Dad," I told him. "With Jesus being our Savior, we will see you someday there when we arrive. But Jesus isn't only our Savior, he's also our Healer. Would you like us to ask Jesus for a miracle? Shall we ask him to heal your liver?"

Dad responded, "Yes, I would like that."

I stood up, placed my hand over his liver area and prayed several passages of Scripture to encourage and build up our faith. Then in Jesus' authority, I commanded Dad's liver to be well and to be healed. After several minutes I said, "Amen."

Dad was very tired. I told him to rest well and said that I would see him in the morning.

The next morning I greeted Dad and asked how he slept. He said he slept great, that he hadn't slept so well for months.

Then he said, "What's for breakfast?"

I was thrilled with such a question after a week of trying to get him to eat anything at all.

"Eggs, fried potatoes and bacon sounds good," Dad said.

"We will make it right up!" I said. Dad ate it all.

When June went in to drain his abdomen, only 450 ccs came out. We immediately realized that was quite a change from the 1100 ccs she'd drained the days before. We decided not to draw any conclusions yet, and June actually wondered if something had gotten plugged up. We would wait to see how much fluid would be drained the next morning.

From this point on, Dad improved daily. Each day less fluid needed to be drained from his abdomen and each day his appetite increased.

After three weeks, Dad removed his oxygen and said, "I don't need this anymore." We began getting Dad out of bed with the hoist that hospice care had provided.

Six weeks after the evening of prayer, Dad was doing so well that we felt some responsibility to consider returning the hospice equipment since we weren't using it. We called the hospice doctor and requested another liver test for Dad.

The doctor responded graciously but denied the request, reminding us that the agreement in hospice care is that no more tests are done. We understood the doctor's position and ended the call simply reiterating that Dad seemed to be doing much better and it appeared there had been a change in the condition of his liver.

A few weeks later, at the two-month mark, the hospice doctor made a house call to see how we were all doing. After examining Dad, the doctor decided another liver test was called for.

The next day one of the hospice nurses came by the house to draw some blood. A few days later we received a phone call from the doctor. She said, "This is very unusual. Your dad's liver has improved greatly. Medically we can't explain it."

June and I shared with her how we had been praying for him. She said, "Praise God. We don't see things like this happen very often."

Dad continued to get stronger. He asked if we could bring him to the church service on Thanksgiving Day. Though he was still weak, we wheeled him into the sanctuary where he received a warm welcome by the surprised congregation. (Not everyone knew about the healing that had taken place.)

A week-and-a-half later, Dad wanted to try walking into the sanctuary with a walker. We stood one on each side to support him. Each week he grew stronger. The following Sunday he used the walker all on his own. Soon he needed only a cane.

After three months Dad was doing so well that the family released us to return to Kenya. After four months the external tube was removed. Since then Dad has been living with a healed liver. He's returned to driving and to normal life activities.

2015

About four years after Jesus healed Dad's liver and at a time when he'd been doing well, June and I received a message from our family in the United States: Dad had collapsed in the house and had been unable to get up. He'd been taken to the hospital by ambulance. One side of his body was paralyzed and he was unable to talk.

The diagnosis was an intermediate severe stroke. Given his age, he was not expected to walk again. The doctors said Dad would likely be bedridden and need 24-hour care the rest of his life. Dad's health insurance would pay for three weeks of physical therapy; doctors recommended he be transferred to a hospital that would focus on rehabilitation.

The rest of the family had begun discussing how to manage Dad's care once he returned home. Living halfway around the globe in Kenya, we had to travel first to the capital city and then on toward our children's school where internet access made it possible for us to call.

On Monday evening we were able to connect by FaceTime with

my older sister, Linda. Dad had just settled into his new bed at the rehabilitation hospital and Linda was there with him. We could see and speak with Linda and Dad together through our phones.

We asked Dad to tell us what had happened. Because his tongue felt thick and heavy, speaking required a lot of effort for Dad; Linda filled in the gaps to help us understand what he was trying to say.

After hearing his story, I asked, "Dad, do you remember what Jesus did for you when he healed your liver? Would you like to ask him for another miracle to heal you from the effects of your stroke?"

Dad responded immediately with a strong "yes."

Because unforgiveness sometimes blocks healing, I asked Dad if there was anyone he had not forgiven. He responded, "Nothing comes to mind."

I reminded Dad that Jesus gave us, his disciples, power and authority to heal the sick, raise the dead, cleanse those with leprosy and drive out demons as we boldly proclaim the Gospel. I shared other Scripture passages as well.

Linda was standing beside Dad's bed; I asked her to place her hand on his head. From thousands of miles away, I asked Jesus, who was present with each of us, to extend his hand once again and do another miracle, to take all the trauma of the stroke from Dad and heal him. Then I said, "In the name and authority of Jesus Christ of Nazareth, I command all the trauma to leave, all the internal bleeding in Dad's head to stop, and all the brain tissue and blood vessels to be healed. If any unclean spirits took advantage of this trauma, in Jesus' name I command them to leave. In Jesus' name I command Dad's body to be strong and restored."

We waited with Linda's hand on Dad's head for a while, and then I said, "Amen."

Each day Linda sent us a report on Dad's status and each day he improved. The side of his body affected by the stroke got stronger; more movement was restored hour by hour.

To the amazement of the hospital staff Dad walked out of the hospital five days after arriving. There was no evidence that he'd had a stroke.

The next day Linda took Dad out on the road to see how he would do driving. He did well; she concluded he could safely drive on his own.

The following week Dad had an appointment with his family doctor.

The doctor was amazed at Dad's recovery. He said that he doesn't normally see patients Dad's age fully recover from strokes as severe as the one he suffered.

Some weeks later I asked my sister Linda when she had first detected improvement in Dad's condition. After thinking a moment, Linda said improvement had begun right after we had prayed together over FaceTime that Monday. The first thing she noticed after we hung up was that Dad's speech wasn't slurred anymore. Then there was one improvement after another over the next few days. The medical staff were amazed; every time they examined him or did any physical therapy with him he was able to do something more.

Once again God's grace and power had been poured out upon Dad. Praise be to the Lord God Almighty—Father, Son and Holy Spirit!

Update (October 14, 2020)

Dad is now 88 years old. He has slowed down a lot, but he's still driving and doing all the cooking for himself and Mom. During our various visits, I've asked Dad how he's doing in keeping his repentance. His answers are consistent: he expresses his gratitude to June for taking care of him during his illness and to God for all he has graciously done for him. He also says that he has not touched a drop of alcohol nor has he had any desire for it since that day we prayed together. God had healed him physically as well as spiritually. His hunger for the word of God has increased and he is steadily abiding in Jesus.

All glory to God!

HENRY

And he called to him his twelve disciples and gave them authority over unclean spirits, to cast them out, and to heal every disease and every affliction.

MATTHEW 10:1 ESV

And proclaim as you go, saying, "The kingdom of heaven is at hand." Heal the sick, raise the dead, cleanse lepers, cast out demons. You received without paying; give without pay.

MATTHEW 10:7–8 ESV

14

....

Jarso

March 20, 2013

Duma, Kenya

Several of our team members had been fasting and praying for a few days. We were asking the Lord for clarity while working on translating portions of the Bible into the local language. After several days of sitting and working, I felt the need to stretch my legs while visiting some of our neighbors. I walked to the main village center to visit whoever I could find, and I prayed specifically for the Holy Spirit to lead me wherever he wanted me to go.

As I passed the home of our neighbor Jarso, I saw his wife sitting outside in the shade of the house. I greeted her from a distance, asking if her husband was at home. To my surprise, she answered yes, her husband was in the house. So I went in to greet him.

When I entered the dimly lit mud and stick hut with its grass roof, I was shocked to see that Jarso's head was swollen to the point of extreme disfigurement. I greeted him, but he could only respond with a grunt. I blurted out, "What happened to you?" Jarso said he had a bad tooth.

Jarso was sitting on a goat skin spread on the dirt floor. As I sat on a short handmade wooden stool across from him, I saw that one side of his face was quite alarmingly disfigured by the severe swelling caused by his abscessed tooth. Jarso's head drooped in misery as beads of sweat continued to form and drip like rain from his freshly shaven head.

I asked how long he had been suffering from the bad tooth. Barely able to move his swollen lips he mumbled, "Five days and I have not been able to eat or sleep because of feeling miserable the whole time."

I asked, "What treatments have you sought to get help?"

Jarso related how he had gone to our medical clinic three times and received three injections. He also had beside him some traditional medicine of boiled tree bark to help with the pain. But nothing had helped. He continued to get worse as the days went by.

For about 10 minutes I sat quietly observing and praying in my heart. I was asking Jesus what he wanted me to do.

I had been learning a lot at that time about how Jesus had given his authority and power to his disciples and commissioned them to heal the sick while boldly proclaiming the kingdom of God.

Although I'd shared the Good News of Jesus and the kingdom of God with Jarso many times, he had never chosen to follow Jesus. In the last few years he had become less and less willing to listen to the Gospel. He had even gotten rid of his Bible. June and I had continued to pray for him, asking God to change his heart.

Finally, I spoke up. "Jarso, I know someone who will heal you."

He raised his head to look at me and asked, "Who?"

"It is Jesus Christ of Nazareth, the one you've heard so much about and who you have rejected up till now. If you want me to, I would be happy to ask him to heal you."

Jarso didn't answer; he sat there on the goatskin thinking. It was clear there was a battle going on within him. Finally, he mumbled, "You can pray."

"I'm not the one who can heal you; it's Jesus of Nazareth, the one you have rejected as Savior," I told him. "I want no confusion; I will not just be praying to 'God'—it is Jesus Christ of Nazareth who is going to heal you—the One who came from heaven, died on the cross and has risen from the dead. Do you understand this?"

Jarso acknowledged that he did.

I got off my stool and knelt down on one knee right beside Jarso. I placed my hand on my friend's swollen and sweaty cheek. I asked God to reveal his love and grace to Jarso and to confirm the message of the Gospel to him. I prayed several Scripture passages out loud—particularly passages that contained Jesus' words, including what Jesus commanded us, his disciples, to do. Then, in the name and authority of Jesus Christ of Nazareth, I commanded the abscessed tooth to be healed and the pain to leave. I waited there with my hand on my neighbor's cheek for about three minutes. Finally, I said, "Amen." Then I sat back down and waited and watched. Neither of us spoke.

After a few minutes, I asked him how he felt.

With his head still bowed, Jarso began to slowly move his jaw from side to side; he opened and closed his mouth to see if there was any pain. He also gently probed his swollen face with two of his fingers.

Then I noticed he wasn't sweating anymore.

"Look at me," I said.

He turned his head toward me and right before my eyes the swelling was going down! In just seconds, it was reduced by half. I pointed at his face and blurted out, "Look what Jesus is doing for you!"

Jarso visibly relaxed. "How are you feeling?" I asked again.

Then Jarso spoke. He said he was better. He continued to test his mouth and jaw, moving it all around, searching for the pain. The pain was gone.

Over the next fifteen minutes, I told him again of God's love for him, and of God's grace. "Jesus wants to do much more than heal your jaw," I told him. "He wants to heal all of you, inside and out, through his death and resurrection. He wants to take away your debt of sin."

I asked again how his mouth felt. He said there was still a little pain in one spot just under his nose, but he was much better. I stood up and went to him a second time, touching that spot. I thanked Jesus for the healing he'd extended so far and asked Jesus to complete the healing. Then I sat back down again.

After another minute of feeling around his mouth with his fingers, Jarso said, "It is very well. The pain is gone."

I walked home deeply grateful to be an instrument for Jesus' healing power. I want more for my neighbors here! Please pray for this neighbor who has resisted coming to Jesus for such a long time. Pray that Jesus will continue to show Jarso his love and speak to him in a powerful way. We yearn for him and his family to share in our inheritance in the kingdom of God.

After this the Lord appointed seventy-two others and sent them on ahead of him, two by two, into every town and place where he himself was about to go. And he said to them, "The harvest is plentiful, but the laborers are few. Therefore pray earnestly to the Lord of the harvest to send out laborers into his harvest. Go your way; behold, I am sending you out as lambs in the midst of wolves. Carry no moneybag, no knapsack, no sandals, and greet no one on the road. Whatever house you enter, first say, 'Peace be to this house!' And if a son of peace is there, your peace will rest upon him. But if not, it will return to you. And remain in the same house, eating and drinking what they provide, for the laborer deserves his wages. Do not go from house to house. Whenever you enter a town and they receive you, eat what is set before you. Heal the sick in it and say to them, 'The kingdom of God has come near to you.'"

LUKE 10:1–9 ESV

15

....

Uren

April 1, 2013

Duma, Kenya

The day after Easter, June and I hopped on our motorcycle to go and visit some distant Amaro villages. That morning we prayed that God would lead us to a "man of peace" who would be willing to gather family members and neighbors to hear the word of God on a weekly basis. Because the Amaro people follow Islam, persecution must be expected when anyone agrees to study the Bible. The "man of peace" would need courage. We also asked God to stretch out his hand to heal and perform miraculous signs and wonders in the name of Jesus—confirming the message.

Our first stop was at a prominent elder's home. We found him in his small cramped hut carving wooden milk jugs, which he sells to the neighbors or gives away to members of his own family. After catching up with the local news, we spent nearly two hours sharing the Gospel. It was a leisurely visit complete with steaming cups of particularly delicious and milky sweet *chai*. After the *chai* was finished, June went out to join a group of women and children under a shade tree.

Just as I was about to find June, intending to move on to the next village, and disappointed that we hadn't received an invitation to return for further weekly Bible studies, the elder said, "I hurt my back last week. It's really painful, and it keeps getting worse instead of getting better."

I responded, "Uren, I know someone who will heal you."

He looked at me and asked, "Who?"

"It is Jesus the Messiah, the one we've been talking about for the last couple of hours. If you want me to, I would be happy to ask Jesus to heal your back." Uren agreed.

Before beginning to pray, I called June to join us back inside the hut. Then I clarified that the one who was going to heal him is Jesus Christ of Nazareth who came from heaven, who died on the cross and rose from the dead three days later. I wanted to make sure he understood that this is not the Jesus he'd heard about from the Qur'an, but the Jesus spoken about in the New Testament.

Uren said he understood.

We asked Uren to lie on his stomach on the mat, while June and I placed our hands on his back. After praying with Jesus' authority and waiting on the Lord for a few minutes, I said, "Amen," and asked Uren how his back felt. He just lay there not moving and looking so relaxed we wondered if he had fallen asleep, so I asked again.

Uren sat up and moved and twisted around, testing his back. Then he declared with a big smile, "All my pain is gone!"

We thanked Jesus together and Uren invited me to return on Monday evening to share with his whole family and his neighbors from the word of God about who this Jesus is.

Put on then, as God's chosen ones, holy and beloved, compassionate hearts, kindness, humility, meekness, and patience, bearing with one another and, if one has a complaint against another, forgiving each other; as the Lord has forgiven you, so you also must forgive.

COLOSSIANS 3:12–13 ESV

And he told them a parable to the effect that they ought always to pray and not lose heart. He said, "In a certain city there was a judge who neither feared God nor respected man. And there was a widow in that city who kept coming to him and saying, 'Give me justice against my adversary.'

For a while he refused, but afterward he said to himself, 'Though I neither fear God nor respect man, yet because this widow keeps bothering me, I will give her justice, so that she will not beat me down by her continual coming.'"

And the Lord said, "Hear what the unrighteous judge says. And will not God give justice to his elect, who cry to him day and night? Will he delay long over them? I tell you, he will give justice to them speedily. Nevertheless, when the Son of Man comes, will he find faith on earth?"

LUKE 18:1–8 ESV

16

....

Anne

Anne's Story of Healing
as told by Anne herself

August 2017–May 2018
In the USA

One day in August of 2017, I stood up from gardening and noticed that the tractor across the street looked blurry, although the trees surrounding the tractor were clear. Being a health care professional, I realized this wasn't normal and was concerned. I suspected this might be the beginning stages of macular degeneration.

Over the next few days I noticed a pattern: every time I bent my head forward and then looked up, the center of my visual field was blurry and my peripheral vision clear. The blurriness went away after a few hours if I kept my head upright. I made an appointment for my first eye exam.

The eye exam in October went well. I didn't have macular degeneration. The ophthalmologist found nothing wrong with my vision, but he was concerned about my symptoms and sent me to my primary physician. He recommended I have my neck checked to see if the blood flow was being occluded when I bent my head forward.

In December I had an ultrasound of my neck and in February a CAT scan of my brain. Both tests came back negative. But the blurriness in the center of my vision was increasing and lasting most of the day. I was able to do normal daily activities, but reading was increasingly difficult.

It was my daughter who prompted me to make these and subsequent appointments. I shared what was happening with my entire family; we were all praying for answers and for healing.

In March of 2018 Wayne Edwards came to visit, staying in our home. I shared my need for healing for my eyes. Wayne and my husband and I spent the evening in prayer, asking the Holy Spirit to reveal any sin in my life that I needed to confess, any people I needed to ask for forgiveness from and anyone I needed to forgive. The Holy Spirit graciously did so.

Wayne had been teaching us that the consequences of generational sin can be passed from one generation to another, if not addressed. The Holy Spirit alerted me to unresolved issues with my second pregnancy. Although I'd wanted more children 'someday,' when I discovered I was pregnant with our second child, I felt it was too soon.

Reflecting on my relationship with my now grown second born daughter, I started to wonder if already in the womb an ungodly soul tie* had developed. Once she was born, I loved her dearly. But I wondered if the severe baby colic and the stomach issues she suffered later had any connection to my difficulty welcoming her conception. Had she been exposed to a spirit of rejection and a spirit of infirmity in the womb?

I asked God to forgive me and decided I would talk with my daughter and ask her forgiveness, too. Then we all prayed for Jesus Christ of Nazareth to heal my eyes. Wayne prayed several times for healing without my experiencing any noticeable change. The next day Wayne again prayed for my eyes to be healed and we all joined him. Again, there was no change that I could tell.

Wayne and my husband went outside for a few hours. In the time they were away, it seemed to me that my left eye was healed. I tested it over and over again. But when they returned I was hesitant to say anything; it seemed too good to be true. Of course, I did tell them. We were all so excited. A miracle of healing! We praised the Lord.

There had been no change in my right eye, so we all prayed again, but the vision in the center of my right eye remained blurry. When Wayne left later that day, he reminded us to persevere and continue to ask God for complete healing in my right eye.

Some time later I was able to travel to meet with my daughter. I shared

---

* see page 117 for explanation of soul ties

everything God had put on my heart, telling her how much I love her and asking her forgiveness. We both experienced inner healing—which was so important for us and which surely helped clear the way for the Lord to accomplish even more healing going forward.

In April both Wayne and June came for a short visit. Once again we spent an evening in prayer, and once again the Holy Spirit revealed things from the past I needed to deal with. I confessed my sin and noted people I needed to forgive and those I needed to ask to forgive me.

Wayne, June, my husband and I again asked Jesus Christ to heal my right eye. There was no change. We prayed several times. We prayed repeatedly again the next morning before Wayne and June left, but I experienced no immediate change. Thankfully my left eye continued to be clear. Wayne and June encouraged us to continue praying for healing for my right eye.

My primary physician suggested I get a second opinion from a retina specialist. As I waited for my appointment, Satan tempted me to doubt that my left eye had actually been blurry as well.

On May 11, 2018 I saw the retina specialist who diagnosed what was wrong with my eyesight. It's a condition called vitreofoveal traction. The vitreous fluid in my eye is more viscous (thicker) than normal and it was pulling on my retina. This condition afflicts only five percent of the population.

The specialist described several treatment options. The least invasive was an injection into my eye with a drug to thin the fluid and hopefully release the traction. The second option was surgery with a scalpel through the white of my eye to cut the traction on my retina. The third was to do nothing, but since my traction was already quite severe, this was risky. If it became worse my retina would detach and I would have a black hole in my visual field.

The doctor recommended the injection option but suggested I find a retina specialist with more experience. He also confirmed that my left eye had indeed had the same condition but the traction had released on its own.

I was thrilled to hear that. Now I knew without a doubt that my left eye had been healed by Jesus Christ in March. I was so overcome with gratitude for this certainty about the earlier healing miracle that it didn't occur to me to seize the opportunity to tell the doctor about it before he had left the room. Later I was really upset with myself! I wished I'd spoken up so that Jesus would get glory and honor for what he had done for me.

On my way home I called my daughter to share what I had learned from this retina specialist. She encouraged me to contact her husband's aunt who seemed to be having a similar issue with her eye. When I called her it did seem that our eye issues were similar. I told her about the miraculous healing I'd received from Jesus for my left eye. She told me that she was seeing a retina specialist five hours away and receiving eye injections; her physician now recommended that she see his partner who was traveling to our town once a week.

She gave me the doctor's number and I called for an appointment right away. God was opening doors for me, confirming that he is in control of all the details.

My daughter called shortly afterward to let me know that her husband's aunt had started asking questions. She was wondering if Jesus really could heal someone miraculously. And so the door opened for sharing what Jesus Christ can do! Praise the Lord!

Two weeks later I had the appointment with the traveling retina specialist. My husband and I had been praying consistently for healing for my right eye. The day before the appointment I told my husband that I was quite sure my right eye had been healed.

I decided to keep the appointment just to be certain. The physician asked me if I had banged my head against a wall to detach the fluid. I replied that I had done just the opposite and had kept my head very still for fear of detaching my retina. He then told me it was my lucky day: the fluid in my right eye had detached from my retina and my vision was clear! The doctor said that with the severity of the traction I had, it was rare for detachment to occur spontaneously. I immediately told him that Jesus Christ had healed my eyes—through prayer! He said, "Chalk one up for prayer!"

Both of my eyes are clear now with no blurriness! I'm overwhelmed with gratitude for God's grace, forgiveness, and miraculous healing— for *me!*

And since then? On December 12, 2020, in an email to Wayne and June, Anne reported that her eyes continue to be well and her healing has lasted. On December 6, 2022, Wayne and June received another email from Anne. Her eyes were still doing great. Thanks be to God!

---

* *The author understands the soul to consist of the mind, emotions and will. Soul ties are mental, emotional and volitional (i.e. decision-based) bonds that occur between two or more people. Soul ties may be godly or ungodly.*

*An example of a **godly soul tie** would be when a mother completely accepts and loves her child, and a healthy bond is established already in the womb. Another example would be the healthy soul bond that can develop between a husband and wife within a pure sexual relationship before and during their marriage.*

***Ungodly soul ties** occur when sinful behaviors and patterns create an ungodly bond between two or more people. For example, this can happen when a child senses, possibly already in the womb, that she or he is unwanted by the mother or father. An ungodly soul tie can also occur when there has been a sexual relationship outside of marriage, even with a couple that later married. In this instance it's possible for a couple to have both a godly and ungodly soul tie.*

Truly, truly, I say to you, whoever believes in me will also do the works that I do; and greater works than these will he do, because I am going to the Father. Whatever you ask in my name, this I will do, that the Father may be glorified in the Son. If you ask me anything in my name, I will do it.

JOHN 14:12–14 ESV

17

....

June

May 1, 2014

Duma, Kenya

June had taken the clinic pressure cooker sterilizer off the charcoal fire. As she carried it into the house, the lid toppled off. Steam and the hot lid burned her arm in two places. The burns—one about two inches by four inches and the other about a square inch—were very painful.

After enduring the pain for two hours, June asked our visitor Bineso and me to pray for her. I reminded us all of the Gospel and the Good News that Jesus is our healer. Then I carefully placed my fingers around the burns and prayed. In Jesus' name I commanded the pain to stop and the burns to heal.

After a few minutes we asked June what she was feeling. June said that at first her arm had been tingling and hurting more, but then it felt a bit better, and then she felt the pain lift off and leave her.

Twenty minutes later June said the pain was completely gone. The pain never returned, even though the blisters and darkened area of skin remained. The skin healed gradually over the next few weeks.

And my message and my preaching were not in persuasive words of wisdom, but in demonstration of the Spirit and of power, so that your faith would not rest on the wisdom of mankind, but on the power of God.

1 CORINTHIANS 2:4–5 NASB

18

....

Dido

June 2013

Duma, Kenya

Dido, one of our night watchmen, had been complaining of stomach problems, poor appetite and burning in his esophagus for some time. We encouraged him to go to the dispensary for treatment.

June was on duty in the dispensary when Dido arrived. It had been a very busy day seeing patients. June examined him and treated him for an ulcer.

The next morning while June was in her quiet time with the Lord, she sensed the Holy Spirit showing her that despite the dispensary being so busy, she should have taken time to pray with three specific patients, one of whom was Dido.

It was 6:15 am. Dido was still on duty, but he would be going home at 7 am. June wanted to respond in obedience right away so she left the house to find him.

June explained to Dido that because she had been so busy the day before she hadn't taken the time to pray with him for healing, but that God had told her that morning to come out to pray for him. Dido had started the medication the afternoon before, but he was still having the same symptoms; he agreed to allow June to pray.

June began praying by expressing her trust in Jesus the Messiah—the Jesus who the *Injil* (the Gospels) tells us came from heaven and died on the cross to pay the penalty for our sin and to provide healing for our bodies, spirits and souls.

"Jesus, you have all power and authority over our enemy, the devil," June prayed. "You rose from the dead, crushing his head!"

June thanked Jesus for sharing his authority to heal with his disciples, including June herself. "So," she prayed, "this healing is in the name of Jesus, and in the power and authority which Jesus has given me."

Since the other night watchman was observing and listening close by, June felt it was appropriate to ask Dido if she could lay her hand on his upper abdomen. She then told the pain and illness to be gone in Jesus' name and authority. "Be healed!" she said. "Be well because of Jesus' healing grace and because of all Jesus has done on the cross!"

After the prayer Dido jumped on his *piki* to go home, about a three minute ride. We learned later that by the time he arrived at his house all the symptoms were gone and he felt well. He also finished all his medication as was recommended.

Rejoice in the Lord always; again I will say, rejoice. Let your reasonableness be known to everyone. The Lord is at hand; do not be anxious about anything, but in everything by prayer and supplication with thanksgiving let your requests be made known to God. And the peace of God, which surpasses all understanding, will guard your hearts and your minds in Christ Jesus.

PHILIPPIANS 4:4–7 ESV

...for I the LORD your God am a jealous God, visiting the iniquity of the fathers on the children to the third and the fourth generation of those who hate me, but showing steadfast love to thousands of those who love me and keep my commandments.

EXODUS 20:5b–6 ESV

The LORD passed before him and proclaimed, "The LORD, the LORD, a God merciful and gracious, slow to anger, and abounding in steadfast love and faithfulness, keeping steadfast love for thousands, forgiving iniquity and transgression and sin, but who will by no means clear the guilty, visiting the iniquity of the fathers on the children and the children's children, to the third and the fourth generation."

EXODUS 34:6–7 ESV

19

....

Bethany

August 3, 2016

Duma, Kenya

After spending almost a month with us in Duma and hearing stories about people who had been healed, Bethany rather timidly approached June about the possibility of receiving prayer herself. She had been struggling with anxiety-induced panic attacks for two or three years. Chest pain and shortness of breath would come upon her suddenly and without warning. She was chronically anxious about her future, especially about finishing nursing school and about whether she would get married. June encouraged Bethany to talk with me, so that the three of us could talk and pray together. She brought it up at dinner that night.

Bethany shared the details of her struggle. She explained that people on both sides of her family tree—her mother, both grandfathers and some of her aunts and cousins—had struggled with anxiety. Bethany said she had assumed it was quite a normal part of life.

We asked the Holy Spirit for wisdom and began to talk to Bethany about the possibility that one or more members of an earlier generation of her family might have given the demonic an opening in their lives and that this liability may have been passed on to her.

When we asked Bethany if she considered anxiety to be sinful, she thought for a moment and then replied, "I thought it was a sickness."

"What does the Bible call it?" I asked.

We opened our Bibles to Philippians 4:6 and read, "Do not be anxious about anything...."

"If the word of God says not to be anxious about anything but to present everything to God in prayer," I continued, "and we don't obey his command, what are we actually doing?"

We read through several more Scripture passages together. It became clear to Bethany that being anxious isn't God's will for us. "It is sin," she said.

Bethany forgave all her ancestors from both sides of her family for passing on a foothold for the spirit of anxiety. She renounced it and surrendered everything to the Lord Jesus, trusting him for her future. She asked God to forgive her for the years she had allowed anxiety to master her, rather than letting the peace of Christ rule in her heart. Then, in the authority of Jesus Christ, we commanded the spirits of anxiety and fear to leave.

Bethany experienced a distinct release from her chest. Tears welled up in her eyes. She told us that two hours earlier, as the time to pray together was approaching, she had felt the spirit of anxiety bearing down on her, generating more and more fear. But now the anxiety had been turned to peace and joy—Jesus' own peace and joy.

August 7, 2016 (Four Days Later)

Following Bethany's deliverance, we prepared her for future temptations to anxiety that were sure to come. James 4:7–8 gives succinct counsel; it says, "Submit yourselves, then, to God. Resist the devil, and he will flee from you. Draw near to God and he will draw near to you." We taught her to refuse to give any ground to the evil one, rebuking him in the name and authority of Jesus Christ, and to bring all her concerns to God in prayer, with thanksgiving, as Philippians 4:6 instructs.

December 10, 2017 (14 Months Later)

We received an email from Bethany. It was full of good news and included the following:

Thank you for checking in with me. That healing is one of my favorite stories to tell! Since then, I haven't had any panic attacks, haven't needed counseling, or needed any medication. PRAISE THE LORD! That's not to say that I have zero anxiety in my life (I feel we all have some portion of anxiety that is "normal"). It seems that the devil knows anxiety is my weak spot, and he will try to attack me there if he can. I read the passage this week about how if a demon is cast out, it gets seven more and comes back even stronger. But the enemy has not succeeded. For I am filled with the Holy Spirit, a holy and dearly loved child of God who has power in Jesus' name. In recent situations where I would expect to be filled with anxiety, I am instead filled with immense peace—peace that surpasses understanding—peace that is only from Christ. I have nothing but positive things to say. The Lord is so good.

Thank you, again, for walking me through the healing and praying in Jesus' name for me.

In Christ,

Sadia :) [Bethany's African name]

This is my commandment, that you love one another as I have loved you. Greater love has no one than this, that someone lay down his life for his friends. You are my friends if you do what I command you....I chose you and appointed you that you should go and bear fruit and that your fruit should abide, so that whatever you ask the Father in my name, he may give it to you. These things I command you, so that you will love one another.

JOHN 15:12–14, 16–17 ESV

20

·······

Dr. John

2016

Nairobi, Kenya

A missionary colleague and good friend of ours who has served as a medical doctor in some very challenging contexts was passing through our nation's capital. June and I were shopping at one of the several city grocery stores when John happened to walk in and see me. As soon as we greeted one another I noticed indications of anxiety or concern on John's face.

John explained that while he was walking from the guest house to the mall to get some exercise (about three kilometers each way), he began to have some chest pains. When he arrived at the mall, he decided to go to the top floor where a clinic office is located. He asked for an EKG and was given one right away.

The technician said there was nothing to worry about, but when John examined the EKG readout himself, it seemed to him to indicate that his heart wasn't functioning properly. Uncertain what to do, he made his way down to the ground floor to leave the mall. As he passed the grocery store on the bottom floor he spotted me waiting for June to finish her shopping.

John, looking a bit ashen, told me what was happening. He didn't want to diagnose himself and asked if I knew any local doctors we could ask about the EKG.

Our son-in-law's father came to mind. Dr. Ted Collins is the head cardiac surgeon at another mission hospital in western Kenya. It took a few calls but we were finally able to reach Dr. Collins who was traveling toward Nairobi. Ted asked us to take a picture of the EKG and send it to him by phone. A few minutes later Ted called, saying that John should get to the hospital immediately; Ted had made arrangements for him to be received by a cardiologist friend from Karen Hospital. We needed to find a way to get John there; the doctors would be waiting for us.

By this time June had finished her shopping and we called for a taxi and waited. It was rush hour and we knew that traffic would be particularly bad in the direction of Karen Hospital. We were sitting in a quiet place at some distance from the walking traffic. Prompted by the Holy Spirit, I asked John if we could pray for Jesus to heal his heart. He immediately agreed.

Aware that any unforgiveness can block healing, I asked John if there was anyone he had not forgiven. John said right away that there was someone who had said some hurtful and offensive words to him recently. Without any prompting John immediately began to pray, telling the Lord all that had happened. Then, by an act of his will, he forgave the person who had offended him. He went on to confess his own sin of staying angry ("Do not let the sun go down while you are still angry" Ephesians 4:26–27 NIV) and said that he would live in a forgiving way with all people and in all situations in the future. We asked if there were any other people he needed to forgive. There were none.

June and I then placed our hands on John, my hands on his chest and June's on his shoulder. After a short prayer, in Jesus' name and authority I commanded John's heart to be healed and to be well. After a few minutes we said, "Amen."

Shortly after that the taxi arrived and we piled in. The traffic jam was bad. Since we were making very little progress, I got out of the taxi, leaving June to go with John to Karen Hospital. I hurried to the guest house on foot to find John's wife and escort her to the hospital. John's wife and I found another taxi and traveled a different route to the hospital, arriving about 45 minutes before John and June, whose 15 kilometer trip took two hours.

The medical personnel were waiting. They administered several preliminary cardiac tests, another EKG, and other blood and lab tests.

After about an hour or so, when all four of us were together in one of the examination booths, a doctor came in. He said nothing as he looked over all the lab and test results. Finally, John asked him what he saw going on. The doctor said that his findings weren't quite making sense. He had the two EKG readouts in front of him. The first one showed that John had something abnormal and worrisome going on with his heart; the second showed a normal heart. The cardiac enzyme results also showed his heart to be normal. The doctor explained that such rapid changes don't normally occur.

We knew that it was God's grace and healing power that were responsible. The doctor wanted to take one more blood sample to check cardiac enzymes eight hours later before he gave the green light for John to travel. John was feeling fine and strong, so we went out for a late dinner, celebrating and thanking Jesus for his gift of healing. John went back to the hospital the next morning; his cardiac enzymes were normal.

Follow up:

After returning to England, Dr. John was advised by his staff and friends to have a thorough examination by a cardiologist. The doctors who looked at the latest EKG and blood test results agreed that they were normal.

And he went up on the mountain and called to him those whom he desired, and they came to him. And he appointed twelve (whom he also named apostles) so that they might be with him and he might send them out to preach and have authority to cast out demons.

MARK 3:13–15 ESV

21

....

Sugo of Tula

March 2009

Tula, Kenya

When June was first called from the clinic in Tula to go see Sugo at his home in March of 2009, it was clear to her that he was a very sick man. He was having seizures, his stomach was bloated, his head was enlarged, he was grunting with every breath and was in a lot of pain. His problems were far beyond the dispensary's capabilities. IV drugs were able to stop the seizures for the moment, but Sugo remained unconscious, still grunting with every breath but with stabilized vital signs. An ambulance was called by radio to come from Kola and meet Sugo and his brothers in Duma. The men carried Sugo to the vehicle June had driven from Duma to Tula and they traveled together to the clinic in Duma. Once there, the men hoisted the still unconscious Sugo from the truck and carried him into the clinic.

Godana, our co-worker and teammate, was visiting me at Duma that day. When he and I arrived at the clinic, we heard Sugo's story from June and the family. I offered to pray, asking the family if they were willing for us to ask Jesus the Messiah to heal Sugo. We summarized the Gospel message and explained more about who Jesus is.

The family agreed; yes, they wanted us to pray. I called everyone together (June, Godana, a Kenyan nurse named Naomi, Sugo's brothers and mother, and others who had come along) and asked them to circle around Sugo to pray. Laying hands on him, we asked God to intervene and heal Sugo.

Sugo continued to writhe in pain, incoherent and moaning continually. His stomach remained distended and his head swollen. We had prayed in Jesus' name, but we hadn't seen any improvement.

Two of Sugo's brothers called me outside to talk. They were seeking financial assistance, not being prepared for the expenses awaiting them in Kola. In addition to the hospital fees, they thought it very likely they would face burial expenses. I agreed to assist them with a loan, and then went back into the clinic to see Sugo.

As I walked to the clinic doorway the Holy Spirit spoke very quietly and clearly, telling me that Sugo had a spirit of death. I stopped and thought to myself, "What am I going to do with this?" Standing there in the doorway, I looked in both directions. Not seeing anyone nearby, I walked inside. June was in the room washing up equipment; she wasn't facing in my direction.

I went up to Sugo, laid hands on him and, in the name and authority of Jesus Christ of Nazareth, I commanded the spirit of death to leave Sugo immediately and not come back. Hearing what I was saying, June turned to see what was going on.

Sugo stopped moaning and grunting and visibly relaxed. In less than a minute, his bloated stomach deflated and the swelling of his head was noticeably reduced. Sugo's unconsciousness seemed to become peaceful sleep.

The ambulance arrived a couple of hours later. We shook Sugo and said, "Wake up. The ambulance is here; you need to go to the hospital." He got up from the clinic bed. With the help of his brothers, he walked to the ambulance and after some initial resistance (since other than being a bit weak, he felt fine) he climbed in.

Distances being what they are in Kenya, we could only wonder what happened after the ambulance left Duma. Then a month later, on April 25th, when I was in Tula walking from the *dukas* (small shops) to Godana and Diram's home, someone called my name from a distance. I didn't recognize the man.

It was Sugo! He looked like a different person! He was healed! He was in wonderful shape. The two of us sat down under a tree and I told Sugo what had happened that day in the clinic. Sugo agreed that what the

Holy Spirit had said was true; he'd had a spirit of death that was trying to kill him. The spirit had a strong hold on him and would not let him go. When the spirit of death was ordered to leave in Jesus' name, it left. Sugo knew then that he had been set free. Sugo opened his heart to learning about Jesus and promised to ask Godana to tell him more in the days to come.

It is by the name of Jesus Christ of Nazareth, whom you crucified but whom God raised from the dead, that this man stands before you healed.

ACTS 4:10 NIV

And they departed and went through the villages, preaching the gospel and healing everywhere.

LUKE 9:6 ESV

22

·······

John

February 2017

Kenya

We have known John for about 30 years. He and his wife serve God faithfully in a very challenging part of the world.

When we were attending a conference together in East Africa, John asked for prayer. He had injured his back on his last home assignment just before returning to the field.

The owner of the house in which John and his family had been staying was in the process of doing some maintenance on the property and had dug a hole at the base of the front doorstep. John walked out of the front door carrying an oversize box of household goods that blocked his vision of what lay directly in his path. He stepped down into the hole with the heavy box in his hands and wrenched his back. John simply kept on working; their personal belongings had to be put into storage.

John and his family traveled back to the African country where they live and serve. Weeks and months went by, with John's back always in pain.

After hearing his story, I asked him, "Whom do you hold responsible for your back pain?" John thought for a while and eventually said he supposed he held the owner of the house responsible. He hadn't warned John about the freshly dug hole.

I asked John if he had forgiven the landlord. He could not recall that he had.

The two of us went to prayer together. John forgave the homeowner and also realized that he himself needed forgiveness because he had let time elapse without forgiving. John determined then and there that if anyone wronged him in the future he would forgive right away. He never wanted to give the devil a foothold again (Ephesians 4:26–27). He thanked Jesus for forgiving him.

I asked John to show me exactly where he was having pain. I placed my hand on his back at that spot and prayed for him. Using Jesus' authority, I commanded John's back to be healed and commanded all the pain to be gone. After a couple of minutes I ended with "Amen" and asked John how his back felt.

He responded, "I don't feel the pain anymore. The pain is gone!"

We both laughed in delight and thanked Jesus together in prayer.

Several years later I ran into John at a guest house where we were both staying. He reminded me of that day when we had prayed together for his back. He said the pain never came back.

Praise the Lord!

Whoever loves father or mother more than me is not worthy of me, and whoever loves son or daughter more than me is not worthy of me. And whoever does not take his cross and follow me is not worthy of me. Whoever finds his life will lose it, and whoever loses his life for my sake will find it.

MATTHEW 10:37–39 ESV

...if you confess with your mouth that Jesus is Lord and believe in your heart that God raised him from the dead, you will be saved. For with the heart one believes and is justified, and with the mouth one confesses and is saved.

ROMANS 10:9–10 ESV

Beloved, do not believe every spirit, but test the spirits to see whether they are from God, for many false prophets have gone out into the world.

1 JOHN 4:1 ESV

23

....

Maaka

April 27, 2013

Duma, Kenya

Maaka grew up hearing the Gospel from a very young age. But she reached adulthood and then married without having yielded her life to the Lordship of Jesus or taking the gift of salvation he offers.

After marriage, Maaka's husband would only allow her to travel to places he was familiar with and had visited himself. He seemed afraid of what might happen to her in a place where he had no control. Maaka was particularly disappointed when he refused to let her go on a trip to a big city for a special occasion, but she submitted to his wishes as was expected of a good Amaro wife.

A couple months later, in what seemed to be an effort to make up for depriving her of that trip, Maaka's husband suggested she go to visit some relatives in a village several hours to the south.

While she was there, tribal clashes erupted in that very village. Men from an enemy tribe, armed with machetes and clubs, came to raid and kill. She hid, crouching with her baby, in a large hut crowded with mothers and children. They could see the men killing ruthlessly and setting huts on fire. The terrified women did their best to keep the children quiet while expecting the marauders to burst into the hut at any moment.

Confronted with almost certain death, Maaka realized that even though she knew the truth of Jesus' salvation, she hadn't taken this gift and didn't know where she would go if she died that day. With the chaos and violence surging all around, Maaka prayed from the quiet place in her heart; she asked Jesus to forgive her and to save her from her sin. She surrendered her life to him and entered into God's kingdom.

Inexplicably, or perhaps miraculously, the marauders bypassed that hut full of women and children.

After Maaka returned to her home village some weeks later, she told us about her experience and shared with us her new faith in Jesus the Messiah. Already knowing how to read, Maaka began regularly spending time in God's word and in prayer.

One Saturday morning some time later, June and Maaka studied I John 4 and 5 together. In the afternoon they sat together to explore the need for deliverance since Maaka had grown up believing and following Islam.

Because of the Scripture they had studied together, Maaka agreed that walking in the way of Islam is sin and ultimately rebellion against God; in prayer, she confessed this sin. She forgave her parents for leading her into Islam and repented of practicing it, promising not to participate in Islam again.

Maaka also forgave the *shifta* (armed bandits) for murdering her father while she was still growing in her mother's womb. In addition, she confessed that before she was married she had participated in *Hinesse* (an occultic dance that welcomes and worships evil spirits). Maaka repented of these sins, thanked Jesus for his forgiveness and for his death on the cross and his resurrection.

At this point June and Maaka invited me to join them. They gave me a summary of what they had already covered together.

As I commanded the unclean spirits to leave, Maaka felt manifestations in her heart and then felt them move to the back of her neck and then become a headache. The headache lifted and Maaka was at peace; the spirits had left.

We asked the Holy Spirit to fill Maaka afresh and bring healing to her soul.

Many people who come to Jesus from an Islamic background experience persecution and intense pressure to return to Islam. Maaka however, being delivered from a spirit of Islam, has not turned back. Having this new freedom and being intentional about reading God's word and spending time in prayer every day, she continues to grow in her faith and enjoy her freedom in Christ.

April 2016 (Three Years Later)

After struggling with stomach cramps, loss of appetite and a slow but steady flow of blood for more than a month, Maaka finally confided in June. She was given medication to help with the stomach issues, but nothing seemed to help.

Finally, June and I asked Maaka if she would like to come together to ask Jesus for healing. With a childlike faith, she agreed right away. We sat together in one of the rooms in our house and asked Maaka to update us on how she was doing. She explained that whenever she tried to eat, her stomach hurt even more. The cramping was so uncomfortable that she simply didn't want to eat, so of course she was losing weight. She was still bleeding too.

We reviewed the Gospel message, which Maaka already believed, and then asked her if there was anyone she had not forgiven. After a long pause, and although she had already forgiven this person many times, she finally said yes. Her father-in-law, a verbally abusive man, has repeatedly called Maaka all kinds of evil names and has wounded her deeply. Just a few days prior to our meeting, he had said some nasty and very hurtful things to her. (We know him well and can attest to the fact that he has a spirit of bitterness and often says terrible things.)

Maaka led in prayer and, in obedience to Jesus, forgave her father-in-law. She also asked Jesus to forgive her for holding on to her anger. She repented, choosing to love her father-in-law and live in a forgiving way.

We laid hands on Maaka. I rebuked the spirit of infirmity, and with Jesus' authority commanded Maaka's stomach to be healed and all the pain and bleeding to stop.

When we asked Maaka how she felt, she said that her stomach was well and at peace.

The next day she reported that the bleeding had stopped and her stomach was still well. Maaka's appetite returned and over the next three weeks, every time we asked, Maaka reported that she was continuing to do well. Praise God!

Beloved, if our heart does not condemn us, we have confidence before God; and whatever we ask we receive from him, because we keep his commandments and do what pleases him. And this is his commandment, that we believe in the name of his Son Jesus Christ and love one another, just as he has commanded us. Whoever keeps his commandments abides in God, and God in him. And by this we know that he abides in us, by the Spirit whom he has given us.

1 JOHN 3:21–24 ESV

24

....

Tom

2015

Midwest USA

On January 11, 2015, after leading two morning worship services and Sunday School at one of our supporting churches in the Midwest, I was approached by two married couples, each asking for prayer. Two of the church's elders and one of their wives joined us in praying for Tom and his wife Sally and for Rose and her husband.

Tom explained that in November he'd had an MRI hoping to rule out the possibility of brain cancer. His MRI showed hundreds of small lesions scattered throughout his brain. Thankfully, the biopsy showed no cancer. But there was still reason for grave concern; this same condition had caused Tom's father's death, and the brain biopsy had left Tom's right cheek, hand and foot numb.

In the course of praying for Tom's healing from the trauma of the biopsy, we asked Tom if there was anyone he blamed for the numbness on his right side. He said that he didn't blame anyone. Sally, however, said that she did blame those she felt were responsible. We asked Sally if she was willing to forgive them and we took some time to explain how essential forgiveness is in removing possible spiritual blocks to healing.

Since Tom's dad died of the very condition Tom now has, we addressed the possibility that Tom was experiencing generational consequences. Tom prayed and renounced any sin as well as any consequences that had been passed down to him through the generations, and he forgave his ancestors.

As a group of elders and disciples, we laid hands on Tom and prayed for the healing of his soul, spirit and body.

There was no noticeable change in Tom's condition.

We prayed again. When there was still no change, we decided to focus for a time on Rose's needs—the most pressing being to forgive God and others for past traumatic events and for the times she had been wronged.

Tom was present during this process and witnessed how the Holy Spirit led Rose and her husband during this session. He saw firsthand the freedom Rose experienced by forgiving those who had wronged her.

When we turned our attention back to Tom, I asked him if there was anyone he had not forgiven. He immediately confessed that there were a number of people he needed to ask to forgive him as well as others he himself needed to forgive. In prayer he confessed his own sin as the Holy Spirit brought to mind the various situations in which he had sinned against others. He also forgave by name those who had wronged him. By an act of his will he repented and chose to live in a forgiving way in the future. He gratefully received God's forgiveness.

Again we prayed for healing. There was no outward physical change, but Tom experienced his soul and spirit being set free. We encouraged him to keep asking, seeking and knocking. Tom decided that in the next few days he would seek out the individuals the Holy Spirit had brought to mind—people he had wronged—so he could ask them to forgive him.

Four days later we received a phone call from Tom's wife Sally. She was clearly very excited. She said, "A few days after we prayed together for healing at the church, Tom had an appointment to have another MRI done on his brain. The technician was dumbfounded! He showed us the two MRI pictures and tried to explain them to us. The picture from the MRI that had been done some weeks earlier showed hundreds of lesions throughout Tom's brain tissue. Today's MRI picture showed no brain lesions at all! We know that Jesus has healed Tom and we wanted to call you to share this exciting news."

Almost nine years later on October 8, 2023, I met with Tom and his wife during one of my church visits while in the United States. Tom and Sally were thrilled to report that the MRI Tom had just had a few days earlier showed that all the brain tissue remains clear.

Ask, and it will be given to you; seek, and you will find; knock, and it will be opened to you. For everyone who asks receives, and the one who seeks finds, and to the one who knocks it will be opened. Or which one of you, if his son asks him for bread, will give him a stone? Or if he asks for a fish, will give him a serpent? If you then, who are evil, know how to give good gifts to your children, how much more will your Father who is in heaven give good things to those who ask him!

MATTHEW 7:7-11 ESV

25

....

Headman Kolde

2013

Amaro Region, Kenya

On the morning of October 22, 2013, Luke and I set out on the *pikis* (motorcycles) for a village about ten kilometers away. We would be meeting with the village elders to continue teaching the story of Noah. The day was hot and dry, so we made sure we had enough water and then set out. For the first five kilometers we followed the dirt track road; walking paths took us the rest of the way.

Luke, an American, was doing a one-month internship with us as part of his training while participating in a two-year program in another country. The two-year program was offered by an organization that requires each of their participants to spend a month experiencing life among a different people group.

When we arrived, the elders and I shared the customary greetings. Luke and I were invited to sit down with them on goat skins and mats in the shade of a grass-covered structure built of sticks skillfully bound together to allow good airflow.

As everyone shared the latest news, I in turn told the group that some travelers from Kanchoro's village had told me that Kanchoro had been completely healed within a day after we had prayed for him when he had visited our home in Duma about a month earlier. (See chapter 27.)

Eventually it was time to begin telling the second half of Noah's story. The village headman, Kolde, noted that the people in Noah's day rejected God's word and were lost while those who received it were saved. "But," he added, "only eight people believed and acted upon it."

I explained to the village elders that, like the ark that saved Noah's family from the flood, Jesus is the Ark that saves us today.

Then Kolde said, "My back, thigh and knee have been sick for a while. Pray that Jesus will heal my back and my leg and knee."

I asked him to tell us more about his injuries.

"I was hurt a year ago while lifting a cow too weak to stand due to drought. Over time my condition has become worse. I have pain and my leg is so weak that while sitting I have to use my hands to help straighten my leg to stretch it out and to pull my lower leg back up to bend it."

An essential step in praying for healing is making sure everyone understands that it's Jesus who is the Savior and Healer. After I'd made that as clear as possible, Luke and I placed our hands on Kolde, who was sitting on the mat. I explained to Luke, "This healing belongs to Kolde because of what Jesus has done on the cross. We can be confident that healing is God's will because Jesus revealed the Father's will when he healed everyone who came to him for healing 2000 years ago."

"Now *we* use Jesus' authority," I told Luke, "and we pray for healing because Jesus commanded us as his disciples to do it."

I didn't hurry through this; I wanted both of us to have time to remember who Jesus is and who we are in Christ. I asked Luke to place his hand on Kolde's knee while I placed a hand on his lower back. In the local language, I thanked Jesus for his love and prayed an assortment of his promises and commands. I asked Jesus to extend his power to heal Kolde.

Then, in Jesus' name and authority, I commanded Kolde's back, leg and knee to be healed. A minute or so passed. Then I suddenly felt something move in Kolde's lower back. It was as if a lump moved from one side to the other under my hand. After about three minutes I said, "Amen," and asked Kolde how his back and knee felt. Kolde stood up and tested his knee and leg. He pulled his foot behind him up to his lower back. Then he sat down on the mat and extended and then bent his leg repeatedly with freedom, without the aid of his hands and without pain.

All of us laughed with joy. I encouraged Kolde to thank Jesus in prayer and when he extended his open hands and lifted his face to the sky to thank Jesus for healing him, we all held out our hands, too, and joined him.

"Wives, submit to your husbands, as is fitting in the Lord. Husbands, love your wives, and do not be harsh with them.... Whatever you do, work heartily, as for the Lord and not for men, knowing that from the Lord you will receive the inheritance as your reward. You are serving the Lord Christ. For the wrongdoer will be paid back for the wrong he has done, and there is no partiality."

COLOSSIANS 3:18-25 ESV

Bless the LORD, O my soul, and all that is within me, bless his holy name! Bless the LORD, O my soul, and forget not all his benefits, who forgives all your iniquity, who heals all your diseases, who redeems your life from the pit, who crowns you with steadfast love and mercy, who satisfies you with good so that your youth is renewed like the eagle's. The LORD works righteousness and justice for all who are oppressed.

PSALM 103:1-6 ESV

Behold, all souls are mine; the soul of the father as well as the soul of the son is mine: the soul who sins shall die. Now suppose this man fathers a son who sees all the sins that his father has done; he sees, and does not do likewise....he shall not die for his father's iniquity; he shall surely live.

EZEKIEL 18:4, 14-17 ESV

You shall not make for yourself a carved image, or any likeness of anything that is in heaven above, or that is on the earth beneath, or that is in the water under the earth. You shall not bow down to them or serve them; for I the LORD your God am a jealous God, visiting the iniquity of the fathers on the children to the third and fourth generation of those who hate me, but showing steadfast love to thousands of those who love me and keep my commandments.

DEUTERONOMY 5:8-10 ESV

26

....

Samuel and Purity's Twins

November 11–16, 2013

Johannesburg, South Africa

While ministering in South Africa, June and I taught about Jesus' grace and power while sharing the Gospel of Jesus Christ. We shared our experiences of miracles, healing and deliverance.

After the first meeting, Samuel and Purity asked if they could talk with us about one of their thirteen-month-old twins. They had beautiful twin daughters, but were very concerned about Hope, the second born. She was twitching or jerking in an unusual way both during the day and at night. This had been happening a few times every day since Hope was two weeks old. Hannah, the firstborn twin, had never done this. The parents sensed this might be a spiritual issue.

June and I had dinner with the family and asked various questions as the Holy Spirit led us. We learned that when Purity became pregnant, neither she nor Samuel were happy about it. They were in training with a Christian ministry and living in a harsh and stressful situation in a country not their own. The thought of having to care for a baby at that time was very daunting for Purity. She didn't know how she would cope being away from her family. She hadn't intended to become pregnant and had only skipped her birth control pills the week she'd been ill. Samuel had been angry with Purity for not taking her birth control and he blamed her for the pregnancy. He had spoken some harsh words that weren't easily forgotten.

A few months later they were given the news that not only were they going to have one baby, but two. Their anxiety only increased as they fell into habitually complaining and asking one another, "How are we going to be able to cope while we are in training and so far from our family, home and country?"

Given both Purity's and Samuel's initial reactions to the pregnancy, we considered the possibility that little Hope had experienced fear and rejection in the womb.

Samuel was very humble throughout this exploration. When encouraged to ask his wife for forgiveness, he did so immediately. He humbly confessed the details of each incident of blaming Purity that he remembered. Purity was encouraged to share openly the ways Samuel's words had hurt her, and then she freely forgave him.

Samuel and then Purity each prayed aloud, confessing their sin and asking forgiveness. They renounced any passing on of rejection and fear to their children. They repented, choosing by an act of the will to love each of their twin daughters equally and fully. Then June and I laid hands on Hope and prayed for her to be healed.

The next morning Purity told us that she'd had a rough night; Hope woke often and was fussy. She'd also displayed more jerking than usual during the night. I told them that after we had prayed the night before and all returned to our rooms, I'd sensed I should have commanded in Jesus' authority that any demons leave.

We asked Purity and Samuel if they would be willing to come for prayer again and they were eager to do so. That evening Samuel, Purity, June and I ordered all demons of fear and rejection and any other demons to leave Hope; their rights had been removed by Samuel and Purity's confession and repentance and by Jesus' forgiveness.

No manifestations were seen. We also prayed again for healing—that all the small twitches would cease and be gone. Over the next three-and-a-half days no one noticed any twitching or jerking and Hope slept well each night thereafter. Her parents were very encouraged. It seems that Hope has been healed.

June 2014

Seven months later Samuel wrote that the girls were doing well. Samuel and Purity had seen Hope exhibit only one of those little jerks, and that was just a few weeks after our time of prayer. Since then Hope has been entirely free of them.

Now those who were scattered went about preaching the word. Philip went down to the city of Samaria and proclaimed to them the Christ. And the crowds with one accord paid attention to what was being said by Philip, when they heard him and saw the signs that he did. For unclean spirits, crying out with a loud voice, came out of many who had them, and many who were paralyzed or lame were healed. So there was much joy in that city.

ACTS 8:4–8 ESV

27

....

Kanchoro of Chuba

September 2013

Duma, Kenya

Kanchoro had come to Duma with his relative Abrahim in September of 2013 to seek help for a boy who was very ill with an aggressive infection that was eating into the side of his torso. They'd left the boy at home but had come to ask for a letter of introduction to the Mission Hospital for the boy and his family. The governor of the area had promised to pay for an ambulance to bring the boy the 400 kilometers from their village of Chuba to the hospital.

After Kanchoro and Abrahim had described all the previous treatments the boy had received, June went into the house to write a letter so the mission doctors would have all the pertinent information when the boy and his family arrived.

While June was writing the letter of introduction, I shared the Gospel with Kanchoro and Abrahim as clearly as I could. I also told them about the various miracles of healing Jesus had done around our village area. Kanchoro suddenly interrupted me, saying, "Pray for me. Ask Jesus to heal me. I had a *piki* (motorcycle) accident many months ago and injured my knee and I still have pain in it."

First, I emphasized that *Jesus* is the healer. I stress this so that people understand that it is to Jesus Christ they are consenting to bring their injuries and illnesses. "Jesus loves you, Kanchoro," I told him. "Jesus has come to redeem you. He wants to heal not only your knee but your relationship with God by what he did at the cross for you, 'swallowing' your sin."

Kanchoro was eager to come to Jesus for healing, so I laid my hand on his knee and prayed for healing in Jesus' name and authority.

"How does it feel, Kanchoro?"

He got up and walked around. "It feels good," Kanchoro said, "but the real test is at night and early morning." Kanchoro and Abrahim took the referral letter and then started on the journey back to Chuba.

About a month later I met two people from Chuba passing by on a *piki*. While we were exchanging the news, I asked if they knew Kanchoro. They did, and one of them was a relative. I asked if they knew about his knee problem. They said they did and that his knee was healed.

"Do you know how he was healed?" I asked them. They said they did not.

"It was Jesus who healed him," I told them. "Ask him when you get back."

The two men on the *piki* said, "Kanchoro will be passing through here next week to visit his relative." I asked them to invite Kanchoro to stop in to see us.

Two weeks later, on October 31, 2013, the assistant chief, the retired headman from the village of Chuba, and another of the village elders passed through our area and reported that Kanchoro was completely healed.

"How was he healed?" I asked them.

"You, Wayne, prayed for him," they said.

"But in whose name did I pray?" I asked.

"Kanchoro said it was in the name of Jesus the Messiah."

Update

About nine years later we saw Kanchoro again. As a driver for a *boda boda* (a *piki* taxi), he had brought a patient from a distant village to our dispensary for treatment. I happened to come up to the clinic while he was waiting for his passenger to be seen by the nurse in charge. Kanchoro greeted me warmly, but I didn't recognize him right away. He reintroduced himself and I realized then who he was. I asked him how his knee had been since the day nine years earlier when we had prayed in Jesus' name. Kanchoro said that Jesus had healed him that day and his knee has been good ever since.

As we were going to the place of prayer, we were met by a slave girl who had a spirit of divination and brought her owners much gain by fortune-telling. She followed Paul and us, crying out, "These men are servants of the Most High God, who proclaim to you the way of salvation." And this she kept doing for many days. Paul, having become greatly annoyed, turned and said to the spirit, "I command you in the name of Jesus Christ to come out of her." And it came out that very hour.

ACTS 16:16–18 ESV

And they went into Capernaum, and immediately on the Sabbath he entered the synagogue and was teaching. And they were astonished at his teaching, for he taught them as one who had authority, and not as the scribes. And immediately there was in their synagogue a man with an unclean spirit. And he cried out, "What have you to do with us, Jesus of Nazareth? Have you come to destroy us? I know who you are—the Holy One of God." But Jesus rebuked him, saying, "Be silent, and come out of him!" And the unclean spirit, convulsing him and crying out with a loud voice, came out of him. And they were all amazed, so that they questioned among themselves, saying, "What is this? A new teaching with authority! He commands even the unclean spirits, and they obey him." And at once his fame spread everywhere throughout all the surrounding region of Galilee.

MARK 1:21–28 ESV

28

....

Mohammed

December 11, 2006

Tula, Kenya

After publicly sharing the foundational truths of God's salvation through Jesus—a salvation that includes healing and deliverance from demons—Godana (our colleague who is a missionary pastor) and I met privately with Mohammed.

For several years Mohammed had professed to be a born again believer in Christ and at first had eagerly participated in Bible studies and prayer meetings. But in subsequent years he'd become inconsistent in his witness and unreliable in attending worship services and the discipleship meetings he'd agreed to attend with Godana.

First, we invited Mohammed to share his testimony. Mohammed focused on the truth of the word of God as being of great importance, but he seemed unable to talk about the central core of the Gospel—Jesus and the cross. We spent about half an hour trying to help him, prompting him with a variety of questions, but still Mohammed wouldn't speak of the death and resurrection of Christ.

Finally, we all but spelled out for him how significant these events were to the Good News of Jesus Christ; at that point Mohammed agreed and added words to his testimony about why Jesus had to die. But by then the glaring omission had raised red flags for Godana and me.

After we'd reaffirmed the basics of the Gospel, Godana and I shared with Mohammed what we'd learned about the spirit of Islam—that this spirit could afflict anyone who had followed Islam, and that this spirit didn't always automatically leave when someone became a Christian.

In the experience of missionaries in our part of the world, exploring the need for deliverance from spirits of Islam is essential when discipling a convert from a Muslim background. Even successful deliverance ministry doesn't guarantee that people will mature in their faith, of course, but deliverance can free new believers from the relentless downward pull that the demonic spirits exert. This offers some time and space for growing in the grace and knowledge of our Lord Jesus Christ. Given human free will and the cost of following Jesus in our context, we can never assume that a convert will persevere. We find that Jesus' parable of the four soils reflects many of our experiences.

Mohammed agreed that he wanted freedom. We explained that first he needed to remove the legal right (permission) he had previously given a demon or demons by the sin of following Islam. We read 1 John 4 and 5 together so Mohammed would understand that by the criteria spelled out in Scripture, the Islamic prophet Mohamed had failed to show himself to be a true prophet of God, and that Mohammed's own following of Islam in the past had actually been sin and rebellion against God. We took our time to explain that he could withdraw the permission he'd inadvertently granted the demons by confession, repentance and forgiveness.

Mohammed struggled to pray. Though he had said he wanted deliverance, we didn't see true conviction of sin. We found we had to explain repeatedly and then remind him several times to make a decision of his will to repent. Godana and I began to sense he was just trying to please us.

Finally, I asked Mohammed for permission to order any evil spirit to leave. He gave his permission, but he didn't seem to be seeking, eager or open to the Holy Spirit's conviction, and nothing happened. Mohammed said, "No evil spirits were there."

Afterward, I asked Mohammed if he had ever participated in the *Hinesse* dance—a traditional dance associated with wedding celebrations. (The dancers are usually young people though occasionally some married people also participate. The dance begins with young girls on one side of the area and young men on the other. The leader tells various stories in song; the chorus, which never varies, consists of deep guttural sounds in unison from the throats of all the young men while they jump up and down and clap. The young women are on their knees facing the young men while dancing and moving side by side. The practice is actually an invitation for demons to take control of the young people's bodies. As the dance continues on through the night, demonic power takes over the participants, giving them supernatural strength and endurance.)

Yes, Mohammed had participated in the *Hinesse* dance—quite often, in fact.

Godana and I invited him to confess this as sin before God and to repent. Mohammed said he was willing. But once again he left the decision to repent out of his prayer and was clearly struggling. Finally, after more discussion and explanation, Mohammed told God that he repented from the dancing and would never participate in it again.

Once again I ordered any evil spirit to leave. This time Mohammed described to us how his stomach immediately started to react. But at the same time Godana and I sensed a hardening of his will.

Nothing noticeable happened and Mohammed's stomach settled down. We didn't witness any deliverance.

Godana and I discerned that Mohammed was not being completely open and honest with us and hadn't experienced true conviction of sin. He didn't have clarity of mind. We realized that he hadn't *himself* expressed the need to be delivered. It was only after the two of us had continued to talk with him that he agreed to explore the issue and ask for deliverance. Again, we wondered if he was doing it just to please us and for the sake of our relationship.

I realized that I wasn't sure Mohammed had truly been born again. Godana acknowledged that he felt that Mohammed had always been a rather "slippery guy" and he hadn't seen much godly fruit in his life.

March 3, 2008 (A Little Over a Year Later)

Mohammed was one of four men requesting baptism. Godana and I met with each of the men individually in Tula. When it was Mohammed's turn, we asked him about his testimony.

Godana was concerned because Mohammed had only come

periodically to study the Bible. Just the Saturday before, at Tula's prayer day, Mohammed shared with the group that he had many struggles and requested prayer. I took note that these were the same struggles he had shared a year ago.

I asked Mohammed many questions: Who is Jesus? Why did Jesus come? Why did Jesus have to die? It took some time and prompting for Mohammed to say that Jesus died because of our debt of sin which leads to death.

Mohammed shared that he had many struggles and didn't have peace. I reminded him that last year he had requested prayer for similar problems and that he'd also mentioned these same problems again at prayer day the previous week. I asked him why he thought he continued to struggle with these recurring problems.

Mohammed said it was because of *shetani* that he was struggling so much—demons had been leading him in the wrong way.

I asked him why he didn't come regularly for Bible study and prayer with Godana. He said that when he has many problems in his life, he starts to believe that the problems have come because he's going to church. When things get better, he participates again. I asked him how he'd come to that conclusion. He answered that it must be *shetani* telling him this. He said, "Many times when I'm walking to the church service and am nearly there, I hear demons threatening to harm me if I keep going, so I turn around and go back home."

We asked Mohammed if he wanted freedom from the demons. He said yes, and this time he seemed eager for it.

I told Mohammed that since I hadn't seen good fruit in his life, I thought perhaps he had not given his whole heart to the Lord Jesus Christ. He agreed that he had not.

Mohammed confessed his sin and told Jesus that he wanted him to have 100% of his life. He confessed that he had not been faithful to the Lord. Then, by an act of his will, Mohammed chose to follow Jesus with everything he has and is.

Because I'd heard years before that Mohammed's grandfather had worshiped evil spirits, it seemed crucial to deal with this generational matter. We learned later that his grandfather was a witchdoctor from a cousin tribe, who had moved here from the north hundreds of kilometers away.

Mohammed agreed that his ancestors had worshiped evil spirits and that even his father, Asan, had been involved with the *Ayana* (the practice of worshiping and appeasing evil spirits through ceremonies involving drums, rhythmic dancing, and drinking blood from a dying goat's jugular vein). Asan had also gone to the witch-doctor periodically seeking help for various problems. Although he had at one time confessed Christ as Savior, Asan had turned back and now lives as if he is lost.

We looked at Deuteronomy 18 together so that Mohammed could see clearly that witchcraft and other occult activities are sin before God. In Exodus 20 we saw that idolatry brings punishment to the third and fourth generations. (Often the legal ground on which demons pass from one generation to another is the sin of the forefathers.)

Mohammed was led to forgive his grandfather and father and to renounce what they had done as sin.

He also confessed being involved with Islam again, but he said he had only been involved a little. I pointed out there is no "little;" either you were or you were not. He agreed. But we didn't address that any further at that time.

We asked if there was any other sin the Holy Spirit was bringing to mind that needed to be confessed and repented from.

Mohammed confessed that he had beaten his wife some time ago. He realized it was sin. He confessed this sin in prayer and made a decision never to do it again, but to love his wife. He said that he would ask for her forgiveness that very night.

There were several things Mohammed held against his father. He had divorced his mother and had treated him unkindly as a small child, often being harsh and getting angry at Mohammed.

We told Mohammed he needed to extend grace and forgive his father as Jesus has been gracious and forgiven him (Matthew 6:14–15). He agreed and went to prayer. Mohammed also remembered not being respectful to his mother. He confessed it in prayer and said he would go to his mother and ask forgiveness.

After a long list of things to deal with, the moment came when

Mohammed couldn't think of anything more. I ordered the evil spirits to leave in the name of Jesus Christ of Nazareth, reminding them that their rights had been broken by Mohammed's confession and repentance, and that the debt of sin had been paid at the cross by Jesus Christ.

At first nothing happened. Then Mohammed's stomach started to react. The reactivity moved to his heart, lasted about 30 seconds, and then seemed to dissipate; his body became quiet.

I asked Mohammed if there was anything else he needed to confess. No. What about his great grandfathers? Mohammed prayed aloud to renounce their occult activities and forgave them.

Again, I ordered the demons to leave.

After a few minutes Mohammed's stomach was stirred up again and then his heart; after a few more minutes the manifestation moved to his side and onto the center top of his back toward his neck.

We persisted in calmly commanding the demons to leave in Jesus' name.

After about five minutes Mohammed's body, neck and head arched back. His eyes rolled back, leaving only the whites of his eyes. Then very slowly he moved his head toward the floor while his hands remained at his side. It was all in slow motion. He gently put his forehead on the floor while still sitting on the chair. He stayed in this position for 10–15 minutes as we persistently ordered the demons to leave and as we read Scripture.

Then Mohammed's body moved slowly to the floor and slithered like a snake across the room. He lay in an awkward position with his face pressed against the wall. His arms began to move in unnatural ways, rather like a snake might writhe after being pinned to the ground with a rod.

Godana and I continued to order the demons to leave and to read passages from Scripture such as Revelation 18–21 and Philippians 2. We made no progress. Mohammed remained in this condition for quite some time, slithering in place.

We realized that there must be more footholds giving the demons some legal right to stay.

Finally, I told the demons to either leave Mohammed or go back to his stomach. After a few minutes I saw his muscle tension relax. But he remained on the floor. Then I called Mohammed's name and he immediately answered. I told him to get up.

Mohammed got up and sat in his chair as if nothing had happened. He seemed himself again. I asked him what had happened. He said he didn't know; he'd found himself on the floor but didn't know how he got there.

It was 8 pm and we were exhausted, so we concluded for the day. Godana and Mohammed would resume looking for the additional footholds another time. We were aware that possible areas to explore might include the spirit of Islam and the grandmother's involvement in *Ayana*, as well as anything else God might bring to light. We closed in prayer asking God to reveal the next step.

March 4, 2008 (The Next Day)

Godana and his wife Diram called Mohammed to come to their house to continue with the deliverance the next day. Godana was convinced that other footholds remained.

Mohammed revealed 17 more hidden sins. Godana and Diram carefully led him through confession, repentance and thanking God for his forgiveness for each of these sins.

Then Godana and Diram ordered the spirits to leave. Various spirits manifested as a snake, crocodile, elephant and many other animals. Mohammed remained sitting, but his body moved in strange ways and he made a variety of strange sounds.

Mohammed lifted tables with a strength beyond what is human. The spirits would not leave even after several hours of deliverance ministry. Finally, Godana asked Diram to get Charles (the nurse) and Judah (a Christian school teacher) to come and join forces to pray with them.

While waiting for Diram to return, Godana told the spirits he was going to get more believers to pray and increase the power.

Just as Judah was about to come in, Mohammed jumped up and proclaimed, "They all have left! I am free!" He was so full of joy that Godana believed him. Mohammed looked different and was full of joy the next day as well.

When Godana described all that had happened later when we met again, I asked if they had explored the need for any more deliverances. He said no, he thought the spirits all left at once. I wondered whether the spirit of Islam still needed to be dealt with. Godana and Diram were scheduled to go on a month's leave the next day. We decided we would talk again after their return.

August 2008 (Five Months Later)

Godana reported that Mohammed was still struggling with some evil spirits and bearing only minimal fruit.

Sometime later Godana met with Mohammed again for deliverance ministry and prayer, and more manifestations occurred. Each time Mohammed jumps up and cries that the demons are gone and he thanks Godana for the deliverance. But Godana suspects the evil spirits are trying to trick them into thinking they have left.

Progress has been made, but more work remains. Godana will work more with Mohammed when he returns from his leave.

November 11, 2010 (Two Years Later)

Mohammed is doing very well. He is growing in the Lord and teaching others, even in the midst of much persecution. Praise the Lord!

October 2020

Ten more years have passed. Mohammed has grown enormously in his faith. He is abiding in Jesus. He has become quite bold in sharing the Gospel with his neighbors. It has been wonderful to watch Mohammed grow in his faith and to see him bearing the good fruit Jesus intends for him to produce.

Once again: Praise God!

MOHAMMED

And he told them many things in parables, saying: "A sower went out to sow. And as he sowed, some seeds fell along the path, and the birds came and devoured them. Other seeds fell on rocky ground, where they did not have much soil, and immediately they sprang up, since they had no depth of soil, but when the sun rose they were scorched. And since they had no root, they withered away. Other seeds fell among thorns, and the thorns grew up and choked them. Other seeds fell on good soil and produced grain, some a hundredfold, some sixty, some thirty. He who has ears, let him hear."

MATTHEW 13:3-9 ESV

29

....

Neko

June 2013

Duma, Kenya

One morning at *chai* time, I shared how Jesus had healed various people here in our region in the last few weeks and months. I told the group that Jesus had healed Maaka just the night before.

Neko piped up and said that he had been feeling sick for over a week. He was having fevers, headaches and weakness. He asked me to pray for him. I told him I would be happy to pray for him and made it clear that I would be praying in the name and authority of Jesus Christ—the Jesus of the New Testament.

I got up and stepped over to Neko and placed my hand on his head. I thanked Jesus for his power and for the promises he made when he commanded us to share the Good News of the kingdom of God. I thanked the Lord for giving us his own authority to heal the sick and I prayed that Jesus would extend his grace to Neko.

Then, in Jesus' name and authority, I commanded Neko's fevers and headache to leave and commanded that Neko be healed and his strength restored.

Neko was completely healed that day.

And yet during the days that followed Neko would acknowledge only that God had healed him. This is true of course because Jesus Christ is God the Son, but Neko was in effect denying Jesus. As a Muslim he wanted to give Jesus only the status of a prophet. As shown in the parable of the sower and the seed, the evil one snatches the seed so quickly.

"Beloved, do not believe every spirit, but test the spirits to see whether they are from God, for many false prophets have gone out into the world. By this you know the Spirit of God: every spirit that confesses that Jesus Christ has come in the flesh is from God, and every spirit that does not confess Jesus is not from God. This is the spirit of the antichrist, which you heard was coming and now is in the world already. Little children, you are from God and have overcome them, for he who is in you is greater than he who is in the world. They are from the world; therefore they speak from the world, and the world listens to them. We are from God. Whoever knows God listens to us; whoever is not from God does not listen to us. By this we know the Spirit of truth and the spirit of error.

Beloved, let us love one another, for love is from God, and whoever loves has been born of God and knows God. Anyone who does not love does not know God, because God is love. In this the love of God was made manifest among us, that God sent his only Son into the world, so that we might live through him. In this is love, not that we have loved God but that he loved us and sent his Son to be the propitiation for our sins. Beloved, if God so loved us, we also ought to love one another. No one has ever seen God; if we love one another, God abides in us and his love is perfected in us.

By this we know that we abide in him and he in us, because he has given us of his Spirit. And we have seen and testify that the Father has sent his Son to

be the Savior of the world. Whoever confesses that
Jesus is the Son of God, God abides in him, and he
in God. So we have come to know and to believe the
love that God has for us. God is love, and whoever
abides in love abides in God, and God abides in him.
By this is love perfected with us, so that we may have
confidence for the day of judgment, because as he is
so also are we in this world. There is no fear in love,
but perfect love casts out fear. For fear has to do
with punishment, and whoever fears has not been
perfected in love.

We love because he first loved us. If anyone says,
"I love God," and hates his brother, he is a liar; for
he who does not love his brother whom he has seen
cannot love God whom he has not seen. And this
commandment we have from him: whoever loves
God must also love his brother.

Everyone who believes that Jesus is the Christ has
been born of God, and everyone who loves the Father
loves whoever has been born of him. By this we know
that we love the children of God, when we love God
and obey his commandments. For this is the love
of God, that we keep his commandments. And his
commandments are not burdensome. For everyone
who has been born of God overcomes the world. And
this is the victory that has overcome the world—our
faith. Who is it that overcomes the world except the
one who believes that Jesus is the Son of God?"

1 JOHN 4:1–5:5 ESV

30

....

Omaro

March–April 2008

Amaro Region, Kenya

After studying the Bible with our colleague in another village for several months, on March 3, 2008, Omaro made the choice to surrender his life to Jesus Christ and receive salvation. A month later, on April 3, 2008, Godana said he thought Omaro was ready to be examined in preparation for baptism. We've learned how important it is to explore whether deliverance ministry might be needed.

Omaro gave his testimony, sharing how his new life in Christ had changed him. We enjoyed a time of encouraging conversation about the Scriptures, and Omaro demonstrated a fairly good grasp of the Gospel.

I introduced the question of whether Omaro might have a spirit of Islam. We didn't know if this was the case, but we knew from past experience that it was important to explore the possibility. We explained to Omaro that while he was growing in faith and obedience to Jesus now, if any spirits of Islam were allowed to remain in his life, over time they might attempt to pull him away from the Lord and persuade him to backslide.

We read 1 John 4 and 5 together, asking the question, "How does one determine the difference between a true prophet of God and a false prophet?" Through this study of God's word, Omaro realized that Mohamed was a false prophet and that Islam is based on a lie.

Omaro confessed his previous involvement in Islam as sin and rebellion against God. He made a decision of his will to turn definitively from any involvement in Islam. Omaro thanked Jesus for paying for his sin at the cross.

Realizing that any foothold the demonic could claim had been removed by Omaro's confession and repentance and by Jesus' forgiveness, I then—in Jesus' authority—ordered the spirit of Islam to leave Omaro.

At first nothing seemed to happen. We waited and then repeated the command. After a few minutes, Omaro told us that he felt his stomach was doing something strange. The sensations moved to his heart, then to the ribs on his left side, to his shoulder and to the back of his neck. Omaro heard a whoosh from his ears and instantly knew the demon had gone.

With obvious joy, Omaro told us the demon was gone, that he had seen light and that his heart was much lighter.

Next we asked Omaro if he had ever participated in the *Hinesse* dance. He said that he had. When we asked him if the dance was of God or from the devil, Omaro immediately said, "It is of the devil." We read Deuteronomy 18 together and explained to Omaro that because the Hinesse dance invites demonic spirits to manifest in one's body with supernatural strength, it's a form of demon worship and therefore sin.

After Omaro had prayed, confessing his sin and repenting, and after he realized afresh his forgiveness through Jesus, the spirit was ordered to leave in Jesus' name.

The manifestation started as a tingling sensation in Omaro's left shoulder. It moved down his left arm to his hand and then went out his pinky finger as a feeling of numbness. Omaro knew when it exited and said he felt lighter and could see more light. He was full of joy.

We asked Jesus to reveal anything else that might be a foothold. Then, since we had heard Omaro's testimony and witnessed his deliverance, all agreed he was ready for baptism. Omaro, along with two other young believers, would be baptized on May 18, 2008.

Update (May 2015)

Omaro was not baptized. Soon after our meeting with him, Omaro encountered significant persecution and pressure from his father-in-law (the chief) and from the community. Omaro returned to Islam.

And I, when I came to you, brothers, did not come proclaiming to you the testimony of God with lofty speech or wisdom. For I decided to know nothing among you except Jesus Christ and him crucified. And I was with you in weakness and in fear and much trembling, and my speech and my message were not in plausible words of wisdom, but in demonstration of the Spirit and of power, so that your faith might not rest in the wisdom of men but in the power of God.

1 CORINTHIANS 2:1–5 ESV

31

....

Roba

April 23–25, 2015
Duma, Kenya

June and I have known Roba for over 25 years and have shared the Gospel with him dozens of times.

Early in the evening of April 23, Roba arrived at his post at our home to be our night watchman with Said. As we were visiting with one another, our discussion turned to Jesus and the Gospel.

Out of the blue, Roba told us that he had been suffering for two years with pain in the muscles around his right shoulder blade, his arm and his wrist. He had injured his arm at the wrist a few years ago while using a machete to cut a tree. He'd accidentally whacked his wrist against the tree, which caused it to swell up. For several months he couldn't move it at all without severe pain. Although there was some slow improvement, the wrist remained swollen and had never fully healed. Roba's "*kotu*" (shoulder blade) had also been giving him pain ever since.

Roba declared, "If Jesus will heal me, I will choose to follow him." That was a bold statement for a Muslim; we believed the Holy Spirit was leading him to say it. So we talked more about Jesus the Healer and Savior.

We offered to pray for him right then, but Roba wanted to put off praying until another time. We asked, "Why wait until another time? Jesus is willing to heal you now."

Roba finally agreed and sat down. June and I put our hands on Roba's right shoulder blade area. I said, "The one who is going to heal you is Jesus Christ of Nazareth—not the Jesus of the Qur'an. The Jesus who is going to heal you is the Jesus who came from heaven, and entered this earth born of the virgin Mary. Jesus healed all those who came to him. He is the one who died on the cross for all our sin and rose from the dead three days later."

"Do you understand?" I asked. "It is Jesus of the *Injil* (New Testament) who is going to heal you."

Roba said he understood. He seemed to have a simple childlike faith. He wanted to be free from the pain and immobility. He wasn't trying to figure out how this all works; he just wanted healing. He had heard of many other people in our area being healed by Jesus.

Despite all the healings we have seen, we had never before heard anyone say that if he were healed, he would follow Jesus.

I began to pray, thanking Jesus for his love and grace. I repeated Roba's words to Jesus: "Lord, Roba says that he will follow you if you heal him. Well, Jesus, as you commanded us to pray for the sick in your authority and name, we are here to do so now."

Together we prayed various well-known Scriptures, building up our faith with the truth of Jesus' words (John 14:12–14, John 15:7–8, Matthew 10:1, 7–8). After prayer, June and I commanded the spirits of pain and inflammation to leave Roba in Jesus Christ's name. We next ordered Roba's shoulder to be healed and all the pain and inflammation to be gone.

After about four or five minutes, we ended with, "Amen."

We asked Roba how his shoulder blade was. After testing it, he responded that it was very good. The pain in his shoulder was gone, but his wrist was still hurting.

We prayed again for his arm and wrist. They too became better, but the swelling was still present.

Roba then went to his post to work for the night.

In the morning, Roba was clearly excited. He moved his shoulder back and forth, and exclaimed with delight that his shoulder blade was completely well—and that after two years of pain. But then he stretched out his arm and said, "My wrist is still hurting and swollen." So we prayed again for his wrist.

The next evening when he came to work, we asked him how he felt.

He said that he had no pain at all around his shoulder blade and he could move it freely. The wrist too was some better but a little pain and swelling still remained.

We prayed again, and this time commanded the bones in Roba's wrist, in Jesus' name, to be aligned and healed. I also commanded the spirit of pain to leave.

The next morning Roba declared that his wrist was well and the swelling was gone. He was very happy.

I asked if he remembered what he promised. Roba answered that he'd said that he would follow Jesus if he healed him. Then, as Said, the other night guard, walked up to the veranda, Roba told him that very same thing.

Later in the afternoon, I went to visit Roba at his home. He said again that his wrist was completely well, as was his shoulder. I reminded him again about his promise that he would follow Jesus if he healed him. "Now," I said, "it's important that you learn who Jesus is. When can we begin with the teaching? And Roba, this is not just for you; your whole family needs to be included."

Roba said he would talk to everyone in the family and ask them to join him in studying.

However, Roba's family objected to the plan and began trying to persuade him to stop studying the Bible. After a few months, Roba succumbed to this pressure. I would go to study with him, and he just wouldn't be around. After that happened a couple times, I asked him about it. He explained that his family refused to have him continue his studies.

Roba seems to have become unresponsive to the Holy Spirit's prompting. This grieves us deeply.

We love Roba and we remain friends. We yearn for his whole family, and for him specifically, not only to be healed physically, but spiritually too, in every aspect of their lives. We will continue to pray for Roba to be rescued from darkness and come into the light. May God the Father draw Roba to come to his Son, Jesus Christ, and yield his life to him as his Savior and Lord.

Now many signs and wonders were regularly done among the people by the hands of the apostles. And they were all together in Solomon's Portico. None of the rest dared join them, but the people held them in high esteem. And more than ever believers were added to the Lord, multitudes of both men and women, so that they even carried out the sick into the streets and laid them on cots and mats, that as Peter came by at least his shadow might fall on some of them. The people also gathered from the towns around Jerusalem, bringing the sick and those afflicted with unclean spirits, and they were all healed.

ACTS 5:12–16 ESV

32

....

Hussein

December 11, 2006

Tula, Kenya

On December 11, 2006, Godana and I spent time with three men, teaching them about the Gospel of Jesus Christ; one of these men was Hussein. In the course of our teaching we explained that demons sometimes stay with a person even after conversion. Hussein had been taught that it wasn't possible for a believer in Jesus Christ to have a demon because the Holy Spirit and a demon could not co-exist in a single individual. But he was open to learning from our experience.

Godana and I took Hussein to the back of the house where we would have more privacy. We read 1 John 4 and 5 together and discussed how to distinguish false prophets and teachings from true. When we held the teaching and religion of Islam up to this standard, Hussein concluded that the teaching of Islam is an enemy of the biblical Jesus Christ and a false religion.

Hussein now recognized that by following Islam before he had received Christ he had sinned. Because he hadn't previously thought of it as sin, he hadn't confessed it as such or repented. The Holy Spirit convicted Hussein and we witnessed his grief as he brought this to Jesus in prayer. With an act of his will, Hussein definitively turned away from any practice of Islam. By faith he received forgiveness through Christ's atoning blood.

Now that any legal rights the demons might claim had been removed by Hussein's confession and repentance and by Jesus' forgiveness, we could proceed. Under and with Jesus' authority, I ordered any demon(s) of Islam to leave.

We didn't see any of the obvious manifestations we might have expected, but after a short time Hussein burst out in joyous laughter. We asked him to try to explain what had happened. Hussein said that when I had ordered the evil spirit to leave, his whole body had begun to tingle and then he felt a joy he'd never had before, and so he had laughed with delight.

Given this experience, Hussein now believed that yes, it is possible to have demons and yes, deliverance and healing are available through what Jesus has done at the cross.

During this time of teaching and praying together, Hussein also confessed and repented of watching *Ayana* devil worship. He had been attracted to it as a child. After we studied Deuteronomy 18:9–13 the Holy Spirit convicted Hussein about this. He spontaneously went to prayer and confessed his involvement as sin against God. Hussein repented and voiced a firm decision never to participate in devil worship again and then thanked Jesus for his forgiveness.

We went on to address Hussein's past participation in the dance of *Hinesse*. With conviction and clarity, Hussein confessed this as sin. He chose by an act of his will to repent and to tell the Lord that he would never participate in *Hinesse* again. Hussein thanked Jesus for forgiving him and for paying the debt of sin at the cross.

Once again I ordered any spirits to leave. After a few seconds Hussein burst out with joyful laughter even more exuberantly than the first time.

Then a third issue surfaced; a chronic problem with anger. We asked Hussein if the Holy Spirit was reminding him of anything that might indicate how or when this began. (We were looking for the demonic entry point.)

Hussein described how his uncles had beaten him unjustly when he was a boy charged with shepherding the sheep and goats. He named each of the five uncles. His grandfather had also regularly exploded with anger and beaten him, causing him to miss school.

Hussein wanted to be free from anger and had prayed urgently for deliverance, but he hadn't yet received it. From the time of his conversion he had understood that forgiveness was essential. He had already talked humbly to each of his uncles and to his grandfather, taking part of the blame himself, even though he had been treated unjustly and abused. He asked their forgiveness and told them that he had forgiven each of them.

Godana, Hussein and I read Ephesians 4:26–27 together: "Be angry but do not sin, do not let the sun go down on your anger. Do not give the devil a foothold." Hussein realized that he had been angry for several years about the unjust treatment he'd suffered. Under the Holy Spirit's conviction, he repented and confessed to God that he had held on to his anger, and he gratefully received forgiveness.

When we ordered any remaining spirits to leave, Hussein's sense of relief and release bubbled over into laughter again. He had never before experienced such freedom and joy. He left Godana's home that day as a changed young man who wanted to serve Jesus wholeheartedly.

April 3, 2008

A year and a half later Hussein requested baptism. On April 3, 2008, he spoke with Godana and with me, sharing his testimony of believing and following Jesus Christ. We asked him many questions. His careful answers made it clear that he was ready to be baptized. On May 18, 2008, along with two other believers, Hussein was baptized into our Lord Jesus Christ. Thanks be to God.

Jesus said, "The Spirit of the Lord is upon me,
because he has anointed me to proclaim good news
to the poor. He has sent me to proclaim liberty to the
captives and recovering of sight to the blind, to set at
liberty those who are oppressed, to proclaim the year
of the Lord's favor."

LUKE 4:18–19 ESV

33

....

Rose

January 11, 2015

Midwest, USA

Whenever June and I are in the United States during home assignments, we speak at our various supporting churches, sharing the Gospel and some of our experiences of miraculous healing and deliverance. After the services conclude, individuals who are suffering often ask for prayer; Rose was one of them.

At 63 years of age, Rose had already suffered from both diverticulitis and stage one breast cancer, and she had recovered from both. But when she was preparing to have a knee replacement, doctors discovered that her hemoglobin level was very low, a cause for grave concern.

Rose shared some of her personal history with those of us who were going to pray for her. Her mother, whom she loved deeply, had suffered from seizures and died when Rose was only six years old. Now, 57 years later, as she related the story to us, she added that she still feels the same intense pain today as she had as a six-year-old.

I asked Rose who she felt was responsible for her mother's death. She said she blamed no one. We asked God in prayer to help Rose remember the time of her mother's death when she was six years old, but without the pain of the trauma. Her tears began to flow.

After a pause, I gently asked again, "Rose, who do you hold responsible for your mother's death?"

She looked directly into my eyes. "God!" she exclaimed.

Rose knew, of course, that God is without sin and needs no forgiveness, but in the face of tragedy, grief easily overwhelms rational thought while one thing seems crystal clear: surely God could have prevented this terrible thing.

But finally now, after such a long time, Rose understood and chose to forgive God.

We also encouraged Rose to ask God to forgive *her* for blaming him all these years for her mother's death. Together we prayed that Jesus would take the pain and trauma from her soul and spirit.

After our time of prayer, I asked if there was anyone else in her life that she had not forgiven. She looked at her husband, then back at me, then back to her husband and back at me. She then slowly lifted her hand and pointed to her husband and said, "Him."

I asked, "What's the problem?"

Rose's husband immediately broke in and humbly explained that he had been a terrible husband for the first half of their 40 years of marriage. "I have asked for Rose's forgiveness, and she *has* forgiven me for many things," he said, "but there are some things she's not been willing to forgive."

I asked Rose if this was true. She answered, "Yes."

We reviewed the Scriptures about forgiveness, including Jesus' commands. Finally, as the Holy Spirit brought the truth of God's written word alive, Rose chose to forgive her husband. He responded immediately; he knelt down in front of Rose and asked her again to forgive him for all the terrible things he had done to her so many years ago.

She answered yes; she would forgive him. The presence of God's Spirit was evident to all of us. Rose began to pray, "Lord, help me to forgive my husband."

I interrupted her, "Rose, you don't need to ask Jesus to help you forgive. Jesus himself commanded us to forgive one another; he can be trusted to give us all the help we need. We can simply obey. Will you choose by an act of your will to forgive?"

Rose went on to make the necessary act of her will; she forgave her husband and then asked the Lord in prayer to forgive her as well for hanging onto her anger for so long. It was beautiful to witness the Holy Spirit working in and among us.

Along with the elders, we laid our hands on Rose and asked Jesus to heal her soul and spirit. We then called upon God to raise her low hemoglobin level and to bring her to health.

After prayer Rose reported feeling deep peace and joy.

Three Years Later

When I returned to speak at this same church, I happened to see Rose and we had a few minutes to speak together. She looked healthy and strong. I asked how she had been since that day we and the elders prayed with her. With enthusiasm and energy, Rose described the various ways she had experienced significant inner healing. She's filled with gratitude for the grace God has shown her.

*Is anyone among you in trouble? He should pray.
Is anyone happy? Let him sing songs of praise. Is
anyone among you sick? He should call the elders
of the church to pray over him and anoint him with
oil in the name of the Lord. And the prayer offered
in faith will make the sick person well; the Lord will
raise him up. If he has sinned, he will be forgiven.
Therefore confess your sins to each other and pray
for each other so that you may be healed. The prayer
of a righteous man is powerful and effective.*

JAMES 5:13-16 NIV

34

....

Thomas

January–February 2015

Midwest, USA

When June and I are in the United States for home assignments, we usually spend several months at our home base in the midwest where June grew up. The pastor of one of the local churches there, Thomas, had been supporting our mission work and prayed for us regularly for many years.

Thomas's congregation at First Church loved their pastor who lived with serious health issues and severe pain despite multiple back surgeries.

On one particular home assignment, I visited with Thomas and told him about many of the healing miracles we'd witnessed in Duma and among our friends and family. Thomas wanted his congregation to hear about this work Jesus was doing. Although the church was typically very careful to keep services to one hour, Thomas told me to take as long as I needed.

For two hours, June and I taught the congregation about the Good News of Jesus continuing to heal and deliver people even today. Around this same time June and I were also teaching a five-session class entitled "Jesus Our Healer" in the area.

Thomas's own pain and neuropathy had become so severe and his balance so poor that he could no longer stand to preach without holding on to something. Finally, the day came when he announced to his congregation that he was going to have to retire and go on disability. Many in the congregation wept.

Just before this announcement to the congregation, I received a call from Thomas while I was traveling in another state. He asked if I would be willing to come over when I returned to the area and share more about Jesus as our healer, and also pray with him. We agreed on a time the following week. I spent six uninterrupted hours with Thomas, learning more about Thomas's condition and the traumas Thomas had suffered in life. When all was shared, we counted 18 separate major traumatic events in Thomas's life.

Thomas's History

Thomas grew up in the Netherlands Reformed Church, hearing fire and brimstone preaching with very little grace. Most people in the church weren't sure if they would go to heaven or hell. It was such a severe community that often only nine or ten people from the congregation were permitted to receive Communion.

From the time Thomas was eight years old, he heard his parents fighting. His father was verbally abusive to his mother. Yet on Sundays his father was quite a different man.

Thomas remembers a day when his parents' arguing included threats of divorce. Thomas pleaded with them not to divorce, promising to be good.

One day when Thomas was 16 years old and the family was sitting around the dinner table, he and his brother were surreptitiously flicking a pea back and forth while his father was reading from the Bible. Thomas miscalculated and the flicked pea landed on the Bible. His dad paused briefly as he removed the pea with a grave expression on his face, but he said nothing. Immediately after dinner, his dad told him to stand up and began punching Thomas with his fist in the shoulders and thighs. (This was the way he often disciplined his sons.) Afterward Thomas's father told him to turn around. Thomas was standing in front of the doorway to the basement. His father aimed a forceful kick at his buttocks and Thomas tumbled down the basement stairs.

That same year Thomas's kneecap was punctured by a nail. Two months later he was still in a lot of pain. His dad brought him to the doctor who took x-rays. After several visits the doctor said there was no reason for Thomas to be in pain, that "it was all in his head and that he was making it up." His father accused Thomas of being a liar.

When Thomas was still in pain two months later, his dad said he could go back to the doctor on one condition: if he doesn't find anything, Thomas would have to pay for the doctor's visit. Thomas agreed. The new doctor confirmed that there was a problem in Thomas's knee and he reprimanded Thomas's father for not believing him.

When Thomas was 22 years old, he left the Netherlands Reformed Church and joined the Christian Reformed Church. His father said, "Now I know there's no hope for your soul," and refused to speak to him for the next two years.

A few years later, when Thomas married, his father refused to come to the wedding.

Later in life, when Thomas told his dad that he loved him, his dad responded, "So?" He never told Thomas that he loved him.

Thomas's Account of His Search for Healing

I had surgeries on my lumbar spine in 2005, 2006 and 2008. During 2008–2009, I had several steroid injections and used various painkillers as well as a TENS unit as part of my pain management. But a spinal fluid leak several days after a steroid injection (requiring five days in the University Hospital and a blood patch to stop the leak) meant that I was no longer a candidate for injections. The only alternative was more surgery.

In January, 2009, my spine was fused and rods were inserted. Back at home, I lay in a hospital bed on heavy doses of pain medication. I returned to preaching the week after Easter. I was using a walker and for the next year I sat on a stool to preach both morning and evening.

Within our church we have relatives of Wayne and June Edwards who are missionaries in Kenya. Whenever they're on home assignment, they visit our church and give us accounts of what's happening in their work. I had prayed often that they might see fruit in their labors as well as experience God's blessing on their ministry. None of us knew the connection God had in store for us.

In 2010, I was diagnosed with Diffuse Idiopathic Skeletal Hyperostosis Disease (DISH), a degenerative disc disease which causes vertebrae to fuse together. There is no effective treatment, but I was told it was likely the disease would take 15 years to advance enough to cause additional problems. I was advised to keep riding my bike as long as I could. Yet just four years later, when it was a challenge to manage the pain and stiffness, doctors told me there was nothing more that medicine or surgery could do for me. They advised me to retire early and apply for disability.

I told my congregation what the doctor had said and asked to be released from my pastoral responsibilities; I said I'd work as long as I could while they looked for a new pastor.

On March 25 and May 27, 2013, I had two failed surgeries on my cervical spine. My vocal chords were damaged and I was unable to speak for several weeks. After receiving Botox injections near my vocal chords, I was able to speak but my voice has never been the same.

On August 19, 2013, five vertebrae in my cervical spine were fused. Recovery took some time and I needed Botox injections twice for pain. Sinus surgery followed on March 17, 2014.

Sometime in October of 2014, Wayne stopped over for a visit. Wayne and I spent three hours talking about what God has been doing in his life and ministry. We confirmed a date for him to preach at our church.

I learned that God had called Wayne and June to begin a healing ministry, and Wayne would be talking about it with our congregation. To lay the groundwork, I made plans to preach three sermons in advance of Wayne's coming. The first would be *Jesus as Our Redeemer,* the second *Jesus as Our Healer,* and the third *Jesus as Our Intercessor.* A few of the Scripture passages I studied for the sermon *Jesus as Our Healer* raised questions for me.

On November 18, 2014, I went to the doctor because oxycodone and the medications I was using for arthritis weren't handling the pain and I couldn't sleep. (Lying down was the most painful position. We had a Tempur-Pedic bed with a remote control, which was helpful; I sat up until the drugs kicked in.) My doctor sent me for x-rays of my thoracic spine. I was given prescriptions for 10 mg. OxyContin and 10 mg. Ambien to help me sleep.

I was still riding my bike when weather and road conditions permitted. The riding caused pain, but the overall pain was worse if I didn't ride. I was advised to start using a cane since I was beginning to lose feeling in my right foot.

A week later, on November 25, 2014, I had a follow-up visit with our family doctor. My medication was changed to 20 mg. OxyContin, but I still got only between four and five hours of sleep before pain would wake me up.

On Sunday, November 30, 2014, Wayne and June shared with us some of what was happening in their ministry. I asked several questions about Paul and his "thorn in the flesh," about accepting our lot knowing that "God's grace is sufficient," and about the verses in James 5 that direct the sick to ask the elders to pray over them.

On December 9, 2014, I visited the surgeon to review my x-rays and consider the next step. The surgeon said there was nothing that could be done surgically to help me; surgery would only make matters worse. A prednisone taper showed that steroid injections wouldn't help either. The damage from DISH disease that we'd expected to take 15 years had taken only four. Because the discs were disintegrating, my body was trying to compensate. My spine had grown large spurs on the right side and was trying to fuse itself together.

On Saturday, January 2, 2015, the pain in my back was getting worse, and both feet and parts of both hands were now affected. I had pain in my neck, shoulders and jaw (both sides). I called my doctor to ask what medications I should use and how high a dose I could take. I was advised to go to the Emergency Department at the local hospital immediately. We arrived at 8:40 pm.

After five injections of morphine through an IV and a CT scan of my spine from head to waist, I was sent home with the news that I had multiple nerve impingements due to the severity of the DISH disease. They discovered that I have a very high threshold for pain as well as a resistance to drugs. We arrived home at 2:30 am.

With just over three hours of sleep, I went to church and planned for a very short service. One of the elders read Scripture and planned to close with a few songs whenever I reached the point at which I couldn't go on anymore.

Throughout the years, God had consistently answered my prayers and removed the pain for the duration of the worship services. I always prayed for temporary relief so that my pain would not get in the way of the message. I also prayed that my voice would be restored (I could hardly talk). I was thrilled that God continued to answer that same prayer, week after week. I did not use pain medication until after the services so that my mind would be as clear as possible. That Sunday was no exception. I finished the service and asked the congregation to pray as the future seemed uncertain.

During this first week of the new year, I went through various Scriptures and prayed for healing as I laid my hands on each area of my body. I had full relief from the pain for about 48 hours. Then it all came back full force.

On January 5, 2015, I had a follow-up visit with our family doctor. I was given a February appointment at the Arthritis Clinic. The pain and the sleepless nights continued. The radiologist's report on my CT scan showed that a few of the screws at the base of my neck and another in the lumbar region had come loose. We weren't sure at that point if they were causing a problem or would become a problem.

Account of the Events of January 8 and 9, 2015 (Wayne)
January 8, 2015
Preliminary Meeting

Thomas and I talked together for several hours. Thomas spoke of many of the traumas already mentioned, and other experiences that could have provided foothold opportunities for the demonic and for pain and illness. Because forgiveness is often a prerequisite for healing, Thomas and I carefully noted any additional experiences that might require a decision to forgive, including those that follow.

When Thomas and Maureen were dating, Thomas's dad told him to break up with her. Later Thomas's dad seemed to have accepted Maureen. Had Thomas forgiven this offense?

Thomas's dad was at Thomas and Maureen's house one day when one of their son's black friends was also visiting. Thomas's dad was rude to this friend and called him the N-word. Thomas asked his father to leave the house.

Thomas's sister had once written a harsh letter to Thomas suggesting that his agreeing to have their brother placed in a hospital's mental health unit was motivated by an unwillingness to take care of him. (While there had been reconciliation between Thomas and his sisters, I wanted to make sure Thomas had explicitly and verbally forgiven them.)

Thomas and I thought together about the possibility that particular spirits and/or generational spirits might need to be dealt with—perhaps religious spirits or spirits of rejection, of being unloved, of epilepsy (seizures), of fear, of hatred, of unworthiness, anger or bitterness. We wondered together whether demons could have gained access during any of Thomas's hospital stays, his surgeries and times of being under anesthesia.

Did Thomas perhaps need to ask God's forgiveness for the anger and bitterness he'd allowed to linger in his heart? Were there some ungodly soul ties* with his dad or with doctors or with anyone else that needed to be broken in Jesus' name? We also wanted to pray for healing from any ill effects from medications.

As we were finishing our visit, Thomas said that through the years he had preached on James chapter 5 and the need to forgive, but he had questions about the healing James wrote about in that same chapter.

I suggested to Thomas that we do exactly as James described and asked if he had some church elders who would be willing to meet the next night and pray together. Thomas knew of several and said he would call some of them. Besides bringing June, I asked Thomas's permission to bring an elder from another congregation who we had been discipling.

Before leaving, I prayed briefly for the relief of Thomas's pain. In Jesus' name, I bound any demons, but I didn't try to drive them out at that time, since we hadn't addressed the footholds.

January 9, 2015
The Elders Gather and Prayers for Healing are Answered
Several believers gathered with Thomas and Maureen at their home at 6:30 on the evening of January 9, 2015—elders George and Brian and their wives, Dave, June and I.

I explained the purpose of the gathering and made sure everyone understood that what we were undertaking that evening would require

---

* see page 117 for explanation of soul ties

considerable time. It was quite possible that we would be together until daybreak. We opened in prayer asking Jesus to give everyone discernment through the evening. Everyone was asked to pay attention to whatever it seemed the Holy Spirit might be saying and to be willing to express what they had sensed.

I laid the biblical foundation by teaching from the book of James.

"Is anyone among you sick? He should call the elders of the church to pray over him and anoint him with oil in the name of the Lord. And the prayer offered in faith will make the sick person well; the Lord will raise them up. If he has sinned, he will be forgiven. Therefore confess your sins to each other and pray for each other so that you may be healed. The prayer of a righteous man is powerful and effective" (James 5:14–16 NIV).

"If any of you lacks wisdom, he should ask God, who gives generously to all without finding fault, and it will be given to him. But when he asks, he must believe and not doubt, because he who doubts is like a wave of the sea, blown and tossed by the wind. That man should not think he will receive anything from the Lord; he is a double-minded man, unstable in all he does" (James 1:5–8 NIV).

I explained that the James passages outline what we, believers in Jesus, are to do when we or others are sick. We do this expectantly, full of faith because of Jesus' anointing and mission as foretold by the prophet Isaiah:

The Spirit of the Sovereign Lord is on me,
because the Lord has anointed me
to proclaim good news to the poor.
He has sent me to bind up the brokenhearted,
to proclaim freedom for the captives
and release from darkness for the prisoners... (Isaiah 61:1 NIV).

First, we explored possible generational curses that may have allowed spirits of infirmity to work in Thomas's life. We suspected such generational curses because of his own and his family's health history. We noted his mother's breast cancer and death from a massive heart attack, Thomas's own seizures and those of his grandmother, his father's colon cancer and nervous breakdowns, and his sister's death from breast cancer.

We began by working our way through the Ten Commandments together asking the Holy Spirit to alert Thomas to any his ancestors might have broken. We didn't find this to be very fruitful at the time, although at one point Thomas, like Nehemiah, took responsibility for his ancestors' sins. In prayer, Thomas renounced sin and the consequences of sin that his ancestors may have passed down to him, including any curses, and he forgave them.

Then the elders and I laid hands on Thomas. I asked the Lord Jesus to step in and break all curses that had been passed on to Thomas, particularly curses of infirmity and unworthiness. In Jesus' authority, I commanded any demons to leave.

Then I summarized the things Thomas had talked about the day before, and Thomas very humbly reviewed some of those details about his father and forgave one by one the traumatic experiences he remembered. Thomas also asked God's forgiveness for having held on to his anger toward his father all those years. In each case the elders laid hands on Thomas and asked Jesus to remove the trauma and bring healing to Thomas's soul, spirit and body. After about three hours, we concluded this part of the process by praying together with the elders.

Anointing Thomas with oil and again laying our hands on him, we then prayed for a miracle. We asked God to extend his mercy and grace to heal Thomas's spine and restore his vertebrae and make his ligaments new. We asked the Lord to remove all trauma associated with the surgeries and in Jesus' name commanded any demons that had ridden in on those traumas to leave and not come back.

In Jesus' authority we commanded Thomas's spine to be well. During the time of prayer with all our hands laid on him, we periodically asked Thomas if he was sensing anything happening. He said he was feeling heat in his spine where our hands were on his back. After several more minutes of prayer and waiting, we asked Thomas to stand up and to tell us how he felt. At first he said, "Well, I don't know...," but as he stood there he started turning and twisting a bit, and found he was already experiencing significant relief. His back pain was gone, but he still had numbness, neuropathy and some pain in his legs.

The elders laid their hands on Thomas again. We thanked Jesus for the healing that had taken place, and asked Jesus to complete the healing by bringing relief from the neuropathy in Thomas's feet and hands, including restoring sensation and functionality for his hands.

James 5 refers to Elijah praying for the drought and then praying again for the rain. We looked at 1 Kings 18 to read the entire story. Elijah prayed seven times before he saw the cloud rise up from the sea. So we prayed again. There was more improvement in Thomas's feet. The elders laid hands on him and Dave led in prayer. In Jesus' authority, Dave commanded Thomas's feet and legs to be well and to be strengthened. Thomas got up to test the progress and said, "It's better, but not all the way."

After more prayer for more healing, Thomas started swinging his arms and doing some calisthenics and even a couple jumping jacks. Clearly healing was happening. He was stretching and bending and even got down on the floor to do a few push-ups, at which his wife exclaimed, "Oh, Thomas! Don't hurt yourself!" We all began to laugh with joy, witnessing God's power and grace working in Thomas. We continued to pray with George leading us. Then I followed this up with another prayer. Thomas walked around testing the extent of the healing. He was feeling pretty good.

But the Holy Spirit was speaking to me, bringing to mind what God had done for Elisha and the widow whose small amount of oil filled jar after jar, even jars borrowed from neighbors (2 Kings 4:1–7). So I said, "Let's pray one more time and focus on Thomas's arms and hands."

After this Thomas was feeling even better. All the pain in his spine was gone. He stood with a firm stance and then went up to his tiptoes and back down, telling us that he hadn't been able to do that for years. He felt loose and free.

We concluded our night of prayer and healing, praising God and thanking Him for all he had done that night in Jesus' name.

As the group was getting ready to leave, Thomas wanted to try laying down because that position typically caused the most pain. Dave and I were still in the room gathering up our winter coats, when Thomas lay on his bed and started doing calisthenics while lying on his back, swinging his arms and legs around. We once again began laughing in joy as Thomas was set free, all by God's grace. Praise be to the Lord Jesus Christ, the Father and the Holy Spirit.

Subsequent Interactions between Thomas and Wayne and June
as recorded by Wayne Edwards

January 10, 2015

About 11 o'clock the next day, as June and I were traveling to South Dakota, we got a telephone call from Thomas. He'd had a fantastic night, currently had no pain and felt great. He had decided not to take any pain or sleep medications that evening. He did however intend to put his remote controlled positional bed in what he knew to be the best position for him.

However, the remote wouldn't work. He tried several times, but he finally gave up and just lay flat on his back, praying. He went right to sleep and slept soundly until his wife woke him around 8 am the next morning because he had a meeting to go to. Then he tried the remote and it worked; he tested the batteries and they were fully charged. Thomas told us that he hadn't slept more than four or five hours in a stretch for a very long time, and that he's so thankful to the Lord Jesus for his grace.

January 11, 2015

While we were traveling through Minnesota on the way back home, Thomas called us to tell us about his most recent Sunday services. He said that he was feeling "fantastic," and that he'd told his congregation all that had happened the two days before. Everything seems to be going well. We thank Jesus so very much.

January 16, 2015 (Five Days Later)

We received an email from Thomas. He wrote, "Yesterday, I rode my bike 5.8 miles again! Today I rode 10.6 miles. God is good! For those who have been praying for me, I thank you with all my heart. I ask that you pray for the completion of this healing and that it will be permanent. Our God is an awesome God!"

February 6, 2015 (Three Weeks Later)

Thomas wrote, "Today marks four weeks since my health outlook changed. God has graciously answered prayers for continued healing. I am still sleeping through the night without drugs or pain!

"I am at a loss for words, except to thank Jesus for redeeming me, healing me, and for being my intercessor. I will say that central to this whole process is forgiveness. I needed to forgive some old hurts that I had simply forgotten about or tucked away, but never actively forgiven. I ask forgiveness from anyone reading this whom I may have hurt or offended at any time as well. This experience has brought a whole new dimension to the meaning and importance of forgiveness in my life. Matthew 6:14–15 reads: 'For if you forgive men when they sin against you, your heavenly Father will also forgive you. But if you do not forgive men their sins, your Father will not forgive your sins.' This verse has had a powerful effect on me."

At about the same time, Thomas kept an appointment he'd made some time earlier with a rheumatologist who hadn't seen him before. The doctor asked Thomas to do various movements to measure his range of motion. He asked Thomas to attempt bending down to touch his toes. Thomas did so quite effortlessly.

The doctor just stared at Thomas.

After a long moment the doctor said that he had studied all Thomas's medical records and had been expecting a man who could barely walk. Thomas shared the story of how Jesus had healed him. The doctor, a Christian, exclaimed, "Praise the Lord!" and added, "We rarely see healing of this nature happen."

The doctor went on to say that Thomas no longer had arthritis and could stop his medications. Thomas sheepishly admitted that he'd already stopped taking all his medications except those he was still weaning himself from.

July 10, 2015

June and I received this email from Thomas:

Subject: *Do you know what day it is?*

Today marks six months since I experienced Jesus' healing! Still praising God daily!!

I have had about 60 miles of pain free bike riding so far this week (25+ miles on Wed ;)

I have shared my story at Classis (a regional denominational body), while at a seminar at my old seminary, and at my former church in Virginia, and at a host of other places.

Blessings,

Thomas

If you had faith like a grain of mustard seed, you could say to this mulberry tree, "Be uprooted and planted in the sea," and it would obey you.

LUKE 17:6 ESV

Bear with each other and forgive whatever grievances you may have against one another. Forgive as the Lord forgave you.

COLOSSIANS 3:13 NIV

35

....

Mary

June 15, 2015

Nairobi, Kenya

I had known Stephen for about a year (we were serving together on the board of a Christian ministry) when Stephen and his wife Mary invited June and me to have dinner at their home in Nairobi. The four of us had a lovely evening getting to know each other better. As the evening was coming to a close, Stephen asked us, "How can we pray for you?"

I mentioned some general things about the Amaro people and then described how Jesus has been healing more and more people as we share the Gospel. I also shared the story of Pastor Thomas's healing.

Hearing Thomas's story brought back memories for Mary of her own injury just six months earlier. She had broken her back in January and experienced the trauma associated with it. She said she couldn't imagine the pain Thomas had endured; her own trauma seemed small in comparison. Mary was encouraged to hear that God had healed Thomas and asked if we would pray for her. So we asked her to tell us her story.

Mary works for a Christian non-governmental organization in Kenya. In January, filmmakers came to Kenya to shoot footage of some of the organization's projects. They wanted to shoot some film in the Maasai Mara—the large national game reserve in Rift Valley Province—so a team from the office in Nairobi took the film crew out to the Mara for a few days.

On one of those days, the camera man wanted to be in a *manyatta* (a Maasai homestead) before the sun rose. He wanted to film footage of a woman carrying water with the rising sun behind her. To capture the scene, the camera man had to do the filming while walking backwards. Mary, who was on site with the crew, recognized that the camera man could easily trip and fall on the rough terrain while walking backwards. She quietly volunteered herself to keep a grip on the back of the camera man's shirt so that he wouldn't stumble.

During one of the video shoots, Mary tripped and fell on her back and the cameraman fell on top of her. She heard something crack. The pain was severe; she first thought she had cracked a rib. Whatever had happened, she knew it was serious and so didn't try to get up.

The team lifted her into the Land Cruiser and began the drive to the hospital several hours away. The road was very rough; Mary found she had less pain if she sat up. On the way, they called Mary's husband Stephen. When they arrived at the hospital Stephen was already there waiting.

X-rays showed that one of the vertebrae in the middle of Mary's back was broken. After considering surgery, the doctors decided instead to keep Mary immobilized there in the hospital for a couple of weeks. Then doctors ordered an additional six weeks of bed rest at home. Gradually Mary's vertebrae healed enough that she was able to get out of bed if she wore a back brace.

After a few months the doctors gave Mary permission to return to work wearing the back brace. Certainly, Mary told us, her condition was much improved, but even though almost five months had passed, she was still struggling with residual pain and weakness in her back. By the end of the day she was always exhausted and sore.

I asked Mary who she held responsible for the accident, expecting it would be the cameraman. Mary thought a bit and said, "My supervisor." Mary explained that since she had recently had a very hectic work week, she wasn't scheduled to go out that morning on the camera shoot; she was supposed to have a chance to rest. But at the last minute her supervisor had changed plans and woke her up in the very early hours of the morning to tell her that she had to go.

I asked Mary if she had forgiven her supervisor. She said that she hadn't.

We shared Matthew 6:14–15, "For if you forgive men when they sin against you, your heavenly Father will also forgive you. But if you do not forgive men their sins, your Father will not forgive your sins."

We asked if she was willing to choose to forgive her supervisor. She said yes, she was.

Before we said anything more, Mary went right to prayer. She forgave her supervisor and then asked Jesus to forgive her for holding onto her anger. Listening to Thomas's story had alerted Mary to her own need for forgiveness as well.

We asked Mary to stand, and we asked permission to join her husband Stephen in placing our hands on her back. We thanked Jesus for his grace and prayed John 14:12–13. We asked Jesus to take the trauma of the accident out of Mary's soul and spirit.

In Jesus' name we bound any demonic spirits that might have taken advantage of the trauma. Then we asked Jesus to heal Mary's spirit, soul and body.

In Jesus' authority we commanded any demonic spirits associated with the trauma to leave. Then we asked Jesus to bring healing and wholeness to Mary's spirit, soul and body. After saying, "Amen," we continued on and said, "In the name and authority of Jesus Christ of Nazareth, we command the broken vertebrae to be healed and to be strong, and all the pain to be gone."

After about five minutes I asked Mary if she felt anything. She said she felt heat under our hands.

We waited a while longer and then said, "Amen," and asked Mary how she felt. After moving around and testing her back, she told us that all the pain was gone.

We finished the evening giving thanks together for God's grace and the healing Mary had received.

The Next Day, June 16, 2015

We received a text message from Stephen: "Mary is healed. Completely! Praise be to God."

Five Days Later

We received another text message from Stephen: "Hi Wayne, Mary is healed. No pain. *Kabisa* (completely). Glory to God."

Five Years Later

Stephen and Mary reported that Mary continues in her healing from Jesus. Praise be to God and the Lord Jesus Christ.

The seventy-two returned with joy, saying, "Lord, even the demons are subject to us in your name!" And he said to them, "I saw Satan fall like lightning from heaven. Behold, I have given you authority to tread on serpents and scorpions, and over all the power of the enemy, and nothing shall hurt you. Nevertheless, do not rejoice in this, that the spirits are subject to you, but rejoice that your names are written in heaven."

LUKE 10:17–20 ESV

36

....

Ron

March 13, 2014

Nairobi, Kenya

Ron and his wife knocked on the door of our room in the guesthouse when we were staying in Nairobi for a few days. Ron asked if he could have some time to talk with us. I welcomed them both into our room.

They told us they'd been meeting with a counselor, seeking help with a number of issues. Ron had been mired in self-condemnation since the death of his 21-year-old son from a heart attack four years earlier. His son had weighed 400 pounds and had abused drugs and alcohol. Although Ron thought he had worked through issues of guilt, condemnation and grief, upon coming to Kenya his anguish returned in full force. He struggled with depression and anxiety, obsessively wondering if there was something he could have done to prevent his son's death.

As we talked together, it became clear that the root causes of Ron's pain and bondage went much deeper. As a child and young person, Ron hadn't learned a healthy exercise of his will. His father, a dominating man, both loved and controlled him. Life had been full of rules and criticism with very little affirmation. His father had made time for golf but not for Ron. Ron was left feeling inadequate, unaccepted and unloved.

Desperate and floundering, Ron rebelled both against parental authority and against God. The friends he chose drew him further into danger. During his high school and college years, he abused alcohol and drugs. When drunk he was sexually promiscuous.

When Ron was a junior in college, his girlfriend (who later became his wife) confronted him quite forcefully about his behavior. Ron had grown up attending church regularly, but it was this interaction that led him to surrender his life to Jesus' Lordship.

Ron became serious about following Jesus. Day by day he yielded his life to Christ, and he grew. He stopped drinking, drugging and sleeping around—he was done with all of it.

In 1989, Ron's wife gave birth to their first child, a son they named Tommy. Tommy lived for only three days. In his grief and devastation, Ron was furious with God. For the next year he didn't touch his Bible. Even the birth of his second son, Cory, didn't relieve his anger.

In 1998 Ron came to live in Kenya. In 1999 he had a stroke and was miraculously healed through prayer. Despite this experience of the love and power of God, he continued to struggle with anxiety.

Having heard this much of Ron's story, I asked Ron and his wife to make a list of the ways Ron's father had hurt him and a list of any others who had wronged him.

That afternoon we met again for an hour and a half. I explained how footholds are formed and we looked at God's word together to understand how they can be broken. We also talked about the difference between confession and repentance. I asked Ron if he wanted to be free. Ron said he was very tired and would do anything to find freedom.

First, I asked Ron to forgive his dad for all the ways he'd made him feel rejected. We worked through the list of issues and, with the support of his wife, Ron made the decision to forgive his father for each of them, even though he had been unjustly treated.

Then, with Jesus' authority I broke the ungodly soul tie* between Ron and his father and asked God to heal Ron's mind, emotions and will.

Ron was also led to ask God's forgiveness for his own sin toward his dad; he'd held onto his anger for years and had repeatedly "let the sun go down" on his anger (Ephesians 4:26). Ron was convicted by the Holy Spirit and confessed this and also renounced the anger that had been passed through generations down to him. He decided to never again let the sun go down on his anger but to forgive immediately.

* see page 117 for explanation of soul ties

He forgave each person involved in every situation that came to mind and determined to take specific steps to seek reconciliation and make amends. Ron decided to speak with his dad, both to explain that he had forgiven him and to ask forgiveness for his rebellion and his failure to honor his parents. Ron said he would speak with each of his sons to alert them to the rebellion, anger, and failure to forgive that had defined his own life and had been passed on to them; Ron also said that he would ask their forgiveness and encourage them to break this generational foothold and pattern once and for all.

Ron also worked his way through the list of people who had wronged him, forgiving each one. The process brought to light wrongs he'd committed himself. Ron remembered a previous boss he'd wronged. Ron decided that he would ask for his forgiveness.

During our time with Ron and his wife, Ron confessed that when he was in college, while drunk he'd had sexual relationships with seven different women. Ron asked God's forgiveness for each sexual encounter and repented, determined to live in the purity God wants for him.

I asked the Lord to heal Ron from the ungodly soul ties formed by those seven sexual relationships and, in Jesus' name and authority, severed those soul ties. I asked the Lord to return to Ron all of the emotion, attention, thoughts and energy he'd given to each of the seven women, and asked that whatever the women had given to Ron would be returned to them.

Ron repented from his abuse of alcohol and drugs and resolved never to use them again.

Ron confessed and repented of the many years he had blamed God for the losses in his life, especially Tommy's and Cory's deaths, but other things as well. And then, finally, Ron forgave himself.

Only after several hours—when everything had been dealt with and the footholds exposed and broken by renouncing sin and by confession, repentance and receiving Jesus' forgiveness—did we move to deliverance ministry.

Speaking out loud, Ron renounced Satan and the evil spirits and commanded them to leave. His having forgiven others, his confessing his sin and repenting, and his receiving Jesus' forgiveness had removed any rights the evil spirits had. We affirmed that the blood of Jesus has fully redeemed Ron.

I commanded any spirits of rejection, anger, depression, unforgiveness, self-abuse, adultery, immorality, drunkenness, fear and anxiety to leave. Several different manifestations took place: a spirit leaving through the buttocks with a sensation like a shock, a sense of heaviness, tingling, his head feeling heavy, and a spirit leaving through his legs.

Many demons left via Ron's breath through coughing and yawning. Some lifted from his head. Others exited in a choking sensation followed by a cough.

We tested for a spirit of idolatry. After a major manifestation the spirit left. I went through the deliverance process several times to make sure all the demons had left.

As Ron was delivered, he felt peace and joy. We thanked Jesus for his grace.

As we finished. I asked Ron about his deaf ear. Ron had mentioned earlier that he'd had an infection in 2003 and had lost all hearing in that ear. Doctors had been unable to help, although one doctor had suggested taking a portion of the nerve from the good ear to replace what was damaged in the bad one. Ron declined, unwilling to risk losing his hearing altogether.

I asked Ron if he would like to come to Jesus to receive healing for his ear. Ron told me that he'd had others lay hands on him and anoint him with oil some years ago, but he'd remained completely deaf in that ear. I asked him why he thought he had not been healed; Ron thought maybe he didn't have enough faith. I explained that everyone who came to Jesus was healed. Faith only the size of a mustard seed is needed, just enough faith to come to Jesus. It's all by grace.

Ron said yes, he wanted to come to Jesus.

I placed my hand on Ron's deaf ear, the ear on the right side, and thanked Jesus for this healing that belongs to Ron because of what Jesus has done. Ron was asked to profess the same, and he did.

I asked Jesus to extend his grace to work a miracle, to heal and open Ron's deaf ear.

After a few minutes I felt some warmth and something like a little electricity on Ron's ear.

After we'd finished praying, Ron snapped his fingers by his previously deaf ear and exclaimed, "I can hear, I can hear!" He kept snapping his fingers, stunned. Ron praised God for his grace! He thanked Jesus for opening his ear after 11 years of deafness.

It was almost midnight, so we thanked the Lord together and said goodnight. Even after all these years, I vividly remember watching Ron walk the long corridor to his room, snapping his fingers by his ears, alternating back and forth.

The next morning at breakfast, Ron stood up and asked for everyone's attention. He told the 35–50 people in the dining room that Jesus had healed his deaf ear the night before, exclaiming, "It was a miracle!"

"And if you faithfully obey the voice of the LORD your God, being careful to do all his commandments that I command you today, the LORD your God will set you high above all the nations of the earth. And all these blessings shall come upon you and overtake you, if you obey the voice of the LORD your God.

DEUTERONOMY 28:1–2 ESV

But if you will not obey the voice of the LORD your God or be careful to do all his commandments and his statutes that I command you today, then all these curses shall come upon you and overtake you.

DEUTERONOMY 28:15 ESV

Now the Spirit of the LORD departed from Saul, and a harmful spirit from the LORD tormented him. And Saul's servants said to him, "Behold now, a harmful spirit from God is tormenting you. Let our lord now command your servants who are before you to seek out a man who is skillful in playing the lyre, and when the harmful spirit from God is upon you, he will play it, and you will be well." So Saul said to his servants, "Provide for me a man who can play well and bring him to me."

1 SAMUEL 16:14–17 ESV

His divine power has granted to us all things that pertain to life and godliness, through the knowledge of him who called us to his own glory and excellence, by which he has granted to us his precious and very great promises, so that through them you may become partakers of the divine nature, having escaped from the corruption that is in the world because of sinful desire.

*For this very reason, make every effort to supplement
your faith with virtue, and virtue with knowledge,
and knowledge with self-control, and self-control
with steadfastness, and steadfastness with godliness,
and godliness with brotherly affection, and brotherly
affection with love. For if these qualities are yours
and are increasing, they keep you from being
ineffective or unfruitful in the knowledge of our Lord
Jesus Christ. For whoever lacks these qualities is so
nearsighted that he is blind, having forgotten that he
was cleansed from his former sins.*

*Therefore, brothers, be all the more diligent to
confirm your calling and election, for if you practice
these qualities you will never fall. For in this way
there will be richly provided for you an entrance
into the eternal kingdom of our Lord and Savior
Jesus Christ.*

2 PETER 1:3–11 ESV

*For if, after they have escaped the defilements of the
world through the knowledge of our Lord and Savior
Jesus Christ, they are again entangled in them and
overcome, the last state has become worse for them
than the first. For it would have been better for
them never to have known the way of righteousness
than after knowing it to turn back from the holy
commandment delivered to them. What the true
proverb says has happened to them: "The dog
returns to its own vomit, and the sow, after washing
herself, returns to wallow in the mire."*

2 PETER 2:20–22 ESV

37

....

Bocha

June 2, 2007
Duma, Kenya

Bocha's testimony is that he came to Jesus Christ sometime in August, 2006, when he was perhaps 21 years old, through the ministry of our Kenyan mission colleagues in a village some distance away. While visiting with us in our home, he talked about the ways he was growing in his relationship with Jesus. We enjoyed his openness, transparency and maturity. Bocha seemed to have a good grasp of the basic biblical doctrines and was eager to learn and understand even more.

Bocha reads English very well. He and I were able to enjoy in-depth discussions of God's word. When Bocha told me that he had come to see Islam as a false religion and Mohamed as a false prophet, I was a bit surprised. It's unusual for such a young believer to come to those understandings on their own.

The morning of June 2, I sat under a tree with Bocha and Ben (who was with us for a year serving as a teacher). We were studying 1 John 4 and 5 together. Bocha read the chapters out loud and we took time to spell out some of what these passages teach. We learned that Jesus had come from heaven itself, that God is love and can be known, that any spirit that does not confess Jesus as the Son of God who came from heaven is not from God, and so much more.

We noted that while Islam honors Jesus as a prophet, it denies that Jesus came in the flesh from heaven ("The Word became flesh and made his dwelling among us" John 1:14 NIV), was crucified and rose from the dead. Hearing all that Ben and I were saying, Bocha stated even more clearly that he understood that following Islam was actually sin and rebellion against God.

We explained to Bocha that we had discovered that some followers of Jesus who have received the gift of eternal life may not have been automatically set free of the spirit of Islam. Bocha understood and wanted to make sure that he himself harbored no such spirit. He confessed to Jesus that he now understood his past involvement with Islam as sin; he repented and stated that, by an act of his will, he was choosing never to return to Islam. Bocha thanked the Lord for his forgiveness and for all he had done at the cross.

Once the foothold was removed, we continued. In Jesus' name and authority, I ordered the spirit of Islam to leave.

Bocha's heart began to beat very hard and fast. After a few minutes a strange sensation occurred in his throat and resisted our commands that it leave. Then suddenly it seemed to disappear.

We prayed together, asking Jesus not to allow the spirit to trick us and hide, but to deliver Bocha from the spirit. Once again, we ordered the spirit to leave.

Again, Bocha's heart began to beat very hard and fast. Again, he felt a sensation move to his throat. The sensation moved to his head; Bocha's head became very heavy and felt like it was shrinking. After a few moments the spirit released its grip and Bocha felt freed of it. We praised God and asked for fresh anointing of the Holy Spirit in his life.

Afterwards I asked Bocha if he had any other unconfessed sin. "What is the Holy Spirit saying in your heart and mind?" I asked.

When Bocha said he wasn't aware of any hidden or unconfessed sin, I asked him if he had ever participated in the *Hinesse* dance. "Yes, several times," he said.

We looked at Deuteronomy 18 together and then discussed participation in the *Hinesse* dance as a form of demon worship. Bocha agreed that this is an offense against God, and detestable in his sight. He confessed and repented in prayer and then gladly received God's forgiveness.

I ordered the demonic spirits to leave in Jesus' name. Bocha felt his ears and eyes tightening and shrinking. His eyes became glassy. We persisted in prayer and in ordering these spirits to leave. Finally, the moment came when Bocha knew they were gone.

We explained to Bocha that in spite of the demonic involvement, he had been accountable for his decisions. But with this deliverance he could expect to experience more freedom to make right choices. We warned him against falling back into the sin he had repented from, which could open the door for demons to return.

There wasn't time to explore the possibility of other strongholds before Bocha had to head back to his village. We always feel deep concern for these dear friends who must follow Jesus in what are often confusing and hostile situations. Because Bocha lives quite far away, we won't see him on a regular basis, but we will pray for courage for him and for a hunger to grow in Christ.

June 28, 2008

It had been over a year since we had seen Bocha. Periodically we were privy to a bit of news about him, but sometimes the reports varied.

It seemed Bocha had an opportunity to go back to school with the help of colleagues in their home area, but something went wrong. Some said that after a while he left school and began using alcohol and fooling around with girls.

We do know that later Bocha moved up to a town in the north to live with a cousin for six to eight months. This cousin, who has a butchery business, pressured Bocha to join him in praying five times a day and practicing the ways of Islam. Things went from bad to worse. For several months the thing Bocha was really living for was *miraa* (an amphetamine plant that is grown in Kenya); he consumed it every day with his cousin and friends. He also visited a prostitute a few times; his life was in a tragic tailspin.

One day Bocha, dressed in Muslim attire, showed up with our colleague at a prayer day in Duma. He told us that his life was a mess. He joined us for a small portion of the meeting and we prayed for him.

About a week later he showed up in Duma again and stayed with us for a few days. It was then that I had opportunities to meet with him. In many ways, it seemed to be a repeat of the experience we had shared a year earlier.

I took some time to explain Jesus' authority and the wonder of his rescuing us from the kingdom of darkness. Bocha wanted to turn back to Jesus and confessed his sin in a general way and also repented, but he said that he still had a heavy heart.

We read 1 John 4 and 5 again. Bocha confessed following Islam as sin and repented. He decided by an act of his will that he would never involve himself in Islam again. He thanked Jesus for all he had done on the cross and gladly received the forgiveness Jesus offers so freely.

In Jesus' authority I ordered all evil spirits connected to the foothold of Islam to leave. Bocha began sweating and then both his ears popped. He said, "They have left." Bocha felt some joy at this point and felt lighter. He reported that he could see more clearly and that the pain in his ribs had disappeared.

Next we read the Ten Commandments together from Exodus 20 so that Bocha could understand that his use of *miraa* and misuse of alcohol were a form of idolatry. After Bocha confessed, repented, and thanked God for forgiveness, I ordered the evil spirits to leave. Bocha's feet began to sweat quite intensely and then he reported that the demons had left.

The commandment prohibiting adultery was the basis from which we addressed his fornication with a woman named Halima and his past sexual partners. First, we cut the soul ties* with each of the women he had sinned with and against. Then Bocha came to the Lord, confessing his sin and repenting, followed by thanking Jesus for his forgiveness. I ordered all other spirits to leave. The manifestation started in his chest and moved down his legs to his feet. Bocha was sweating profusely. The demons finally left. Bocha reported that each deliverance brought more light and clarity. His body also felt lighter in weight.

(Note: Although Bocha reported that the demons were gone, I had sensed no clear exiting from his rib cage or feet. He may have been deceived when the spirits stopped manifesting; they may not have exited. His ears popping, however, was a more likely indication of spirits exiting.)

* see page 117 for explanation of soul ties

January 13, 2011 (Two Years Later)

Bocha traveled to our place in Duma to ask for help. He told us that his life had become a mess again and he confessed making many sinful decisions and reopening many demonic footholds. After we'd talked, I asked him if he was serious and if he really wanted freedom. Bocha wept and said he did.

I sent him back to his village to think and pray for two weeks. I invited him to return when he was truly ready to repent from his sin and was serious about wanting to be free.

January 27, 2011 (Two Weeks Later)

Bocha returned to Duma. He told us that he truly wanted to be free.

I reminded him how important it was to be totally honest and to bring everything out in the open. So Bocha confessed that he hadn't been a good child of God and that he had not been faithful to Jesus or loved him in the way he deserved. Hatred and rejection had been allowed to enter into his heart. He had shamed Jesus by his sexual immorality and drinking—particularly while taking a polytechnic course at a Christian organization in western Kenya—and by using drugs like *bangi* and *miraa,* as well as by smoking cigarettes. Bocha also confessed that he'd been dishonest; he had lied to our colleague and he'd lied and cheated while at school and had also broken other school rules.

After quite a protracted time of counseling, Bocha seemed genuinely convicted. After repenting from all of the sins he had confessed to us, and thanking Jesus for his forgiveness, Bocha stated clearly that he would submit to Jesus' Lordship.

I then ordered the demons to leave. Demons of drinking and drugs left out of his ears. A spirit of immorality manifested in his leg and arm, moved through his heart and then out of Bocha's left ear, exiting twice. Two or three demons of dishonesty manifested from Bocha's feet to his torso, then into his right arm, up to his head and out of both ears.

The next morning Bocha said he'd had a rough night. He felt as if someone was fighting with him physically. We talked together at breakfast; Bocha confessed that a few years earlier he had broken into a duka and stolen some goods. Bocha declared his repentance and told us that he would ask the duka owner's forgiveness and do his best to make amends. Bocha also forgave his father for all the stealing he had done. Although there were manifestations in Bocha's arm and thigh, we didn't witness any clear exiting apart from three yawns.

Sometimes people's lives are tragically complicated, messy and full of challenges. Not one of us can rescue, cleanse or heal ourselves. For Bocha to be truly free, it will be essential that he choose, by an act of his will, to definitively make Jesus the Lord of his life. Then he must maintain that commitment by full obedience to Jesus Christ with the reliable help of God's Spirit—the Counselor and Helper, that the Father gives generously to all who ask.

The first epistle of John offers a beautiful and certain hope: "This is the message we heard from him and proclaim to you, that God is light and in him there is no darkness at all. If we say that we have fellowship with him while we are walking in darkness, we lie and do not do what is true; but if we walk in the light as he himself is in the light, we have fellowship with one another, and the blood of Jesus his Son cleanses us from all sin." (1 John 1:5–7 ESV)

After he had finished all his sayings in the hearing of the people, he entered Capernaum. Now a centurion had a servant who was sick and at the point of death, who was highly valued by him. When the centurion heard about Jesus, he sent to him elders of the Jews, asking him to come and heal his servant. And when they came to Jesus, they pleaded with him earnestly, saying, "He is worthy to have you do this for him, for he loves our nation, and he is the one who built us our synagogue."

And Jesus went with them. When he was not far from the house, the centurion sent friends, saying to him, "Lord, do not trouble yourself, for I am not worthy to have you come under my roof. Therefore I did not presume to come to you. But say the word, and let my servant be healed. For I too am a man set under authority, with soldiers under me: and I say to one, 'Go,' and he goes; and to another, 'Come,' and he comes; and to my servant, 'Do this,' and he does it."

When Jesus heard these things, he marveled at him, and turning to the crowd that followed him, said, "I tell you, not even in Israel have I found such faith." And when those who had been sent returned to the house, they found the servant well.

LUKE 7:1–10 ESV

38

....

Walo

October 2018

Tula, Kenya

Walo lived in the village of Tula, but frequently traveled the three-hour drive to the town of Kola on his *piki* (motorcycle). On one of these trips, when Walo was driving slowly down the road, a *piki* traveling at high speed crashed broadside into him.

Both Walo and the other driver went down hard on the tarmac, causing serious injury to both riders and damage to their bikes. Motorists stopped and transported both men to the hospital. The driver of the second *piki* was transferred to another hospital several hours away where he passed away from his injuries.

Walo had been taken to the Government Referral Hospital, but their x-ray machine was not working and they were experiencing a shortage of drugs and other medical supplies. So Walo, with help from some friends, hired a small car to take him back home to his village.

On their way back to Tula, they stopped by our mission village clinic for treatment. By this time Walo's leg was so swollen and painful that our visiting nurse practitioner attended to him while he sat in the front seat of the car. Walo's leg and knee had suffered severe abrasions as well as a nasty open gash. The nurse practitioner cleaned the wound, then treated and bandaged it and instructed Walo to go back to the hospital for an x-ray.

Walo proceeded to travel the final hour down the road toward Tula.

At this point, June and I finally learned that the man who was injured in the *piki* accident was, in fact, Walo, from the village of Tula, a long-time friend of ours. We wished we had known at the time so that we could have gone up to the dispensary to see him.

About a month later, June and I traveled to Tula. June was scheduled to hold a medical clinic and various work projects there needed my attention. After finishing the day's work, we decided to stop by Walo's home to see how he was doing.

We found Walo in his mud walled house laying on a mattress on the ground with his knee raised. The wound had nearly healed over, but the leg was extremely swollen. Walo was not able to walk and was suffering a tremendous amount of pain and stiffness.

We listened to the whole story of the accident and shared with Walo that God loves him very much. Walo had heard the Gospel many times in the past, and though somewhat receptive, he had not fully yielded his life to the Lord Jesus Christ. We once again shared the Gospel with Walo and before leaving, we invited him to go to Jesus together with us and ask Jesus to heal his knee and leg. Walo agreed without any hesitation.

June and I placed our hands on Walo's knee and prayed. Then, under Jesus' authority, we commanded his knee to be healed in the name of Jesus Christ of Nazareth.

Later Walo explained that while our hands were on his knee and we were praying for him, he had felt pain move out of his knee and up into our hands. Immediately afterwards his pain was gone and the swelling was much less.

We thanked Jesus together for his grace.

After saying our good-byes, June and I headed for home.

Update

Later Walo told us that the next day, still pain free and with most of the swelling gone, he had been able to get up and walk. In fact, after having spent a month lying on the dirt floor of his house, he had jumped on his *piki* and rode all the way to the village *dukas* (small shops).

In the weeks, months and years following, Walo shared with others how Jesus Christ had healed him.

Be angry and do not sin; do not let the sun go down on your anger, and give no opportunity to the devil.

EPHESIANS 4:26–27 ESV

(Same passage in a different translation)

In your anger do not sin. Do not let the sun go down while you are still angry, and do not give the devil a foothold.

EPHESIANS 4:26–27 NIV

And Jesus answered them, "Truly, I say to you, if you have faith and do not doubt, you will not only do what has been done to the fig tree, but even if you say to this mountain, 'Be taken up and thrown into the sea,' it will happen. And whatever you ask in prayer, you will receive, if you have faith."

MATTHEW 21:21–22 ESV

39

....

Margret

November 25, 2013
Nairobi, Kenya

Forgiveness

As a missionary pilot, Jack had flown our kids home from their
boarding school and made several other flights to Duma bringing guests
and supplies. On one such trip, Jack shared some meals with us and our
guests and listened intently to stories about some of the healing miracles
we had seen Jesus do.

After returning home to Nairobi, Jack told his wife Margret about the
stories that had been shared. Then he began to re-examine the Gospels
for himself. What he had heard in Duma was challenging and perplexing
to him. He had been raised in a church that didn't talk much about
miraculous healing. But as Jack studied the Gospels now, reading them
in light of the stories he had heard, he saw that Jesus had healed all who
came to him, not turning anyone away.

On one of our trips to Nairobi, Jack and Margret invited us to their
home for dinner. Margret was so eager to know more about healing that
once we'd come through the door, it took about three minutes for her to
begin peppering us with questions.

This wasn't just curiosity. Margret had been sick with various illnesses
for some time, including some chronic diseases. She had stomach
problems and was lactose and gluten intolerant; she also suffered from an
autoimmune thyroid disease. Before we met Margret, she had received

radiation which had nearly destroyed her thyroid. For the last three years, Margret had been deaf in one ear and she hadn't ovulated for several months. She and Jack hadn't been able to conceive since the birth of their little girl.

The four of us talked at some length about the Gospel accounts of Jesus announcing the kingdom of God, healing people and delivering them from evil spirits and eventually sending out his disciples to do the same. Then Margret asked for prayer for healing for herself. She said that they had prayed many times in the past, but she hadn't been healed.

I asked her why she thought she hadn't been healed before this. Margret said God had taught her a lot in her walk with Christ through these troubles so she thought he must have a good purpose for allowing them.

We wanted to give Margret a biblical framework that would make it more possible for her to receive healing by addressing any doubts, so we looked at various passages together. We wanted her to see that Jesus healed all who came to him, and that he revealed the Father's will in all he did and said.

Before beginning to pray, June asked Margret if there was anyone she hadn't forgiven.

She paused and pondered deeply before she responded. This question opened a floodgate. Margret told us about the pain she was experiencing from a broken relationship. She wanted to forgive and had asked God to help her forgive, but she felt thwarted because the other person didn't repent and seek forgiveness.

She also had some hard feelings towards her parents. They had been good parents, but they'd also been critical, and Margret had never felt that her dad wholeheartedly accepted her.

As various Scriptures came to mind, we let them speak to us and to Margret's need. Ephesians 4:26 urged us not to hold on to anger, to refuse to "let the sun go down" while staying angry for another day. In Matthew 6, Jesus told us that only if we forgive will our heavenly Father forgive us, and in Matthew 18 he urged us to forgive our brothers and sisters from the heart.

The Scriptures were living and active for Margret. She had received God's grace and she wanted to extend grace to her friend and her parents;

she wanted to forgive as Jesus had forgiven her.

When Margret began to pray, asking God to help her forgive, I realized she didn't have clarity about how to choose to forgive by an act of her will. I explained that Jesus can always be trusted to help us forgive; what was required now was a decision on her part. She would need to choose, by an act of her will, to forgive her friend and her parents.

Margret understood. She stated out loud and clearly that she was choosing to repent from resenting the person who had wronged her. Because of the Scriptures, she now understood that holding on to unforgiveness was sin, so she was choosing to love and pray for her and to do good to her. Margret also repented from the sin involved in her relationship with her parents. She stated her intention: she would talk to her parents, express her forgiveness and ask them to forgive her.

June asked Margret if she loved herself. That question seemed to stop her in her tracks. Tears began to flow as she overcame her hesitation. With great vulnerability, she described how she perceived herself and how she continued to struggle to accept herself. She said she certainly *didn't* love herself. We talked at length together about God's thorough acceptance of her—knowing her completely and understanding every aspect of her struggle—and about how deeply God loves her. This seemed to impact her deeply, and before we finished, she said that she had chosen to forgive herself and to see herself as God saw her, and even to love herself.

Deliverance

We spent extensive time teaching from God's word and praying together. After Jack and Margret gave permission, we began to explore whether demons were involved in Margret's illnesses and troubles. We spent more time in intensive prayer eliminating any footholds the unclean spirits had claimed in Margret's life.

When spirits of fear and rejection were first ordered out, Margret's stomach began to ache and she became very cold and then very hot all over. Then, although there was no clear sign of the spirits leaving, a tremendous sense of peace came upon Margret.

Healing

We asked Margret to sit in a chair so that Jack and June and I could lay hands on her. We asked the Lord to open Margret's womb and bless her with more children. We prayed together for healing for Margret's thyroid disease and other illnesses and for her deaf ear. Jack tested her ear by whispering into it. She could hear nothing but a few crackles inside.

We prayed again. She began to hear more. As midnight came and went and we completed our time of praying together, Margret told us that she felt something going on within her ear.

On the Saturday following our meeting together, June telephoned her. Margret held the phone to her previously deaf ear. Although she could hear, she said it sounded like she was in a tunnel; she had received partial healing but more was needed. Margret told June that in addition to the physical healing she'd experienced, which in itself was very wonderful, she was amazed and so thankful to realize that she felt free inside. God had healed her soul.

We asked the Lord to continue to clarify for Margret and Jack his willingness to heal, and we asked him to complete Margret's healing.

Follow-up

The following week we saw Margret at a conference, during which one speaker's perspective was that Paul's "thorn in the flesh" was a physical illness or disability. This raised doubts in people's minds about healing. It certainly raised doubts for Margret. But despite these doubts, on Friday, December 6, 2013, the results from Margret's thyroid test came back normal.

On February 14, 2014, Jack and Margret came to Duma for the day when they brought our son Edwin home for midterm break. Margret told us that her hearing was around 75% better in the previously deaf ear. She expressed deep gratitude to Jesus for the inner healing that had taken place and for setting her free.

Margret's most exciting news was that she had become pregnant soon after we'd prayed back in November. She joyously gave thanks to Jesus and thanked us for the part we had played. All glory goes to Jesus!

January 2017 Update (Three Years Later)

By 2017, Margret had three children—one girl and two boys. Margret's experience demonstrates something we've found to be true: the more bold and eager to come to Jesus a person is, the more they receive from Jesus, whether they understand very thoroughly or not. How gracious he is! Thanks be to God!

2019 Update (Two More Years Later)

In a telephone conversation, Margret said, "I am grateful for all the healing of my thyroid, for the hearing restored in my deaf ear, and for becoming pregnant soon after we prayed together. We have more children in our family and a newborn baby. Yet with all the healing that I received from the Lord, the most significant was the healing of my inner being, my heart."

A few days later she sent me this text: "My endocrinologist's words were that I had some of the worst labs (hyperthyroidism/Graves' disease) she has ever seen in her career, and now I'm one of the most healthy/stable people she has seen. To God be the glory!"

For if someone comes and proclaims another Jesus than the one we proclaimed, or if you receive a different spirit from the one you received, or if you accept a different gospel from the one you accepted, you put up with it readily enough.

2 CORINTHIANS 11:4 ESV

40

....

Alan

June 20, 2014

Duma, Kenya

Alan and Marcia, a pastor and wife from Oklahoma, came to Duma to visit us for two nights, along with Brad and Phil, two missionary colleagues who serve elsewhere. We spent the two days walking around the village and describing the work here. Evening discussions revolved around Jesus and his role as our healer.

On our guests' final night with us, at 9 pm (which for early-rising missionaries feels very much like midnight) as we were about to say good night, Alan suddenly began to speak with a sense of urgency. He said he knew that if he didn't say something right away, he never would. Alan had been praying and talking with his wife all day about the possibility of asking us for help; the subject of deliverance was new to him, but he suspected that he himself needed it.

Before going to seminary Alan had been a lay youth pastor for seven years, and after ordination had served for four years as a pastor in a Lutheran church. But the shame he had struggled with since childhood still haunted him, as did his own history of secret sin. Alan did his best to lay out for us everything that might possibly need to be addressed.

His father, despite experiencing a conversion while in college, had continued to struggle with anger, drinking, drugs and sexual relationships. And although Alan has no memory of being abused himself, he knows that one of the pastors he had when he was small was later convicted of child sexual abuse.

When Alan was in second or third grade, a neighbor boy named Mark convinced him to take his clothes off and the boys touched each other. In fifth and sixth grade a step-cousin paid him to touch his penis. In sixth and seventh grades, Alan and another cousin and the cousin's sister all touched one another. Another cousin named Bob introduced him to pornography and masturbation at the family's lake cabin. Alan became addicted to pornography and despite confession and seeking forgiveness over and over again, he hasn't been able to stay away from it. For the past ten years, gambling has also been an active addiction.

Alan told us that he's always struggled with identity and self-worth. Even though academics and sports came easily for him, throughout his school years he continually heard inner whispers of condemnation.

In high school Alan had sexual relations with two girlfriends. While in college he had sexual intercourse with a girlfriend named Joanna and he wanted to marry her. He had already purchased a ring when he found Joanna in bed with a close friend of his. The pain and anger were deeper than anything he had known before, and Alan confessed that he had not forgiven that betrayal. Alan said it seemed that his entire life had been painful, secretive and shameful.

When we were ready to begin the work of deliverance—which can be lengthy and exhausting—I invited our colleagues to leave, but Alan insisted they stay and participate. He was desperate for help and freedom. So June and I led the session along with support from these fellow missionaries.

First, I clarified the differences between confession, repentance and forgiveness. While confession had been emphasized in his upbringing and education, repentance was unfamiliar to Alan. His understanding of Lutheran theology was that it taught that the human will has very little power to withstand temptation. Asking for forgiveness during the weekly worship service had been the primary way sin and failure were addressed, so Alan was grateful to learn that God had provided a way for us to definitively turn away from sin.

As he continued to confess his sin and to repent by an act of his will, June and I helped him renounce sin, receive God's forgiveness, and forgive by name each person who had wronged him.

Alan told us that he had confessed his problem of pornography to his congregation on a few occasions. Although after each confession he would do better for a while, eventually he always fell again. I explained that the will alone can go only so far; it can't change the heart. But if our will is joined with the power and grace of our Lord Jesus Christ, profound change is possible.

While we were talking, I took notes so that Alan's deliverance could be as thorough as possible. The unclean spirits I suspected we would need to confront included lust, shame, guilt, pornography, sexual immorality, idolatry, anger, gambling and deception.

We worked through each of these issues during the evening, testing to see if deliverance was needed. Lust and sexual immorality were tested first, but no manifestation occurred. Alan said he had received a lot of healing already in this area.

Within a minute of our testing to see if a spirit of pornography was present, Alan began grinning in a bizarre way and breathing very deeply and forcefully (the sound reminding me of a steam locomotive). The manifestations continued for several minutes. Alan described tingling going from his hands and feet up to his head. There was one big yawn and the manifestations ceased. It seemed that the unclean spirit had exited. We tested two more times without eliciting any manifestations.

We prayed that all ungodly soul ties* would be severed and that Alan's mind would be cleansed from all pornographic images. We completed the rest of the tests for other unclean spirits without seeing any more manifestations. Afterwards Alan reported experiencing a very deep peace—a peace he said he had never had before.

June 21, 2014

Alan was still enjoying that deep peace the next morning. We thanked Jesus for his grace and deliverance and suggested that Alan and his wife read Peter Horrobin's book *Healing Through Deliverance*. After breakfast the guests left to continue their journey.

* see page 117 for explanation of soul ties

Personal Questions and Reflections

Given the limited time we had with Alan, significant healing through deliverance had been received. However, a thorough exploration of whether further deliverance was needed wasn't possible before he, his wife and the other guests left to continue their journey.

Although Alan had told us he had already experienced significant healing in matters relating to sexuality, it surprised me that we didn't see any manifestations when we tested to see if Alan needed deliverance in the areas of sexual immorality and lust. I doubt that we identified all the footholds and demons; more exploration of generational curses was also needed.

Alan said he had asked one woman (Joanna, I believe) to forgive him. Given his sexual activity in high school, it's likely he will need to ask forgiveness as well from the two other women. (Alan said he had just 'checked in with them to see if everything was good'—not at all the same as extending and receiving forgiveness.)

We will wait and watch for what John the Baptist called "the fruit of repentance." We find that if freedom is fully received and repentance consistently engaged, the peace and joy of living in freedom is experienced. If something is left unaddressed and still needs healing, this too will become evident. Healthy, long-lasting fruit is what we look for.

A few years later

We learned that Alan had left the church and his wife for another woman.

Partial deliverance can offer a taste of freedom that one hopes will lead the sufferer to seek further deliverance. The overall objective, of course, is complete deliverance from all unclean spirits and a life of fruitfulness and freedom in Jesus Christ.

ALAN

But you will receive power when the Holy Spirit has come upon you, and you will be my witnesses in Jerusalem and in all Judea and Samaria, and to the end of the earth.

ACTS 1:8 ESV

41

....

Dube

December 8, 2022

Amaro Region, Kenya

I jumped on my *piki* (motorcycle) and traveled to a large village about 15 kilometers away. The brother of a friend of mine had visited our village a few days earlier and told me that Dube, the headman from there, had been sick for about a week.

When I arrived, I found Dube in his mud-walled, grass-roofed home. He welcomed me and invited me to sit on a mat on the cleanly swept earthen floor. Soon two of Dube's brothers came in, one joining us on the mat and the other sitting on a stool that stood about four inches high. We talked about the recent rainfall and other local news.

Then Dube began to describe symptoms he had been experiencing for the past week. His hip and leg hurt whenever he tried to walk, and he had been suffering from severe fevers, headaches, back and stomach pain and general weakness.

I asked Dube what type of treatments he had tried. "Did you go to the medical dispensary in your village?"

He answered no; the nurse in charge was not around.

The day before, his brother had gone to another dispensary about five kilometers away hoping to buy something to help Dube, and then in the evening had brought a small package of tablets to him. Dube told me he had been instructed to take two at night and two in the morning for five days. He had just taken the second dose as I arrived, but he was still feeling miserable.

As we visited together, Dube's brothers reminisced about the many times June and I had come to their home to treat their respected father for various illnesses. He had suffered from diabetes in his old age and June had treated him for that and related conditions. Before his death, their father had told them, "You can trust Wayne and June, so always welcome them into your homes."

Chai was served and I was asked to lead in prayer. While praying I began to refer to Dube's illnesses, but I sensed the Holy Spirit prompting me to wait. I obeyed. I realized that this time it was important to share the Gospel message before praying for Dube's healing. So as we drank *chai*, I explained that there are two kingdoms—the kingdom of light and the kingdom of darkness—and that ever since Adam and Eve fell into sin, everyone born on earth is born into the kingdom of darkness. We discussed the type of fruit people produce as part of the kingdom of darkness and how people have tried to change their dark condition— sometimes by embracing different religions to try to gain forgiveness and find a way to heaven.

We talked about God's love and provision in sending the Messiah Jesus to redeem us by paying the whole of our debt of sin on the cross and then rising three days later. We discussed the great blessings of having been rescued from the kingdom of darkness and brought into the kingdom of light: not only full and free forgiveness, but a restored and reconciled relationship with God. And it's not a formal, distant relationship; we're adopted into God's family to share the joy and love of the Triune God. Then being born again into a new and eternal life, we produce godly fruit in our lives through the power of the Holy Spirit.

I explained why I was sharing the Good News with them; I was compelled by my love for them and by God's love for them. I also felt compelled to warn them about the consequences of remaining in darkness when God is offering entrance into the kingdom of light—something only possible because of Jesus' death and resurrection.

The brothers were appreciative and said they would think about the things I'd shared. They didn't have an answer right then.

At about noon, I heard some thunder in the distance. The dirt road can become muddy and slippery once the rains begin, which is especially treacherous when riding a *piki*. Since the visit was nearly at its end, I turned to Dube and said, "If you are willing, let's go to Jesus to ask him for a miracle to heal you from all your illness."

Yes, Dube was willing.

With his brothers and several children looking on, and with his permission, I got up from my side of the mat and knelt beside Dube. I placed my hands on Dube's stomach and lower back. Because I always find it helpful in building my own faith, I incorporated several of Jesus' commands in my prayer. I asked the Lord to extend his hand to Dube and to heal his body of all the symptoms. Then in Jesus' authority, I named each symptom and commanded each one to leave, and commanded Dube's body to be healed.

I was prompted to use Jesus' authority to drive out the unclean spirit of infirmity, ordering it to go wherever Jesus would send it. Then once again, in Jesus' name and authority, I commanded Dube's body to be well, to be healed.

I was conscious of more thunder. It was getting closer, but we waited a few minutes before I finally said, "Amen," and sat back down. I asked Dube what he felt and sensed. At first he seemed a bit dazed, but answered that he felt better. Soon afterwards we said our goodbyes and I headed for home.

At about 6 pm that same day I noticed I had missed a 3 pm call from Dube, so I called him back. Dube said he had called to tell me that Jesus had completely healed him.

I said, "What exactly did he heal you from? How are your fevers?"

"All gone!" he answered.

"What about your stomach?"

"There is now no problem with my stomach; it is at peace and I am eating again."

"What about your back pain? What about your thigh and leg pain?"

"There is now no more pain; it is all gone. I am well!"

I responded, "Praise God! Look what Jesus has done for you! Jesus not only wants to heal your body, Dube, he also wants to heal your spirit and soul. I want you to keep talking to your brothers about all of you coming into the kingdom of light by placing your faith in Jesus the Messiah."

December 9, 2022

The next day at 12:15 pm, I called Dube to greet him and ask for an update. He told me he slept very well last night. The fevers had not come back and all the pain and discomfort were gone. He was up and walking around completely well. Praise be to the Father and the Lord Jesus Christ! Before ending the call, I reminded him to talk to his brothers about receiving the gift of forgiveness God has provided through Jesus and coming into the kingdom of light. Dube said he would talk to them.

December 26, 2022

A few weeks later I was traveling through Dube's village on my way to another village some distance away. I stopped briefly to greet a few people at the *dukas* (shops). I greeted Dube's younger brother who happened to be there and who was at the house the day when we had prayed. I asked about his brother who had been sick. With a big smile, he reported that Jesus healed him that day. "He felt well right after you left," he said. "Even now he is out digging a new well for the animals."

Whoever conceals his transgressions will not prosper, but he who confesses and forsakes them will obtain mercy.

PROVERBS 28:13 ESV

For though we walk in the flesh, we are not waging war according to the flesh. For the weapons of our warfare are not of the flesh but have divine power to destroy strongholds. We destroy arguments and every lofty opinion raised against the knowledge of God, and take every thought captive to obey Christ....

2 CORINTHIANS 10:3–5 ESV

42

·······

Pete

September 27, 2017

East Africa

On one visit to Nairobi, our friends Jeff and Gail invited June and me to come to pray with their son Pete. Jeff had written to us previously about Pete, describing him as a great kid, well-liked by peers and in a good relationship with his parents, though his desire to please his parents and others was often obsessive, and he was constantly afraid of offending others. He also struggled with anxiety, insecurity, sexual thoughts and perfectionism. Pete took prescribed medication for Obsessive Compulsive Disorder (OCD) and was receiving professional Christian counseling at a respected counseling center.

Pete was 15 years old and had just entered 9th grade when we met him. As a child, he had lived in another African country with his parents who were in ministry there. Pete attended the local French-speaking school. When he was about to enter 3rd grade, he began attending boarding school in Kenya with his older brother. While he had very good dorm parents and didn't find the schoolwork difficult, he sometimes struggled with perfectionism in completing assignments.

When he entered 7th grade Pete began experiencing a variety of compulsions and occasional thoughts of self-harm and was diagnosed with OCD. Pete felt compelled to do everything perfectly. He did homework assignments and dormitory chores meticulously and with angst. Even simple things like bringing a glass of water to his dad became very challenging because a decision of some sort—like exactly where to place the glass—was required. Over the next two years, Pete's compulsions and anxieties worsened and he struggled with low self-esteem. His parents finally moved to Kenya temporarily to help care for and support him.

The afternoon we visited with them, the five of us sat gathered in the family living room and began by asking God to lead our time together. Then they shared their story. After listening, I felt led to ask Pete, "Have you and your friends ever done something that you knew was wrong? Have you done anything that you have not forgiven yourself for?"

Pete said, "When I was young, two of my local friends were from Muslim families in the village. They were one or two years older than me. We played a lot together and they came to our house for sleepovers." Pete went on to explain that once in a while they would lie naked on each other, kiss one another, and try to insert their penises into each other's anuses. The boys devised a secret signal to use whenever one of them wanted to suggest this activity; even Pete's older brother knew nothing about it. Sometimes they used the privacy of a little playhouse tent in the boys' room. At other times, if they were in the house during the daytime when their parents weren't home, they went into the guest room and locked the door. A day came, Pete told us, when he realized he didn't want to continue doing this, so he told his friends and it came to a stop.

After hearing Pete's story, we reminded him that God's grace is infinitely greater than all our sin and shame. God's love has provided a way for us; he calls us to confess and repent and he is ready to forgive us. I invited Pete to confess his sin to God in prayer and to repent by making a firm decision to avoid all sexual immorality in the future. Pete did so and thanked Jesus for paying the debt for his sins at the cross. He forgave his two friends for their part. Then I asked Pete if he had forgiven himself. He had not.

When we encouraged him to do so, he understood the importance of this intentional decision and agreed, choosing to forgive himself.

His parents then began to speak, asking Pete to forgive them for not protecting him when he was a small child. They were distressed because they had no idea any of this was going on. Pete assured them that he forgave them.

We then asked Jesus to cut the soul ties* between Pete and his two friends, to return to Pete the parts of his soul that were taken from him and to return to the other boys' souls anything that had been taken from them. We asked Jesus to remove the effects of the trauma Pete had suffered and to heal him. As a group we stood in Jesus' authority and commanded all unclean spirits that might be there to leave, naming those we could identify.

Pete felt something move from his stomach to his chest and later up to his throat. We didn't see any signs indicating the spirits had left. We also considered and addressed any rights that might have been given to evil spirits by past generations. In prayer, Pete renounced any ancestral sin and forgave his ancestors for any ungodliness that had been passed down to him.

Again we commanded any unclean spirits to leave, but the knot in Pete's stomach didn't move. It wasn't until Jeff, in his position as Pete's father, spoke up, taking authority in Christ's name over the spirits and himself commanding them to leave, that the knot loosened and Pete described feeling much better.

September 28, 2017 (The Following Day)

The five of us—Pete, his parents Jeff and Gail, and June and I—had such a short time together, that I decided to send a follow up email the next morning. I wanted to affirm Jeff and Gail's godly parenting and tell them how I appreciated Pete's honesty and humility. It had been beautiful to witness Jeff speaking boldly in his God-given authority as Pete's father, proclaiming freedom in Christ Jesus for his son.

I also wanted to offer whatever guidance I could, since there hadn't been time to be thorough. Even though Pete had felt much better when we finished the previous evening, we hadn't seen any clear manifestations of any unclean spirits exiting; but that didn't mean it hadn't happened. I knew that deliverance, if necessary, would offer Pete greater freedom to say yes to godly choices and no to ungodly choices. I also wanted to try to articulate the questions that remained. I wondered if the sin that

* see page 117 for explanation of soul ties

had now been confessed and forgiven might have played a part in the obsessive compulsive symptoms Pete experienced. It seemed there might be a spiritual link between Pete's inability to accept himself and both his fear of offending, and his obsession with pleasing others. I also wondered again if demonic spirits might have passed into Pete's life from the sexual activity with his two friends, or if there was other past trauma that should be explored. I wrote that June and I would continue to pray for Pete and his parents and hoped to receive updates.

That same day we got an update from Jeff. He said that Pete had been lighthearted and even jovial after our prayer time the day before, almost dancing in his new freedom. The family had enjoyed dinner together, and Pete had slept soundly that night. The next morning he seemed happy and at peace during their regular family devotions.

Later that day Gail, Pete's mom, also sent us an email. She let us know that the day had held some tough moments for Pete, but she was quite certain God continued to be at work in his life. He had asked his dad to talk with him about the issue of sexual thoughts.

The "P.S." attached to Gail's email made us smile. She wrote, "Pete said, 'If you end up writing the Edwards an email, tell them thanks again from me!'"

September 29, 2017 (The Next Day)

Jeff emailed to tell us that Pete was continuing to experience difficulties with both his sexual thoughts and perfectionist compulsions. Jeff and Gail prayed with him and then he and Pete went upstairs to talk more about the problem of sexual thoughts. Jeff said he urged Pete to call out to Jesus for help on the spot, as soon as temptation comes. Gail and Jeff were encouraged that at Pete's initiative, some of his dorm buddies had already been joining him to pray together most evenings.

September 30, 2017 (The Next Day)

In responding to Jeff and Gail, I encouraged them to continue helping Pete learn to rebuke the evil one whenever wrong thoughts surface. We also raised the possibility that the side effects of the prescription medication Pete took could be a factor in his ongoing struggles.

We encouraged them to keep believing that Jesus wants Pete well.

We pointed Jeff and Gail to some of the passages we have found most helpful. John 15 invites us to abide in Christ. Just as none of us can bear fruit by ourselves, neither can Pete fight this battle by himself. It will be those weapons Paul writes about in 2 Corinthians 10:3-5—those with divine power to demolish strongholds and take every thought captive to obey Christ—that will be effective. And since it is Jesus who is our complete and perfect righteousness (Ephesians 6), Pete can now let go of any need to be perfect himself.

We also suggested that they may find Peter Horrobin's books helpful, particularly the two volumes of *Healing Through Deliverance* and *Healing from the Consequences of Accident, Shock and Trauma.*

October 3, 2017

A few days later, I sent one last suggestion: that Jeff and Gail and Pete ask the Lord to bring to Pete's awareness any trauma he may have suffered but has no conscious memory of. If anything should surface in answer to that prayer, it could be addressed.

That same day Jeff let us know that the last few days had gone well for Pete. He seemed joyful and at ease. He was also making progress in calling out to Jesus for help right in his moment of need.

February, 2023 (Six Years Later)

I happened to run into Jeff and learned that Pete was doing very, very well. We both gave thanks to the Lord.

July 19, 2023 (Five Months Later)

After Pete and his parents read through this account and gave permission for us to tell their story, Pete's dad sent us an email to fill us in on further developments. Edited excerpts follow:

> Pete continued to struggle with OCD during his 9th and 10th grade years. In 11th grade, things got even worse. The upcoming Junior-Senior banquet was a source of stress, and Pete had begun to develop "anticipatory fear" about going to college. Gail and I had begun that year (2020) with 40 days of prayer and fasting especially for Pete. At the end of the 40 days, he was worse than ever and I was discouraged.

Gail and I moved to the boarding school to help Pete in his struggles. One day early on the three of us were walking past the prayer chapel on campus and went in to pray and talk. I encouraged Pete to surrender all of his life and reputation and future to the Lord, no matter what condition he was in. If he was only at 10% of normal capacity, he could dedicate that 10% to the Lord. But Pete wasn't ready. (Later he explained that surrendering everything to the Lord would mean that suicide was no longer an option; he was in such a state of angst and tension that he was unwilling to let go of that possibility.) We stayed in the prayer chapel for several hours that day, but there was no breakthrough.

We continued to live at the boarding school with Pete, trying to help him complete his class work. Sometimes he felt able to go to class; at other times he wasn't able to concentrate. Gail and I often sat on the couch with our arms around Pete, praying for him and telling him how much we loved him and that God had created him, and loved him so much more than we ever could. We told him that we didn't understand why he had OCD and struggled so much, but that God had an ultimately good plan for his life.

In March of 2020 the boarding school closed early because of the coronavirus, so Pete and his two brothers came home and our family was able to go through Neil Anderson's "Freedom in Christ" course. We also began meeting online with a counselor who was an OCD specialist. But Pete continued to be anxious and tense. His eyes had lost their sparkle and even our simplest routines were stressful for him.

One evening we had decided to watch a family movie in our living room, but Pete felt so anxious that he and I went upstairs to color together in a Dr. Seuss coloring book with soft music playing. I began to wonder if we would need to move back to the United States and simply hold Pete's hand for the rest of his life. Pete had told us he was "no good to the world," and that it would be better if he didn't go to college, but just became a homeless bum on the streets.

Around April, Gail and Pete decided to make the guest room into a special prayer room so that whenever we had no guests, any of us could spend time there praying or reading in the peace and quiet. One morning in late April or early May of 2020, Pete was in the prayer room and decided to fully surrender everything to the Lord—his future, his reputation and all that he is.

Pete didn't tell us about this until later, but over the next week or two his OCD symptoms began to subside. Over the next few months Pete was weaned from all medications. His counselor "graduated" him saying that he was doing so well that she had nothing more to contribute. We noticed that the light and joy that we had seen in his eyes when he was a kid was back! He seemed free and energized and alive.

It's been three years since that time. Pete has just finished his first two years of college and is playing on the university soccer team. He still has the occasional OCD thought, but he is able to renounce it and move on. The whole OCD experience humbled Pete, and gave him compassion for others who suffer with mental health conditions.

Pete has become a great blessing to his college dormmates, classmates and teammates, and he just completed a short-term mission trip in North Africa. We wait in anticipation to see what sort of future God has planned for him.

And he called the twelve together and gave them power and authority over all demons and to cure diseases, and he sent them out to proclaim the kingdom of God and to heal.

LUKE 9:1–2 ESV

43

....

Phoebe

December 10–19, 2022

Duma, Kenya

Phoebe loves the Lord Jesus Christ deeply. She has a missionary's heart and wants to participate in the kingdom of God by serving as a medical professional. Since graduating from nursing school a year-and-a-half ago, she has been serving on our Amaro mission team running the dispensary and treating the sick in and around her village.

A few months ago she began having pain and itching in her inner ears, and last month her ears bothered her so much that she traveled to an ear doctor. The examination revealed pus and inflamed ear drums. The doctor flushed out her ears and started her on antibiotics. Her ears improved over the next few days and she was more comfortable. But two weeks later the pain and itching returned—the itching returning with such a vengeance that she felt like she was going crazy with the need to scratch deep inside her ears. All of this made it nearly impossible to sleep.

On Saturday, December 10, Phoebe and other colleagues came to our home to spend the day praying, worshiping and studying God's word together. Phoebe told everyone about her ears and asked for prayer. She would be staying with us the next two nights, since she was planning to travel from Duma to Nairobi on Monday.

The following day, Sunday, we worshiped together and rested. After our evening teaching time we focused our attention on Phoebe and her ears.

We started our time together in prayer for God's clear leading. I prepared us all by asking Phoebe some questions that would refresh and encourage us with the truth of the Good News. "Has the Gospel changed in the past 2,000 years?"

"No," Phoebe said.

"Has Jesus changed?"

"No." Hebrews 13:8 states, "Jesus Christ is the same yesterday, today and forever" (NIV), so Phoebe had no doubts about this.

I asked Phoebe, "Is there any reason Jesus would not heal your ears tonight?" She couldn't think of any reason. But when I asked, "Is there anyone you haven't forgiven?" Phoebe paused.

After a moment she answered that someone had come to mind—her stepfather. Phoebe explained that several months earlier her mother had become ill and Phoebe believed she needed to go to the hospital. As she was trying to talk respectfully to her stepfather over the phone, he got angry and rebuked her harshly. Phoebe hung up on him. They hadn't spoken to one another since.

We reviewed Jesus' words in Matthew 6:14–15. "For if you forgive other people when they sin against you, your heavenly Father will also forgive you. But if you do not forgive others their sins, your Father will not forgive your sins."

Ephesians 4:26–27 was also helpful: "In your anger do not sin. Do not let the sun go down while you are still angry, and do not give the devil a foothold."

Phoebe prayed aloud, telling the Lord that, as an act of her will, she would forgive her stepfather's harsh words. She would also forgive him for appearing to have so little concern for her mother when she was ill. Phoebe asked Jesus to forgive her for holding on to her anger and bitterness. Knowing that Christ is faithful to forgive, she thanked him for this forgiveness, and promised that in the future she herself would forgive right away just as he had commanded.

We asked if there were any others she needed to forgive. There was no one else, so we asked Phoebe's permission to lay hands on her. I placed my hands over her ears, while June placed a hand on one of Phoebe's shoulders, and Melody (a short-term volunteer) placed her hand on the other.

I thanked Jesus for his presence and grace. I recalled some passages of Scripture and prayed them out loud. I asked Jesus to heal Phoebe's soul. After prayer, being reminded of the authority Jesus gives to all his disciples, I commanded any unclean spirit of infirmity to leave and go to the place Jesus sends it. Then, in Jesus' name, I commanded Phoebe's ears to be well, all infection to be gone, and her ears to be healed. June added to the prayer we were offering, and after a few minutes of waiting for Jesus to pour his healing power upon Phoebe, we closed with, "Amen."

We all sat down. I asked Phoebe how her ears felt. She said that they weren't itchy anymore and the pain was nearly gone. We all exclaimed, "Praise the Lord!"

The next morning we shared breakfast together before Phoebe and Melody boarded the small mission plane to Nairobi. I asked Phoebe how she'd slept and how her ears felt. She said she had slept very well and her ears felt much better.

"On a scale of one to ten with ten being the worst pain, what number would describe the pain in your ears yesterday before we prayed?" Phoebe rated it a nine.

"And after prayer last night?"

"A four."

After breakfast we placed our hands on Phoebe again and prayed. We thanked Jesus for the significant improvement and we asked for more. When we asked her what she was sensing, Phoebe said that now her pain level was closer to a two.

She had a good flight, but during the evening she wrote that she had a bit of pain and some itching in her ears. I called her mid-morning and asked how she was doing. In the conversation she felt her ears to be about a three on the scale. We prayed again over the phone.

On December 14, Phoebe wrote that her ears were doing very well; there was just a bit of itching at times.

December 19, I sent a WhatsApp message asking Phoebe how her ears were doing. She responded, "Morning Wayne, my ears are doing fine, thank you."

I sent a message back asking, "On a scale of one of ten, with ten being the worst, what number would you give the pain in your ears?" Phoebe responded that her ears were at a one on the scale.

Thanks be to God.

When the unclean spirit has gone out of a person, it passes through waterless places seeking rest, but finds none. Then it says, "I will return to my house from which I came." And when it comes, it finds the house empty, swept, and put in order. Then it goes and brings with it seven other spirits more evil than itself, and they enter and dwell there, and the last state of that person is worse than the first. So also will it be with this evil generation.

MATTHEW 12:43–45 ESV

44

....

Hasan

A note before you read: This is a troublesome story to tell. These events occurred in the beginning stages of our learning how to deal with the demonic and the rights the demonic can claim in a person's life. A person's will and God's grace and provision need to work together. For some, the cost of following Jesus seems too high.

October 29, 2006
Duma, Kenya

On Saturday afternoon, two of my Amaro friends who had professed receiving Jesus as their Savior, but were showing signs of returning to Islam, walked up to our house from different directions. No one else was on or around our front porch—a rare occurrence—so we sat chatting together. Then, in response to the Holy Spirit's prompting, I quite directly called both men to repent and come back to walking closely with Jesus. The one friend refused, saying bluntly, "I don't have anything to repent from!" He seemed disgusted with me and walked away. Hasan, on the other hand, being convicted by the Holy Spirit, said, "You're right, and I'm ready."

Hasan and I met privately the next day, Sunday afternoon, by the teacher's house. I was concerned for him. He had professed faith in Christ a year earlier, but I'd seen many new believers turn back to Islam. I wanted to do whatever I could to help Hasan stay on the path to life.

I laid out as clearly as possible the need for confession, repentance and forgiveness. After we'd read verses from 1 John 4 and 5 together, we talked about the ways Islamic teaching about Jesus differs from that of the New Testament. While Islam teaches that Jesus was created by God, the

Bible reveals a much richer mystery: "In the beginning was the Word, and the Word was with God, and the Word was God" (John 1:1 NIV).

That this Word became the person we know as Jesus, that his presence was so compelling that men left their livelihoods to follow him, that he loved humankind and willingly suffered and died for us—none of this is fully understood or believed among Muslims.

Along with the incarnation, Jesus' death and resurrection are essential saving truths for Christians. Islam, on the other hand, teaches that Jesus did not die and did not rise again. These errors indicate that Islam comes from a false spirit. Hasan came to understand that since Islam misrepresents God, continuing to follow the way of Islam would be sinful. I invited him to confess, repent and ask for forgiveness.

After Hasan had confessed his sin, repented and received forgiveness by the blood of Jesus' redemptive work, I commanded the spirit of Islam to leave.

The demon moved from Hasan's stomach into his heart, causing palpitations and a rapid, pounding heartbeat. I kept calmly ordering the spirit to leave. The demon moved to Hasan's throat and seemed to get stuck there. When I said, "Let it go," Hasan opened his mouth and the spirit left with a cough.

Although it was nearly nightfall, Hasan said, "It is so bright out here!"

I was very tired at this point, and we had a busy evening ahead, as we would be praying and worshiping with our mission team. But I sensed the Holy Spirit prompting me to ask Hasan a question, which was unpleasant to ask, "Do you have any other hidden sin in your life that should be brought out into the open?"

Hasan had just experienced the power of Jesus' deliverance, so he accepted the question humbly. "Yes, there is," he said.

Hasan confessed to adultery and to burning the body of a *shifta*, an armed robber, many years ago. We looked at what God's word said on these matters. When he had confessed, repented and thanked Jesus for his forgiveness, I ordered the demons that were present to leave. Hasan's head jerked from side to side and he felt a demon leave out of his ear. Another demon came up into his throat and exited through his mouth.

After I encouraged Hasan not to involve himself with any Islamic practices so that no additional entry points for evil spirits would be created, Hasan confessed that he hated and wanted to murder two people who had done something egregious some time ago. We read Matthew 5:21–26 together. Hasan confessed his hatred and murderous desire as sin, repented and sought forgiveness in prayer. As part of living out his repentance, Hasan chose to go to the two men he had hated and ask for their forgiveness. Once again, I tested and ordered out any demons that had claimed rights because of this sin.

Three more manifestations occurred. Hasan said one demon had come out of his right ear, then another from his left ear. The third demon exited from his throat with a big cough. After each deliverance, Hasan said he felt much lighter, that a lot of light had filled him and he was experiencing so much peace.

November 1–4, 2006 (The Next Week)

We stayed in close touch with Hasan for the next few days so that he could let us know whenever the Holy Spirit had shown him anything more he needed to deal with. Over the course of four days God revealed several more things to him. Hasan confessed and repented of habitual lying and failure to keep his word, of elevating the opinions of others over obedience to God, of acquiring a charm from the local Imam, and of participating in the *Hinesse* dance.

After Hasan brought the charm to us, burned it in our presence and received God's forgiveness, we ordered any demons to leave. Hasan experienced the demon coming into his chest and then into his throat. He involuntarily released a huge cough and then felt lighter. We asked God to cleanse Hasan and to fill the space the demon had occupied with the Holy Spirit.

When Hasan confessed, repented and asked God's forgiveness for participating in the *Hinesse* dance, and we ordered any demons to leave, Hasan began shaking his head and coughing. He experienced a very loud ringing in one ear as demons left. We ordered them not to return.

On another day, while I was helping Hasan memorize Colossians 1:13–14 and 1 John 1:8–9, I explained that the Muslim cap he was wearing identifies a person as a follower of Islam. He said the cap belonged to his father; he had been using it for protection from the sun, but he would return it to his father. I gave him a ball cap to use instead.

January 3, 2007 (Two Months Later)

Ben (our nephew and volunteer teacher) and I went to Hasan's home this morning. He had missed worship on Sunday without sending word and it was the day the whole village celebrated *Iddī* (Eid), commemorating Abraham's sacrifice of his son (who, according to Islam, was Ishmael rather than Isaac).

During our visit, I told the story of God's promise to bless all the nations of the earth through Abraham's offspring.

Hasan acknowledged to us that he had, in fact, participated with his family in celebrating *Iddi* in the Islamic way. I reminded him that a few months ago he had repented from following the ways and practices of Islam. Hasan was convicted and immediately confessed his sin.

I explained how the devil will try to get a person to open an entry point so the demons can return, and then I asked Hasan what he thought he should do. He wanted to pray and confess and renew his repentance, and seek God's forgiveness through Jesus. Hasan prayed from the heart. Then, in Jesus' name, I ordered any spirits to leave, declaring that their entry had been closed by Hasan's confession of his sin, his repentance and Jesus' forgiveness. In a very short time, demonic manifestations began with Hasan shaking his head, coughing several times, blinking his eyes and shaking his head back and forth. When the spirits were gone, Hasan knew what had happened. He explained that the spirits had come from his stomach, shoulders and chest. He counted four demons that had left through his mouth, eyes and ears, and said that while they were leaving his ears had been ringing.

I wanted to make sure all the evil spirits were gone, so I tested and continued to order the demons to leave and not come back. There were no more manifestations. Hasan told us that he could see light again and that he realized he had fallen into darkness. I reminded Hasan that the first time he was delivered from demons, he had said that everything was brighter and that he could see so much more light. I asked him how long that had lasted. He said it had lasted until about three days ago, when he'd celebrated the Islamic feast, and that just now, after prayer, the light had returned.

I asked if the Holy Spirit was showing him any other sin to confess.

He said, "Yes, there is." He confessed that he had promised to come to worship on Sunday and he hadn't kept his word. Hasan went to prayer and confessed, repented and was forgiven. Testing didn't reveal any demonic manifestations.

April 3, 2007 (Three Months Later)

Hasan came to Godana and me to request baptism. He gave his testimony and after we had asked him several questions, we felt that he was ready. Hasan's baptism and the baptisms of two other believers from Tula were scheduled to take place on May 18.

April 14, 2008 (One Year Later)

Last Sunday evening two village elders invited our family to a non-Islamic traditional feast/prayer event to ask for God's blessing and for rain. "Like in the old days," they said, "we as a village want to ask God's forgiveness for our sins."

I told them that if I came to the feast, I would like to explain the meaning of sacrificing animals. (As years passed, fewer people understood what the event meant.) I wanted an opportunity to share from God's word why the Hebrew people of ancient times had been commanded to use 'clean' animals like sheep, goats and cattle in their sacrifices. I hoped to help everyone see that the animals' lifeblood being poured out was a picture pointing to the Anointed One—Jesus—whose lifeblood was poured out for sin. The animal giving its life as the *dumana* (redeemer) wasn't necessary anymore; Jesus has already given his life for the sin of the world! Animal sacrifice was commanded for God's people only until Jesus made the final and effective sacrifice on the cross.

On Monday morning, the day of the feast, I arrived early. There were only ten to twelve elders present and they were in the midst of slaughtering the three sheep. They told me they were good and clean sheep. I asked them why they were sacrificing the sheep. "To pray for forgiveness," they answered. But they did not know how or why God had given the command; they said they were following their cultural practices.

I explained from God's word that since Jesus was the last and final sacrifice, animal sacrifices are no longer needed. God calls each of us to confess and repent from our sin and run to Jesus asking him to save us.

I had hoped to help them understand that Jesus as the Lamb of God has paid the debt of our sin in full.

I was called away to another meeting at my home, but I told the elders I would come back. I asked that when the rest of the people from the village arrived later, I might be given the opportunity to share the same message with everyone.

Upon returning to the acacia trees by the riverbed about two hours later, I found 35–40 men there, as well as several children and some women who were cooking. I sat under the tree with the men waiting my turn to speak.

Soon the feast/prayer event took a turn I hadn't expected. Two Muslim teachers from our village were present, as well as another Muslim teacher from a neighboring village some distance away. What I'd assumed would be the very old traditional meeting became something quite different under the leadership of these Muslim teachers.

The teacher from the more distant village addressed the gathering for over an hour, speaking about the greatness of Islam and explaining the various rules for prayer. I sensed that a fierce spiritual battle was being waged. I focused on praying as clearly as I could that God would break the grip of the powers of darkness on these people I'd come to know and love.

I found it very hard to concentrate, but I persevered. Eventually others were invited to speak and pray. Finally, I asked permission to speak. Several people objected. After a lengthy discussion it was decided that I should be allowed to speak since I too had been invited by the elders.

Someone yelled, "We do not want to hear about your *dini* (religion)."

"I am not here to tell you about a religion," I answered. "But where I go, I bring my God with me."

The Muslim leaders from our village along with several other people got up and left. When I began to speak about Jesus shedding his blood for our sin more people left.

I struggled to present the Gospel, all the while feeling that I wasn't doing it adequately. Both the open disrespect and the intensity of the spiritual battle were unnerving. I did my best to call everyone to confess their sins and repent from them and run to Jesus to save them.

After I finished speaking, those who had left came back to the shade and sat down. An elder from a distant village was invited to pray. He came forward to sit in the middle of the gathering and began to pray in Amaro, praising Mohamed. Suddenly what seemed to be a demonic manifestation took control. The elder began both snorting and crying out very loudly.

The Muslim teachers immediately began singing the praises of Islam and of Mohamed. After about ten minutes the elder calmed down and became docile. I continued watching his facial expressions, however, because they were clearly not his own. They kept shifting dramatically throughout the singing. His face went from big smiles to expressions of deep sadness, back and forth, as he moved in rhythm with the singing.

I was very concerned for Hasan who was sitting across from me in the back of the group. He didn't move forward into the tight circle the Muslim leaders had called the people to form, but he was in attendance, despite the decision he'd made to avoid participating in any Islamic practices. Of course, neither of us had known that this meeting would become a gathering so tightly controlled by the Muslim leaders.

During the singing in praise of Mohamed, I noticed Hasan being pulled in a few times. It didn't seem to be intentional; it just happened. This is hard to explain, but the fact that my own spirit was very troubled during this time, demonstrates the strange darkness and the power it exerted at this event.

After the meeting, I went back home; I was eager to talk with Hasan. Later that afternoon when an opportunity presented itself, I asked Hasan to talk with me about what he had seen at the *ebbā* (feast) and his thoughts about it. He said his heart had been very troubled, that it was not a good meeting, and that he hadn't realized the meeting would become so Islamic in nature.

I asked him then if he had been drawn into praising Mohamed during the extended time of singing with its hypnotic repetition. He said no.

Since nothing seemed to be clear to Hasan, I decided not to say anything more. We prayed together, reminding one other to be alert to the devil's schemes: "Be self-controlled and alert, your enemy the devil prowls around like a roaring lion looking for someone to devour. Resist him..." (1 Peter 5:8–9 NIV).

April 15–16, 2008 (The Next Day)

My spirit continued to be troubled for Hasan during the morning Bible study time he and I shared with another man. I noticed the lack of clarity in his answers as we studied the word of God together; some of his responses were very Islamic in nature.

During our April 16th Bible study, I sensed the same troubling things. Hasan walked with me to the house afterwards, and once we were alone I asked him how his heart was doing.

He told me that his heart had felt very heavy and unsettled ever since the *ebbā* (feast) a few days back. So I ventured asking again whether he had gotten drawn into singing praises to Mohamed when all the others were doing so. He said yes, he had sung along; he hadn't intended that to happen, but somehow it had.

Despite Hasan's sin being unintentional, demons had taken advantage of the moment. Retreating to the quiet space behind our house, Hasan and I again walked through the process of confession, repentance, and receiving forgiveness. Then we explored the need to cast out demons in the name of the One who died for us.

Demons manifested and left in a variety of ways, but once the deliverance was complete, Hasan said, "Thank you, thank you, thank you, thank you, thank you, I am free! They are gone." He told me that once again the light had returned and he felt light-hearted. We praised God together and asked the Lord to give Hasan a fresh anointing of his Spirit. We also agreed to ask the Lord to reveal any other footholds and unrepented sin. We planned to come together again after Hasan's return from a security trip to investigate a report of *shifta* (bandits) in the area.

July 2008 (Over Two Months Later)

A delegation of eight Muslim teachers arrived at Hasan's home to condemn him for following Christ and for trying to persuade others to follow Jesus as well. Since then, his wife Hagana and his son Dube had been exerting tremendous pressure on Hasan to turn from Jesus and return to Islam.

One Sunday morning, Hasan's son Dube walked up to our house while we were worshiping together with Hasan on our front porch, and glared at us. He asked, "What are you doing, talking?"

"No," we answered, "we're worshiping God. Come and join us."

Dube turned and walked away to express his anger to the watchman. About 30 minutes later Hasan's wife Hagana walked up and glared at us and asked what Hasan was doing. We told her that she was welcome to join us in worshiping God.

She started yelling at Hasan, "Don't even come home. You stay with the Christians. You are no longer a part of our family; we are not together anymore."

During one of my visits to Hasan's home, Hagana told me to leave her family alone. She said, "I want no part of the '*dini* of Christo' (religion of the Messiah). We have our own customs to follow." She talked angrily at some length, even praising *Ayana* (devil worship).

We continue to pray and meet with Hasan nearly every day, hoping to encourage him. This is a tremendous test of his faith. We've been told that a lot of the pressure on family members to persuade Hasan to turn away from Jesus comes from areas beyond our village.

On July 31, 2008, after Hasan and I met in my office to read the Scriptures and pray together, he said he needed to go to the clinic. His stomach and head had been "experiencing a lot of pressure and worry."

I prayed for his healing and then felt led to order all the evil spirits causing worry and pressure to leave. Hasan clutched his stomach and massaged it as the pain increased. When the sensation moved to his chest, he kneaded that area. The manifestation moved to his throat. This was especially agonizing and he stiffened with pain. Only after several minutes of ordering the spirits to leave, did they exit through his ears and mouth with ringing and buzzing.

Once again Hasan was free; he praised God for this deliverance. I cautioned him to stay alert and on his guard, and asked Jesus to anoint him with a fullness of his Holy Spirit.

August 2008 (A Month Later)

Through the month of August we saw Hasan repeat patterns indicating a slow return to Islam. Feeling under siege from his community and family, Hasan no longer attended worship regularly. He asserted that he could worship God anyplace and anytime, but that when nothing prevented him, he would attend worship with the rest of the new believers. My efforts to explain how important corporate worship is for my own life, and my reminding him of the lies of the enemy as well as the call he and I share—to represent Jesus in our village—only resulted in a noncommittal statement about attending if nothing else got in the way.

We learned that after the Muslim leaders had visited his home, Hasan had agreed to return to the mosque and to stop attending Christian worship. His subterfuge about this, as well as about other meetings and monthly prayer days, felt like a roller coaster ride for the rest of us.

Hasan and I met again and again. Each time there would be confession, prayer, deliverance and promises, followed by a return to Islam. Hasan is a very young believer who has suffered trials and persecutions. He needs regular teaching and fellowship in order to grow. At the same time, with the free will God has given us, each of us either chooses actions and activities that increase our love for God or we choose otherwise.

Clearly the devil wants to swallow Hasan alive. But Jesus is Lord. He has given us all we need for life and godliness (1 Peter 1:3–11).

September 21, 2008 (A Month Later)

During the week-and-a-half that we were away in Nairobi, a Muslim evangelist from Meru came to our area and preached for several days, asserting that the Bible is full of falsehood. Also, within that brief time, some community leaders summoned Hasan to a meeting. They told Hasan that they are no longer with him and that his wife and children will be taken away.

When we got back to the village, Hasan avoided us. When we saw him, he was wearing his Muslim hat and was keeping the Ramadan fast. When I asked Hasan about it, he said that the Muslim evangelist from Meru had spoken about having been a Christian and a pastor at one time, but he had turned to Islam because he saw Islam as true. Hasan said that he himself didn't know what was true anymore, but that he was examining things.

My heart sinks when I think that Hasan may once again have exchanged God's power and grace for the Muslim way of earning salvation by works. His confusion about what is true must also be complicated by his fear of losing his family.

Hasan's family watches him closely every time he comes to work here at the mission compound. They watch most carefully on Fridays; they want to make sure he goes to the mosque.

Then last Wednesday, right in our mission compound at our workshop, Hasan publicly declared that Jesus cannot save anyone and that the Bible is false. It was a painful blow to me.

That night there was a medical emergency at a village eight kilometers away. Before heading there in the truck with Hasan, June and I, using English, took care to bind all evil spirits in Hasan and we commanded them in Jesus' name to be silent so that we could talk freely with Hasan himself.

While June was treating the patient, Hasan and I sat in the truck and talked for two hours. The results were remarkable. Hasan was himself again! He spoke freely and was very open. It was as if he was another person altogether from the person he had seemed to be the morning before. He said that the Gospel was true, that Jesus is the Savior.

When we told Hasan what he had said publicly—denying the Lord Jesus and the Christian faith—he hardly seemed to remember it.

The next day we received a medical call out at Limu and had to go to Kola again to bring the patient to the hospital. So we had another opportunity to spend time with Hasan as he rode along. We talked more about the kingdom of God.

We didn't know how long the window of opportunity would be open for us to have access to Hasan. We knew that it was crucial that Hasan repent and be delivered so we invited him to come the next day to talk more. We hope to ask him to repent—if he comes. (The demons will surely try to keep him away).

Lord, move your Holy Spirit within him to come! May his heart consent to be fully yielded to you. Deliver him from the evil one!

September 28, 2008 (A Week Later)

We in our village have seen tremendous persecution and many trials the last several weeks. But the Lord has taken what was meant for evil and turned it to good.

For Hasan especially, it has been a real battle. Hussein, a Christian believer from Tula, came for a night in order to talk to Hasan, and on Saturday, September 27, after a few hours of discussion, Hasan was ready to confess and repent from his sin.

He confessed breaking the promise he'd made to have nothing to do with Islam. He confessed the sin of returning to the mosque and practicing the Ramadan fast. He made a renewed act of his will to avoid everything related to Islam. We encouraged him to be specific in his prayer, and it seemed to come from the heart.

Then in Jesus Christ's name and authority, Hussein, June and I ordered the demons (the spirit of Islam and spirits of fear and of lies) to leave. Within a few minutes the demons had manifested, making Hasan very stiff and able to move only very slowly. Hasan's hands were extended and his ears were ringing. He was kept in this condition for about five minutes. Then suddenly the demons left.

Hasan said there had been many, and that they left from his mouth and ears and through his hands and feet. After they left, Hasan said it was like waking up. The light of God replaced the darkness. He felt joyful and light.

Hasan joined us for worship the next day, and yet we feel some apprehension.

We're struck by the truth and importance of 1 Peter 5:8–9, "Be self-controlled and alert. Your enemy the devil prowls around like a roaring lion looking for someone to devour. Resist him, standing firm in the faith!"

Lord, teach us what we don't yet understand.

October 7, 2008 (A Week Later)

Hasan has seemed to be holding back. When he came for breakfast this morning, we had an opportunity to share our concerns with him. We discerned that he wasn't giving his entire heart and life to Jesus and wasn't yielding to Jesus' Lordship. Old habits from the past had surfaced too, like lying, as well as promising to come for worship, but not showing up.

Hasan agreed with us. He said that he felt there was darkness in himself and that other demons were troubling him. His attitude was very humble and he asked June and me to pray with him in the back of the house. He confessed his sin in detail and told Jesus that he would turn around and make him Lord.

In Jesus' authority I ordered any evil spirits to leave. Hasan became rigid. His whole body shook for some minutes until they released him. He once again said that the light had come back in.

We left later that morning for Nairobi, wondering why we weren't seeing long term, lasting deliverance for Hasan as we had for other young believers. Is it fear? He says he's not afraid of people, but his actions seem to say otherwise. Is he afraid of rejection? Is he afraid to die? He doesn't seem able to hold on to his new status and new place: Hasan belongs in the kingdom of God.

May 1, 2009 (Almost Seven Months Later)

A few days ago I spoke privately with Hasan. June and I had been fasting and praying for him because he seemed to have turned back from following Jesus. Hasan's demeanor was very hard.

Last night we sat with him for about three hours. June told Hasan she had noticed that he doesn't come around much anymore and doesn't come to worship or prayer meetings. I made the observation that his life looks just like the lives of those who are Muslim, not like the life of a follower of Jesus. We haven't seen the fruit of the Spirit in his life for the last three or four months.

Hasan was much calmer than when I'd talked to him earlier and there were no demonic manifestations. After a long discussion we urged Hasan to confess his hidden sins and repent. He said, "It is late; we will talk tomorrow."

We said, "If a sheep becomes lost, do you wait till tomorrow to look for it? No!"

When Hasan complained of a headache, we said, "It is demons doing this, trying to make you leave."

Finally, Hasan relented and told us that when some other Muslim missionaries had come to our village recently, he had been summoned to the mosque. There at the mosque, in front of many people, the Muslim leaders asserted that Christianity is a lie and urged Hasan to return to Islam. Under this pressure, he gave in and agreed and performed the Muslim prayers in front of them all. Since then he has been attending the mosque regularly.

He confessed that he has been lying a lot, has a lot of anger, and hasn't forgiven many people. The demons always tell him not to go to Sunday services and prayer meetings. Hasan said that he is full of darkness and very heavy; he has no peace. In his misery, Hasan confessed his sin in prayer and repented. He thanked Jesus for his grace and forgiveness.

Since the rights demons claim had been canceled by Hasan's confession and repentance, I ordered all demonic spirits to leave in Jesus' name and authority. Many, many demons left; it took a very long time.

Hasan confessed more as the Holy Spirit showed him more. He confessed his deceptions and made a decision with his will to always tell the truth as Jesus would want. Hasan said demons had exited from his mouth, nose, ears and hands; there were too many to count. When we were finished, Hasan said he was set free and at peace. Now his great need is to be in God's word and growing in his relationship with Christ.

Lord, help him to cling to You and stand faithfully with You!

May 2, 2009 (The Next Day)

June and I talked with Hasan about thinking ahead, about envisioning the situations and pressures he's almost certain to encounter—times when elders want him to give *fita* (prayer praising Mohamed) at the beginning or close of a meeting, or times when family and friends exert pressure on him to go to the mosque for prayers. Making strategic decisions now about how he will respond could be very helpful.

January 4, 2010 (Eight Months Later)

For the past several weeks, Hasan has been *duliting* (the Islamic way of praying) and going to the mosque. He's been absent from worship and fellowship times and is reported to have told another man that Christianity is a false religion. For two or three weeks we have been praying for Hasan and calling him to repentance. While he has agreed that he's living in darkness, he very much wants to please his wife and neighbors.

Godana and I talked with Hasan this morning, once again calling him to repent. At first, he said he was not ready, but then he made the decision to repent. We sat and prayed with him. Hasan confessed his sin and repented. So many demons came out with so many different manifestations that we lost count.

In this process we learned that though we had previously driven out the spirit of Islam, there are several other Islamic spirits tied to various aspects of Islam. The spirit of *duliting* (praying) for example, is distinct from the spirit of fasting during Ramadan and from the spirit of *Iddī* (Eid) celebrations.

We also addressed the sin of adultery against God, sins of deceit, and other sins. Manifestations were many and presented themselves in various forms. We plan to meet again tonight. It seems there must still be a root issue that we need the Lord to reveal.

March 14, 2010 (Two Months Later)

In today's Sunday worship service, the message was about being truthful and putting off falsehood. Hasan was there with us and seemed to be uneasy during the Scripture lesson. Afterwards, Hasan told us that he had a heavy heart because of his problems with lying and with not fulfilling his promises.

We invited him into the office and looked again at Ephesians 4, which urges believers to get rid of falsehood. Hasan confessed that this has been a problem for a long time. Once again we shared the Good News that Jesus came to free us from the bondage of the kingdom of darkness—to free us now! Our part is to be careful to live in the light; Jesus has given us the power and authority to be able to do this.

We dealt first with the lying spirits. Hasan confessed that he lies regularly, and he made a decisive act of his will to repent and to tell the truth in every situation. Hasan thanked Jesus for forgiving him at the cross.

I asked permission to drive out any lying spirits. Hasan gave the go ahead, so with Jesus' authority and power I ordered the spirits to leave and commanded them not to come back. For about 15 minutes spirits named Lying, Deceit and Fear argued back and forth about whether to stay or leave. Manifestations began moving from Hasan's thighs through his stomach to his chest. He had trouble breathing as the battle stalled there for several minutes. Finally, Hasan told us that all three had left together—out of his ears and up through his throat, and then out of his mouth with a cough.

Hasan seemed a little dazed but said the demons were gone. He felt that a heavy burden had been lifted and light had come.

April 15, 2010 (A Month Later)

Hasan's freedom lasted only a week; we recognized the signs that demons had returned. When I visited Haji Dadicha's home, I found Hasan *duliting* with the other men at a funeral.

At the first opportunity I asked Hasan when the demons had come back. He said it had coincided with his becoming angry and with his return to *duliting*. He confessed to feeling heavily burdened again. He said he would think about his situation overnight, and he would tell me in the morning if he truly wanted to repent and find freedom. I ordered the demons to be silent for the night so that Hasan would be able to hear the voice of the Holy Spirit.

In the morning Hasan said that he did want freedom and that he had been confessing and repenting through the night. Already he felt much better. Since Hasan had done the groundwork of confessing and repenting and receiving God's forgiveness through Jesus, what he needed from me was help with the deliverance.

We went behind the house and began. For about an hour all sorts of manifestations were seen and maybe 50 to 100 demons left, some in groups. It was a nearly constant stream; some coming out quickly, others a little slower. In the pauses, I asked which demons had left. Hasan was able to identify most of them.

Some of the spirits were:
- *Dulino* (Muslim prayer)
- *Sosbit* (deceit)
- *Dofino* (a 'wanting to hide' spirit, a spirit of secrecy)
- Anger
- *Gamachis* (making people happy)
- Wife Pleaser
- Elders Pleaser
- People Pleaser
- Fasting
- *Maulid* (celebration of Mohamed's birthday)
- *Inafa* (jealousy)
- *Naden dibifut* (spirit of the desire to take another wife)

- Fear (there were many)
- *Tabaliki* spirits (spirits that were passed on to Hasan by Muslim missionaries)
- Religion of Christ (the Holy Spirit told me to command even these to leave; many came out)

Several times after demons had been cast out, Hasan said that there were no more demons that he was aware of; I kept pressing on, and more continued to manifest and then come out. There were so many! I ordered the demon with the most authority, the "strong man," to leave as well. Afterward Hasan told us that some of the spirits that had come out had been hiding within him for many years, but that he hadn't known this until the Holy Spirit revealed them.

After this extensive deliverance, Hasan felt very joyous and full of light.

October 2010 (Six Months Later)

The freedom, joy and light lasted only a few weeks. Hasan began to compromise and then returned to practicing Islam. It was very sad to watch him. We called him to repent, but he refused. He began spreading rumors about us and after being bribed, he went to the County Council in an attempt to take the church's land.

Later he reported to a group of us that on the night of October 16 he couldn't sleep. He was very restless and then had a dream in which Jesus came to him and questioned him. Jesus was full of light and this pierced Hasan's heart. It was so real! Hasan told us that when his eyes were closed, he saw Jesus in a state so bright that there is nothing on earth to compare it with. In the dream Jesus said, "Hasan, I love you. Why did you return to Islam? I have saved you; I have given you light."

"It was very strange," Hasan said. "I was sleeping but awake."

When Hasan asked the man in the bright light, "Who are you?" the man answered, "I am Jesus. I've prepared a good place for you. Why did you return to the dark path of Islam? I am calling you to return."

Hasan went on, "When I opened my eyes, I did not see him; it was just dark. But when I closed my eyes, the house was full of very bright light with Jesus standing there, saying 'Come!' I was very afraid. I have never seen such a beautiful person before."

"He said, 'Get up and come.' I got up and opened my eyes, but then I did not see him anymore. It was dark. When I closed my eyes, it was as bright as the middle of the day. Again he said, 'Get up and come. Why are you shaming me? Why are you going to the mosque? Why are you lying? Why are you *duliting*?' Then he showed me the lake of fire Islam is leading to. I was so afraid! He said, 'If you do not turn around, the lake of fire will be your end! Come back to me.' I was being called to repent.

"Afterward I was so afraid that I turned on the torch (flashlight) in the house and in the morning turned it off. I did not sleep. I got up and could not stay at home. I got up early and went to Wayne and June's house. I wanted to worship God. I arrived early and joined them for breakfast. On my own initiative I set up the worship place mats. I was so hungry to hear God's word. I was hungry for the people to hurry and come together to worship. During the service, in the time of prayer, I confessed my sin. I confessed that I have strayed. I asked for forgiveness."

After reporting this experience, Hasan agreed to "clean house" by addressing the footholds he has given the evil one, and going through deliverance.

January–April, 2012 (Over One Year Later)

Hasan has lived for many months in fear, deception and anger. We have encouraged him to repent once again, to rid himself of competing loyalties and give his whole heart to Jesus. After four more months of talking with him and praying for him, we were grateful when Hasan himself was finally burdened to repent.

On April 29, 2012, Hasan confessed several sins and chose to repent. We hadn't pushed for any deliverance until this time, because we saw signs that he lacked total commitment to Jesus. But now the Holy Spirit was once again working in his heart, so it was possible to offer deliverance ministry. Many of the spirits were ones that had returned after the deliverance on April 15, 2010, but with the addition this time of a "spirit of the Muslim hat."

Just a few minutes prior to this time of deliverance, Hasan had taken off his Muslim cap and burned it. During the deliverance, the spirits kept asking, "Where is my hat?"

Spirits exited from all over Hasan's body—from his mouth, ears, feet, head, nose, arms, knees and hands.

Once again, we urged Hasan to be faithful to Jesus and not to be double-minded or divided in his loyalties. We're perplexed; there must be something we are not seeing or not understanding in Hasan's case. Others have found consistent freedom. But Hasan has slipped back into bondage every time so far. Lord, what is it that we don't yet understand?

February 28, 2013 (Ten Months Later)

Hasan returned to following Islam. He said it began when he visited Haji Dadicha, a local Muslim leader.

Within the past three weeks, Hasan had another dream in which Jesus came to visit him in what he described as a very dark place. Jesus spoke to him, asking why Hasan was shaming him by returning to Islam. When Hasan asked, "Who are you?" Jesus answered, "Jesus, who saved you."

Then a few days ago Hasan had another dream of Jesus coming to him. Hasan said that Jesus was very bright and the place was like paradise, unlike any place he had seen before.

January 22, 2023 (Ten Years Later)

For several years now, Hasan has chosen to follow Islam. He no longer speaks of being a follower of Jesus. When asked, he says he knows he lives in darkness, but the cost of following Jesus seems to him to be too high.

This long story spanning so many years has helped us begin to understand that for some people, the spiritual battle that Ephesians 6 talks about will be especially intense. How desperately Hasan has needed an undivided heart given completely to the Lord Jesus Christ. How desperately he needed the whole armor of God.

Since our first encounters with Hasan and the demons oppressing him, it's been a long and steep learning curve for us. Because of our experiences with Hasan, our discipleship process with new believers now routinely includes testing whether deliverance from the spirit of Islam is needed. So far, every young believer we've tested has required this deliverance. Most of them have been faithful to Jesus Christ and have grown and matured in their faith.

How wonderful if we could see the same results for Hasan!

And immediately he left the synagogue and entered the house of Simon and Andrew, with James and John. Now Simon's mother-in-law lay ill with a fever, and immediately they told him about her. And he came and took her by the hand and lifted her up, and the fever left her, and she began to serve them.

That evening at sundown they brought to him all who were sick or oppressed by demons. And the whole city was gathered together at the door. And he healed many who were sick with various diseases, and cast out many demons. And he would not permit the demons to speak, because they knew him.

MARK 1:29–34 ESV

45

....

Abrahim

August 7, 2016

Duma, Kenya

As we sat in the shade of a tree having our Sunday service, we saw Abrahim, a young believer and longtime family friend, limping toward us. We learned that he had been in a *piki* (motorcycle) accident nine days before. In addition to several scrapes and bruises, his heel had been cut open. He had gone to our mission medical clinic in Duma and received five or six stitches in his heel. But his foot was swollen and still very painful and showed signs of infection.

During the time of prayer in our worship service, seeing that Abrahim was in pain, I asked if he would like Jesus to heal his foot and, half joking, I added, "Or do you want to continue living in pain with an infected foot?"

Abrahim didn't hesitate; he wanted Jesus to heal his foot.

We asked Abrahim to sit in the middle of the circle and allow us to lay our hands on him. Praying in the Amaro language and reciting Scriptures like John 14:12–14, where Jesus invites the disciples to ask anything in his name so the Son will bring glory to the Father, we commanded Abrahim's foot to be healed and all the pain to be gone in Jesus' name and authority. After several minutes we said, "Amen," and asked Abrahim how his foot felt.

Abrahim said that before our time of prayer his foot had been throbbing, but now there was no pain. I asked him to get up and walk around. Without hesitation Abrahim jumped up and walked. The limp, the swelling and the pain were entirely gone.

Abrahim stayed for lunch and then joined us in the wild Sunday afternoon basketball game that June and I love to compete in. He ran all over the court, energetic and strong. The next day his stitches were taken out; the foot was well.

December 10, 2016 (Four Months later)

Abrahim and I sat together reading 1 John 4 and 5 and praying. The epistle lays out so compellingly God's love and the beauty of the salvation available in Jesus Christ; in just those two chapters Abrahim saw many ways in which his practice of Islam was a rejection of God's great gift. He began to pray, renouncing Islam as a false religion and Mohamed as a false prophet. Abrahim forgave his father and grandparents for burdening him with Islamic vows, and also confessed his own sin in following Islam in the past. He repented by deciding that in the future he wouldn't participate in any of the practices of Islam, despite their being ubiquitous in the culture of his tribe.

I explained to Abrahim my concern that because his parents and grandparents followed Islam, evil spirits may have entered him even in the womb and at birth. I asked his permission to explore deliverance and to cast out any spirits of Islam in Jesus' name and authority. Being very humble and open, Abrahim was willing. So I commanded the spirits of Islam, as well as Fear and Deception, to leave.

Abrahim's heart began beating very fast and he started sweating profusely. He experienced tingling beginning in his abdomen and then exiting with his breath. I repeated the deliverance, commanding the spirits of Islam and all spirits of lying or deception that still remained to bind themselves together and leave.

This time Abrahim experienced stomach pain. As we persevered, the pain rose through his body and exited from his head. When it was all over, he said he was experiencing deep peace and joy. We ended by asking the Lord Jesus to heal all the places the unclean spirits had claimed and to fill them with his Holy Spirit.

December 13, 2016 (Three Days Later)

I asked Abrahim how he had been doing since the deliverance he'd experienced last week. "Good!" he said, "I no longer have fear."

We talked together for about half an hour and we discussed the possibility that further deliverance might be needed since Abrahim's stepmother leads *Ayana* occult rituals in his father's home. Abrahim told me that as a boy he was often taken along when the shaman called together the various women who participated in *Ayana* so that he could watch as the shaman 'treated' people with the worship of Haji Abdella (the head spirit) and other spirits. After coming to Christ, Abrahim realized that this was wrong.

I confirmed this by showing Abrahim that in Deuteronomy 18, going to spiritualists or mediums is forbidden; God's people are to seek counsel and direction from the Lord. Even though Abrahim had done these things in ignorance and innocence, he understood that participating in such practices can give 'permissions' or create 'footholds' for evil spirits.

Abrahim went to prayer, confessing his sin. He repented and renounced the practices he had engaged in, and then thanked Jesus for going to the cross to forgive him.

Afterwards, Abrahim and I explored whether any *Ayana* spirit or other evil spirit might be hiding inside him so that we could drive it out with Jesus' authority. When commanding it to leave in Jesus' name, a manifestation came up into his chest and stayed there as I persisted in ordering it to leave. Finally, the manifestation disappeared. It seemed to me that it may have left with a sigh on his breath, but Abrahim described it differently, saying that it lifted off of him.

To make sure there were no unclean spirits lingering, I repeated the command twice, but we saw no more manifestations. When I asked Abrahim how he felt inside, he said, "I have much peace and joy. It is like I have a double amount of joy!"

December 25, 2016 (Two Weeks Later)

This morning Abrahim came to our house to join Edwin, Hasan, Hadija, June and me in worship. He hadn't come to the Christmas feast the day before because he had a headache.

During the service I asked Abrahim if he still had the headache. He said it was better, but one side of his head was still in pain. I asked him if he wanted to keep the headache or come to Jesus for healing.

Right away Abrahim smiled and said, "I don't want the headache! I want to come to Jesus."

June, Hasan, Edwin and I placed our hands on Abrahim. I reviewed the Gospel with him, as is my practice before asking for healing. We prayed, and then in Jesus' authority I commanded Abrahim's head to be well and all the pain to be gone. I ordered any spirits of infirmity to leave and go wherever Jesus tells them.

When we asked Abrahim how his head felt, he said, "All the pain is gone!"

"All of it?"

"Yes, all of it."

Abrahim thanked Jesus for healing him.

The Spirit of the Lord GOD is upon me,
because the LORD has anointed me
to bring good news to the poor; he has
sent me to bind up the brokenhearted,
to proclaim liberty to the captives,
and the opening of the prison to those
who are bound....

ISAIAH 61:1 ESV

46

....

Layla

June 2020

Duma, Kenya

Layla is a 32-year-old native Kenyan woman who survived an extremely abusive home situation. She became a believer in Jesus Christ when she was 16 or 17 years of age and has been serving Christ in ministry since November 2019. A registered nurse, Layla has completed a year-long mission training program.

Layla's demeanor is very humble, gentle and sweet in spirit. This, along with the remarkable boldness of her faith in Christ, has made it a delight getting to know her. Layla is very capable and loves Jesus deeply. Her regular participation in times of prayer has shown us that her abiding in Christ is deep and strong.

A few months ago, after hearing some of our accounts of healing and deliverance, Layla asked for prayer. She has lived in fear of her father all her life. Her father, who is not a believer in Christ, practices herbal/spiritual medicine, treating people living in his home area. Not only his family, but many people in the vicinity fear him. He has had three wives concurrently, though today most of the family have separated from one another. Layla is one of six children from one of her father's wives.

Layla's life story had been filled with hurts and trauma. As we talked about what she had experienced, Layla noted there were many places of bitterness she had never dealt with and things she needed to forgive, such as being denied the opportunity to attend school when she was young and her father's verbal abuse, harshness and rigid control.

She willingly forgave her father. She also asked Jesus to forgive her for having held on to her anger (see Ephesians 4:26–27). With Jesus' authority, June and I commanded the spirit of fear to leave. No manifestations occurred, but Layla knew she had been set free. For months she had been afraid to talk to her father even over the phone. Now she called him without fear.

June 27, 2020

A couple of weeks later, after listening to a Sunday night message about footholds resulting from sexual partners outside of marriage, Layla asked for more prayer.

Layla's father had not allowed her to get to know her mother's extended family while growing up. When she did meet her cousins a few years ago, they alerted her to some generational tendencies that seemed related to her grandmother's name which had been given to Layla, as well as to 11 other cousins. Her aunts explained that none of the 11 cousins named Layla had ever married and each seemed to have some difficulty making or keeping commitments, whether in employment or marriage.

Layla realized that she herself has a fear of committed relationships, and for most of her life has had an aversion to men. When reading newspaper accounts of rape, great fear has always come over her. While going to college she found that whenever a man wanted to go beyond friendship to develop a deeper relationship, she would feel full of fear and break the relationship off.

"Something in me is repulsed," she said. "I could be friends with guys, but if they proposed a relationship, I would feel hatred towards them."

Finally, I knew I had to ask her a very sensitive question. "Have you ever been sexually abused?"

After some internal struggle, Layla finally said, "Yes," and the story came pouring out. When she was young—maybe between six and eight years of age—her stepbrothers had forced themselves on her and raped her. At first she tried to fight them off, but was overpowered and finally gave up trying to fight. Sexual abuse at the hands of her stepbrothers or others visiting the home continued for several years. They would come into her room at night or drag her into a closet during the day and force her to have sex. If she resisted, she was beaten. Her family lived in terrible darkness.

As we listened, our hearts sank. We grieved for her as we continued to listen.

When she was 12 years old, Layla consented to sexual relations with another stepbrother. He had moved into the family home, although he was not her father's son. By the time she was in her mid-teens, Layla's life was in such a miserable state she didn't know where to turn. She lived in constant fear because of the strife in her family. Since her mother and other parents were often away, it was the responsibility of the older stepsisters and stepbrothers to raise her; instead they were cruel and regularly beat her.

Then some neighbor girls who had returned home for their school break invited Layla and her sisters to go to a worship service at a local Presbyterian Church. After several weeks of altar calls, Layla went forward and received Christ as her Savior and Lord.

June 28, 2020 (The Next Day)

During the next evening, June and I sat with Layla for several hours. We heard how she had become a follower of Jesus and how she had relished the sweet fellowship she experienced in the church's youth group. When I asked Layla if Jesus Christ was Lord of her life today, she said yes. We can see the fruit in her life demonstrating that this is so.

Then came the hard work of praying through the awful experiences one by one. Bringing them out into the light, along with the shame, was the way Jesus was choosing to bind up Layla's broken heart. The Holy Spirit himself gently helped Layla choose to forgive each person. Then we asked Jesus to break all ungodly soul ties* and to heal Layla's spirit and soul.

Dima was an older stepbrother from the first of her father's wives. He raped Layla in front of other stepbrothers and a friend. Over the next few years he would periodically grab Layla, pull her into a room away from the rest of the family and force her to have sex. Layla had always blamed herself for this evil. We reminded her that we have an enemy, and one of his names is 'the accuser of the brethren' (Revelation 12:10). We assured

---

* see page 117 for explanation of soul ties

her that these atrocities were not her fault. We also suggested that if she had been chronically struggling with guilt, it may be important for her to forgive herself. In the future she could stand against the accuser like Jesus did, simply stating, "Get behind me, Satan! That has already been dealt with at the cross!"

Layla chose to forgive Dima, renouncing the sin. She asked God to forgive her for holding on to her anger all through the years, and told God she would readily forgive in the future. I prayed, asking Jesus to heal Layla's soul and to sever all ungodly soul ties with Dima. I ordered all demonic spirits that came through Dima's evil acts to leave. No manifestation occurred.

Mani is another stepbrother who often forced Layla as a young child to have sex at night. If she did not comply, he would beat her.

Bito was a friend of the stepbrothers; he also raped Layla.

When she was 12 years old, Layla consented to a year-long sexual relationship with one of her stepbrothers named Evans. Mele, too, was a stepbrother with whom Layla had a consensual sexual relationship. Already at this point, even before she had reached her teens, Layla's spirit and will seemed to have been broken; the demonic met little resistance in luring her into more harmful and ungodly situations. (It seems clear that the enemy uses these types of horrible abuses to break a person's will, so that eventually the conscience is seared and the moral compass damaged.) The Holy Spirit led Layla to confess her own sinful choices mixed in with the abusive situations, and to thoroughly turn away and flee from any future impure sexual relationships.

We explained to Layla that there is no way to avoid the pain of this kind of honesty and confession. It is necessary for achieving full healing and freedom from past shame and bondage.

Layla wanted that full healing, so we persevered together through the mire. Her obedience and trust in Jesus as she chose to forgive each person involved were beautiful to see. We reminded her over and over of Jesus' grace toward her, and of the privilege that was hers in this opportunity to follow in Jesus' steps by extending grace to those who had wronged her. We rejoiced together in the goodness and wonder of Jesus' forgiveness and all that he had done for her on the cross.

Layla then told us about the things that happened when she ran away from home to live with her aunt. A teacher named Wally, who taught in her aunt's school, regularly groped Layla and tried to have sex with her, but she was able to fight him off.

During the three months that Layla was employed treating the leg wound of a prominent man in his fifties who suffered from diabetes, he repeatedly made advances and fondled her. She allowed the fondling but refused to have intercourse with him. When Layla told us that even now he still calls her, offering her jobs in the county where he now works, June and I strongly urged Layla to have no further contact with him.

Layla also remembered that when she was very young, her father brought a man home to "bless all his daughters." The man spread a type of oil on each of the girls' private parts. June and I broke any curses passed to Layla during this encounter.

June 30, 2020 (Two Days Later)

Our friend Rob Douglas, who is a pastor, had introduced us to a tool that June and I hoped might prove helpful to Layla, given the extent of the abuse and demonization in her life. The tool is called *The Spiritual Test*** and it consists of a series of spiritual truth questions that help confirm the presence of evil spirits and identify them. Once identified, the unclean spirits must respond to the command, made in Jesus' authority, to reveal both their claim to a person's life and what their function has been. After confirming this information (aware that the demons may be lying), the footholds or rights the demons claim are addressed, and the person is guided through the process of removing those rights through prayer. Finally, the demons are driven out by the authority of Jesus Christ.

During the afternoon of June 30, June and I began using this tool for Layla's deliverance. The first demon that came to our attention was named Elena. Elena had entered Layla at birth via incest and the witchcraft practiced by Layla's father and extended family. Elena's function was to promote incest and hatred of men.

** Spiritual Test adapted by Rob Douglas from Joel Mondary, John and Helen Ellenberger, and Rob Reimer. To request a copy, please use the email contact at the end of the epilogue.

At this point Layla realized that she needed to forgive her stepsisters for the many beatings and for the fear she felt growing up. Responding to this leading from the Spirit, we helped her follow through on this insight.

Next, we learned that the demon Elena reported to another demon called Masha who together reported to Gatha who said that he was reporting to Lucifer (which we doubted).

Layla expressed her surprise that the demons were speaking to her mind when commanded to do so as we worked through the Spiritual Test. "I have devoted myself to obeying Jesus Christ these last several years and have been abiding in him," she said. "How can it be that I can also have an evil spirit as well?"

We took a break from the deliverance work to address this question, realizing it would be difficult for Layla to move forward without more understanding. Later in the evening, another strong Christian woman shared her own experience of deliverance. I also gave Layla a paper that laid out a biblical foundation for deliverance ministry and explained why even followers of Jesus might need deliverance.

July 3, 2020 (Three Days Later)

When we were able to come together again, I explained more about how a believer in Christ can become demonized. Layla was satisfied with her level of understanding and was ready to proceed.

We reviewed what we had learned so far. In our last session, three demons had been exposed. The highest in the chain of authority was Gatha, a generational spirit of incest that Layla received at birth. Next was Masha, a spirit of guilt and shame and hatred, and then Elena, a spirit of witchcraft, of incest, of masturbation, and of the hatred of men.

We called Elena to attention. Elena again said that he reported to the demon called Masha, whose function was promoting guilt, shame and hate. At this point Layla went to prayer. She renounced the sin of masturbation and extended forgiveness to the men who tried to grope her in public while she was walking and while traveling by public transport.

After the footholds had been removed, the demons confessed that they no longer had any right to lay claim to Layla's life. We proceeded with deliverance.

After we'd commanded Elena to leave a few times, the demon eventually moved from Layla's stomach to her chest and then to her throat, finally leaving on a very extended breath. Masha manifested in the back of Layla's neck and around her shoulders and arms, but then the sensations stopped and the demon went into hiding. After I commanded again, the demon finally came out on an extended breath.

I recognized that Gatha was the most powerful demon we had encountered thus far. He tried to hide and would not manifest and leave. Finally, in the authority of Jesus, I commanded the Strongman (the head demon, later identified as Ammi), to release Gatha. As I persisted in proclaiming the truth that the blood of Jesus has paid for Layla's full redemption, the demon manifested in facial sternness and in sensations in Layla's jaw and Layla's hands took on a rigid claw shape. Finally, the demon left with three coughs and an extended breath.

After each of these deliverances, I asked Jesus to fill the areas in Layla's life in which the demons had previously taken up occupancy—to fill her afresh with the Holy Spirit.

Layla felt set free in a new way.

We decided that the next time schedules allowed, we would go through the Spiritual Test again.

July 7, 2020 (Four Days Later)

A few days later the three of us had an opportunity to meet. As we'd agreed, June and I went through the Spiritual Test again with Layla.

A spirit called Ammi presented itself. Its function was promoting hatred, and both Masha and Elena reported to this spirit. When asked what grounds it had to be inside of Layla, it first answered, "Nothing." The second time we commanded the demon to answer, it said, "Rape."

When we asked again on what grounds Ammi had entered Layla, the demon answered that Layla's father and mother presented grounds. Layla's father abused her mother. When Layla was a little girl, she overheard her mother tell a friend, "Bad things happen in marriage; sexual abuse happens in marriage."

Layla prayed and renounced the sin and abuse in her parents' lives and marriage and forgave them.

When we asked again on what grounds the demon Ammi claimed rights to Layla's life, it first answered "None" again; the second time we asked, the answer was "Incest."

The generational incest was renounced and forgiven, and Layla confirmed that she had already renounced and forgiven her stepbrothers' incest.

In the deliverance, the spirit Ammi manifested in Layla's chest and head and left through her ears.

For a second time that day we worked through the Spiritual Test.

A spirit called Trauma revealed itself. Layla recalled the traumas she'd experienced as a child.

Layla had been told that when she was very young she almost died from an illness. She'd had something like an abscess in her neck and had come to the point of death, but then she had recovered. Layla still has a scar on her neck from that abscess as well as various scars on her legs from boils or abscesses.

For two or three years, beginning in 1998, Layla suffered from swelling in her left leg and an infection that caused blisters that would not heal. Her mother and her father, who combined his practice of herbal medicine with the occult, would not bring her to the hospital. Layla remembered her leg always smelling bad through 6th and 7th grades.

More trauma occurred when, as a very young girl playing with a little ball, a dog named Danger jumped on her. There was also a goat with horns, who was greatly feared. Sometimes the goat escaped and chased Layla; Layla fell and bruised her legs. In kindergarten she was chased by bees and was stung. She also remembered falling down from some stools.

We prayed through the traumas, asking Jesus to take the consequences of these traumas from Layla's soul and spirit and to bring healing to her soul. No demonic manifestation occurred, but Layla experienced the gift of peace.

July 8, 2020 (The Next Day)

The next day as we worked through the Spiritual Test again, a spirit named Mishial was revealed. Like other demons before, Mishial first said there had been no grounds for his entering Layla, but the second time he was commanded to speak, he named the grounds as fear.

At first he denied reporting to any other spirit, but the second time he was commanded to speak, he acknowledged that he reports to Ammi. *(Note: Sometimes demons will lie to create smoke screens and bring confusion.)*

As I bound Mishial together with Fear and Anxiety, Layla's ears became blocked and then opened. When the spirit was commanded to leave it manifested with acid regurgitation and then seemed to disappear.

We again commanded it to leave. After we commanded four more times, the demon manifested with Layla's very wide and continuous yawning. After another five minutes or so, Layla gave a huge yawn and the spirit left.

We asked the Lord to fill those spaces previously occupied by demons with the freshness of his Spirit.

July 11, 2020 (Three Days Later)

After a few days had passed, we went through the Spiritual Test once again. A spirit first claiming to be Masha (who had already been sent out) eventually confessed his name to be Anger. We commanded Anger to stand at attention and learned that the grounds on which it had entered Layla's life were past hurts, jealousy and envy.

Layla explained that she had been very discontented growing up. "Many times I would think it was only me who had not had a good life," she said. "Others seemed to be okay, while I had a hard life. I compared myself with my siblings. I struggled a lot." Layla paused to reflect on those early years.

"I did not have a friend my same age growing up," Layla told us. "My sisters would say, 'You should stop seeing yourself' (an idiom for envy), but I felt that I didn't fit anywhere."

Layla described feeling angry at herself for not having what others had. She was angry at God too, saying to him, "You do not love me like others. Why are all these bad things happening to me?" At the same time, she blamed herself, saying, "I do not measure up in God's sight."

Layla felt that she wasn't important to God. "I began to serve God very much so God would love me," she explained.

Layla prayed and voiced her forgiveness to God (who, she knew, needs no forgiveness). She also asked God to forgive her for being angry at him for so long. She repented and determined that in the future she would see God as her loving Father in heaven.

Then we prayed that Jesus would bring healing to Layla's entire soul: emotions, mind and will. We commanded Anger to stand at attention again and learned that it was Layla's sense of being rejected and her self-hatred that had been the grounds for this demon to enter.

Layla went to prayer. She forgave herself and committed to loving herself as God loves her.

When we learned that there were no more grounds giving Anger access and that there were no other demons reporting to Anger, but that he had been reporting to Mishial, I stated that since Mishial had been driven out already, Anger would have to leave too.

In Jesus' authority, we commanded Anger to leave. Layla yawned extensively for several minutes, and the demon finally left on her breath. We double-checked; Layla said the demon was gone and no more manifestations occurred.

The next day Layla felt a new freedom, a freedom she had not experienced before.

November, 2020 (Four Months Later)

Four months later, during a break, Layla traveled to Nairobi to see some extended family. After she returned, June and I reconnected with her and asked how she was doing.

Layla explained that she was doing very well, that she had truly been set free and had been healed of the many things that used to drag her down. She is living in a freedom she hadn't known was possible. She praised the Lord Jesus Christ for his grace and healing. She is no longer afraid of men and now has freedom to pursue marriage with the young man who hopes to marry her.

June 24, 2021 (Seven Months Later)

After another seven months, we reconnected with Layla and learned that she continues to live in freedom and peace. She told us that she is abiding closely with Jesus and is so grateful to him for the freedom in which she lives. This week she is finishing up a two-week discipleship program that includes training on inner healing and deliverance to further equip her to serve others.

Aug 21, 2022 (A Year Later)

Layla and her fiancé have set the date. She continues to do well.

May 3, 2024 (Almost Two Years Later)

Layla and her husband are married and doing well.

Let all bitterness and wrath and anger and clamor and slander be put away from you, along with all malice. Be kind to one another, tenderhearted, forgiving one another, as God in Christ forgave you.

EPHESIAN 4:31–32 ESV

And whenever you stand praying, forgive, if you have anything against anyone, so that your Father also who is in heaven may forgive you your trespasses.

MARK 11:25 ESV

47

....

Gina

October 13, 2023
USA

We had been staying with Gina's parents for a few days while fulfilling a speaking engagement during our home assignment, when Gina and her husband Duke came over to ask if June and I would pray with them. They explained that Gina has suffered repeated episodes of strep throat and colds over the last 12 months and their children had been getting sick regularly too. Multiple courses of antibiotics had caused gastrointestinal problems for Gina, and although she might improve for a week or two, she invariably got sick again with one illness or another. Her immune system seemed to have been seriously compromised, and now Gina had strep throat again, every swallow feeling like glass shards cutting her throat.

When we asked Gina about any unusual stress in her life, she said she was "worrying a ton," some of that worry being about her four-year-old son Steve, who was about to have genetic testing for a drifting eye. Gina added, "Last January while fasting I sensed that God wanted to teach me something with all the illnesses, but I wasn't quite sure what that was."

When I asked if there were other stress factors, Gina told us about her sister-in-law, Betty. Everyone in the extended family was committed to loving each other, but over the last ten years all of the sisters-in-law had struggled in their relationships with Betty. Several family members have been hurt by her unkind words and actions. No one seemed to be certain about what God wanted done in this situation, and forgiveness hasn't always been forthcoming.

June and I began to explain the necessity and the great power of forgiveness. We told her that failing to forgive is like drinking a cup of poison and waiting for the other person to die. The New Testament, however, calls us to a beautiful way of life that actually participates in the life of God's kingdom, with Colossians 3:13 urging us, "Bear with each other and forgive one another if any of you has a grievance against someone. Forgive as the Lord forgave you." Especially compelling, we said, is Jesus' own cry from the cross, "Forgive them, Father, for they do not know what they are doing." We who are followers of Jesus Christ are always called to forgive.

Gina began to pray. She forgave Betty and committed herself to loving her and doing only good to her. She resolved to speak honestly with Betty in the way that Matthew 18 illustrates, and then going forward, to consistently speak and act with love. Unprompted, Gina also confessed the times she had gossiped. She decided not only to take steps to guard herself from it, but also to talk to her sisters-in-law so that together they could present a united front against the schemes of the enemy.

Gina confessed and repented of holding on to anger instead of forgiving Betty right away. She resolved that in the future she would forgive immediately. Gina expressed deep gratitude that her debt of sin had been paid by Christ's death on the cross, and she thanked God for his free and lavish forgiveness.

Then June, Duke and I placed our hands on Gina, and prayed that Jesus would heal her soul, emotions, mind and will from all the wounds in her past. With Gina's permission, we explored any need for deliverance from spirits of anger, unforgiveness and infirmity. Then we prayed for Gina's physical healing. Using Jesus' authority, we commanded her throat to be well.

After a few minutes I asked Gina how her throat felt. She said it didn't hurt anymore.

We encouraged Gina to be on the alert for attacks from the evil one, reminding her that she is in Christ and can use Jesus' authority to command the attacker to leave.

After Gina returned home her throat did begin to hurt some again, but not like the broken glass feeling she had experienced before praying.

October 16, 2023 (Three Days Later)

The next time Gina came over to her parents' home, we asked her for an update. She said her soul was at peace and her throat was much better, although she still had some pain when swallowing.

We asked her if we could pray again, and she agreed. We thanked Jesus for healing Gina's soul and for relieving so much of the pain. Yet we were asking for more. Following the instructions in James 5:14–16, I anointed Gina with oil and June and I laid hands on her neck and back. In Jesus' authority, we commanded the pain to be gone and Gina to be made well.

I asked Gina if she was sensing anything. The left side of her neck in the area of her tonsils, she told us, was "burning hot." After a few more minutes, I asked Gina again how she felt. She said, "The pain is completely gone."

Thirty minutes later she still had no pain. When she opened her mouth wide to look into her throat with a mirror, she could still see pus in the back of her throat, but the pain was gone.

Two days later Gina reported that all the pus was gone, and that she was completely healed and felt great. All praise and honor to the Lord Jesus Christ.

Trust in the LORD with all your heart,
and do not lean on your own understanding.
In all your ways acknowledge him,
and he will make straight your paths.
Be not wise in your own eyes;
fear the LORD, and turn away from evil.
It will be healing to your flesh
and refreshment to your bones.

PROVERBS 3:5-8 ESV

48

....

June's Ongoing Story

A note before you read: I asked my wife June to write this last and most personal chapter. We both believe that Jesus vividly demonstrated the Father's will as he proclaimed the kingdom of heaven and healed all the sick who came to him. It's clear to us both that Jesus authorized us, as his disciples, to heal the sick while boldly proclaiming the Gospel and calling people to repentance. And yet we have not seen everyone healed.

June's experience has played a significant role in teaching us to hold and steward this mystery. I often say, "We don't know what we don't know." So we continue to ask, to seek, to knock and persevere in our prayers.

June: After our daughter Jane first read this book through from start to finish, she asked us, "Where is your story, Mom? I think it would really add to the book, and I always like it when an author is open and transparent about their own lives."

It's hard for me to be transparent. Concern about how I appear to others has been a struggle for much of my early life and continues to be an area of vulnerability. Several years ago, I heard one of my colleagues on the mission field share a message called "Wearing Masks," about how she had tried to hide some of her own struggles. Her words impacted me very deeply as I realized that was exactly what I had done for so many years.

The truth is that I know what it feels like to be the one who needs healing, the one on the receiving end. Whenever people have requested healing prayer, Roger and I have asked them to share their stories with us. It can be very challenging to open up in that way. Now it's my turn.

In 1998 I was diagnosed with an autoimmune endocrine disorder called Addison's disease. It took some years for doctors to figure out what was going on as my health steadily declined. I had to be airlifted out of our village for medical care twice. My body was attacking my adrenal glands, leaving me unable to handle stress well or maintain my blood pressure and electrolytes. To manage this condition, I take steroids daily to replace the normal stress hormones that my body can't secrete.

Eight years after my Addison's disease diagnosis, we naturally began seeking healing for my illness since God had brought us into this journey of healing and deliverance. We asked the Holy Spirit to reveal anything we needed to know.

As I reflected on my life there were several areas I sensed God was asking me to address: past trauma, an instance of sexual abuse from childhood, generational issues, sin in previous relationships, unforgiveness and anger. So we spent a couple of weeks working intensively through each of these areas one by one.

These weeks were exhausting and emotionally draining as we dealt with deeply emotional and personal issues, one after another, but they also brought a sense of lightness. Through each of the Holy Spirit's victories, my desire for full healing and freedom in all areas of my life grew even stronger.

Whenever issues resurfaced in our ongoing quest for healing, we applied the foundational biblical tools of confession, repentance and forgiveness to everything God's Spirit brought to mind. This proved to be oh, so important. I experienced significant spiritual and emotional healing in my soul as well as deliverance from a generational critical spirit I hadn't even realized I had, despite chronic well-masked struggles in this area for as long as I could remember.

We are confident that God is full of grace and mercy, but we have come to understand that our enemy the devil is very legalistic. So we tried to be as thorough as we could and remove any footholds he might claim.

It's hard to know if you've been healed from Addison's. Taking steroids suppresses the production of your own stress hormones (the job of your adrenal glands), which means you can't abruptly stop taking your steroid replacement medicines because you could go into a crisis very quickly.

One time, early on in the process of working through various issues and receiving significant healing in my soul and spirit, we tried carefully going off my medications. We watched closely for any symptoms, well aware that an Addisonian crisis is a true medical emergency. By the second morning I felt weak, sick and disappointed, as I started back on my medicines.

As weeks turned into months and years, a low dose of medication was all I needed. I was nearly always content, abiding in Christ, thankful for the medicines, and living in the peace of God's grace. But periodically I would begin to wrestle again, wondering why I hadn't been healed. Whenever the Spirit brought something to mind – often during my quiet time – Wayne and I would pray and ask again for more healing.

For example, the memory of my mom's death in 1992, when I was 31 years old, had been an ongoing source of pain. Mom had gone to the hospital emergency room on a Friday evening very ill with an acute abdomen (an indication that this is a very serious abdominal pain that needs urgent attention). I thought the doctors should have rushed my mom straight to surgery, but they didn't. During the night she grew worse; surgery the next morning revealed that a cancer in her colon had ruptured and peritonitis was already severe. Mom didn't make it through the day. I didn't even have a chance to say goodbye.

Now, all these years later, as I asked the Holy Spirit to reveal any unforgiveness in my life, I realized that I had never forgiven the doctors who had decided to wait until morning for Mom's surgery.

Through my tears, I thanked Jesus for his grace in my life. Then I chose to forgive Mom's doctors. It was a significant step toward emotional healing for me, and I thought it might have removed a block to receiving more physical healing.

I also remember times when the Holy Spirit spoke very specifically to me during sermons we heard while visiting the capital city to restock supplies. My response to each experience of conviction was confession and repentance.

After helping one of our friends make their way through some generational consequences, the Holy Spirit seemed to be bringing generational sin to my attention. I grew up in a large and truly wonderful

Christian family, but since "all have sinned" (Romans 3:23), we didn't assume I was immune from consequences of potential generational sin. So I thanked the Lord for all the blessings I received through my ancestors and then forgave them for anything that might have negatively affected my life, renouncing any known or unknown sins. We searched again for unhealed traumas the kingdom of darkness could be exploiting. We prayed again, in Jesus' name and authority, and commanded my adrenal glands to be restored.

We didn't see any change in the weeks or months that followed. Life and all it requires went on as usual, very full and demanding, so thankfully I wasn't constantly sifting through my memory to see if we'd missed something.

Whenever we were given insights from the Scriptures, other books or the experiences of our brothers and sisters, we again went to Jesus to seek healing, sometimes fasting and praying for revelation and clarity. Were we being asked to be persistent like the widow in Luke 18? Sometimes I imagined myself in the crowd surrounding Jesus 2000 years ago, thinking, like the woman who had been bleeding for 12 years and had tried everything, "If I just touch Jesus' garment, I'll be healed!" But time and again I was disappointed. What were we missing?

One morning the Holy Spirit revealed to me that I had forgiven the people involved in the sexual abuse I experienced as a child, but I had never forgiven myself. I understood that I was the innocent party, but I still felt guilty. This had resulted in significant struggles with self-image and self-critical thoughts.

Knowing that in autoimmune diseases the body attacks itself, we wondered if my self-condemnation might have opened the door to an attack by the evil one. I prayed through this until I could accept myself and wholeheartedly thank God for making me just as he had chosen. I spoke words of grace to myself, forgiving and releasing myself from the guilt of the sexual abuse. As I was praying and relishing the emotional relief and joy of having forgiven myself, I felt sharp pains on both sides of my stomach – right where my adrenal glands were.

Wayne and I began calmly commanding any spirit of infirmity to leave. The sharp pains over my adrenal glands intensified as Wayne commanded the spirit of self-condemnation and infirmity to leave me. I sensed a clear exit and then the pain was gone. We were ecstatic. With great expectation and faith, we prayed for the Holy Spirit to fill me afresh and asked Jesus to heal my adrenal glands so that they would function well.

Carefully, and with the help of my doctor, we decided again to test if my adrenal glands were working. I scheduled an appointment for the next time we were going to be in the capital city. This same doctor had diagnosed me with Addison's in 1998 and managed my care since. We explained why we believed I may have been healed and we shared the Gospel with him. We told him that we wanted to test my adrenal function safely and we needed his help. It took a lot of convincing. He kept saying, "Addison's isn't something you get healed from." Finally he agreed to help us.

This was a Friday and we were going to spend the weekend with our kids at their boarding school. We planned that I would stop taking my medications over the weekend, and on Monday morning we would come in for lab work to check my cortisol levels. Usually I took 4 doses of meds a day. Skipping them on Saturday felt freeing and exciting. I felt confident I had been healed and found myself daydreaming about announcing the good news to my kids, family and Dr. T.

However, by Sunday afternoon I had a terrible headache and didn't want to admit how weak I felt. We called Dr. T and he said, "Take a dose of steroids immediately, and we'll see what the lab work is in the morning." I felt very sad about my symptoms and about having to take meds, but still felt hopeful that perhaps there had been at least a partial healing and the adrenal glands were kicking in a bit. I woke up in the night praying and reviewing the truths of God's word to try to drive away my doubts.

I was suddenly flooded with the assurance that God is my Father, my "Abba," and I felt comforted and strengthened. It was almost like getting a hug from God himself! As I continued to ask Father for healing in Jesus' name, and as I pondered and wondered in his presence about this healing, I was again reassured that it was okay. I was free to simply take joy in him no matter what. I went back to sleep feeling very thankful, and woke on Monday morning with great peace about whatever the outcome would be. I was grateful to find that I felt amazingly better than I had the night before, and that again gave me hope.

The Monday morning lab work, however, showed that my cortisol level was zero! My adrenal glands were not functioning at all. I felt deflated, drained emotionally and terribly let down and baffled. Yet at the same time I was able to rest in God's presence and trust him. I was grateful that in just a few days I recovered from the lightheadedness and exhaustion. Dr. T was very sympathetic and encouraging, reminding me that I was on the lowest possible dosages of medication. I realized again that God had supplied these meds. I was thankful and able to move forward in peace.

I've experienced Jesus miraculously healing me physically from other ailments through the years, but as of today, in July 2024, I still require that small dose of steroids for Addison's disease. Sometimes I wonder why, but I don't wallow in my wondering or get swallowed up in it. Wayne and I thank God for the medical community that provides the medicines and compassionate care that have allowed me to live a normal active life, even deep in the rural bushlands of Amaro. We thank God for all the ways I've been set free and healed emotionally and spiritually.

Through our own personal experience of living with Addison's, and the disappointments of not being completely healed in the ways we desired, the Good Shepherd has led us into heartfelt empathy for fellow believers who haven't received healing after asking for it. We walk forward in the partial understanding we've been given, confident of God's faithfulness and love, and with humility seek to continue stewarding this mystery of his healing grace.

Epilogue

Thank you for reading these stories.

I hope this book encourages you to dig ever deeper into God's word and daringly put into practice what you find there. It's okay not to have everything figured out; as fellow disciples of Jesus, June and I also continue to ask, seek and knock. We are still learning and still have questions—especially when we do not see what we are expecting. May we all grow in faith by simply taking Jesus at his word, trusting him with the results. One of the ways Jesus calls us to love him is by obeying what he commanded, modeled and commissioned. May we walk in step with the Holy Spirit as we serve one another and the world—the world God loves so much that he gave his Son to be our Savior, Healer and Deliverer.

May we remember the power, authority and beauty of the One we serve!

"Therefore God has highly exalted him and bestowed on him the name that is above every name, so that at the name of Jesus every knee should bow, in heaven and on earth and under the earth, and every tongue confess that Jesus Christ is Lord, to the glory of God the Father" (Philippians 2:9–11 ESV).

Contact Information:

For additional information, email us at: *Godshealinggrace@gmail.com.*

Bibliography

Douglas, Rob. Adapted by Rob Douglas from Joel Mondary, John and Helen Ellenberger, and Rob Reimer, *Paper on Spiritual Test.*

Doyle, Tom. *Dreams and Visions: Is Jesus Awakening the Muslim World?* Nashville: Thomas Nelson Publisher, 2012.

Fountain, Daniel E. MD. *GOD, Medicine and Miracles.* Colorado Springs: WaterBrook Press, 1999.

Holy Bible, English Standard Version (ESV). Wheaton: Crossway Publisher, 2001.

Holy Bible, New American Standard Bible (NASB). LaHabra, CA: The Lockman Foundation, 1995, 2020.

Holy Bible, New International Version (NIV). Grand Rapids: Zondervan Publishers, 1984.

Horrobin, Peter. *Discover Healing and Freedom.* Lancaster, England: Sovereign World, 2021.

Horrobin, Peter. *Healing through Deliverance: The Foundation of Deliverance Ministry Vol. 1.* Lancaster, England: Sovereign World, 2003.

Horrobin, Peter. *Healing through Deliverance: The Practice of Deliverance Ministry Vol. 2.* Lancaster, England: Sovereign World, 2003.

Horrobin, Peter. *Healing from the Consequences of Accidents, Shock and Trauma.* Lancaster, England: Sovereign World, 2016.

Horrobin, Peter. *Journey to Freedom Year Long Program.* Lancaster, England: Ellel Ministries, Online Program.

Martin, EJ. Editor. *Where There Was No Church.* UK: Learning Together Press, 2010.

Bibliography, Cont'd

Miller, Neil. *Agents of Healing: Learning To Do What Jesus Did.*
Toronto: Swordfish Publisher, 2024.

Murphy, Ed. *The Handbook for Spiritual Warfare.*
Nashville: Thomas Nelson Publishers, 1996.

Reimer, Rob. *Soul Care: Seven Transformational Principles for a Healthy Soul.* Franklin, TN: Carpenter's Son Publishing, 2016.

Sapp, Roger. *Beyond a Shadow of a Doubt.*
Spring Town, TX: All Nations Publication, 2004.

Scott, Lynda. *Lynda: From Accident and Trauma to Healing & Wholeness!*
Lancaster, England: Sovereign World, 2010.

Shaw, Sarah. *Sarah: From an Abusive Childhood and the Depths of Suicidal Despair to a Life of Hope and Freedom.*
Lancaster, England: Sovereign World, 2009.

Trousdale, Jerry. *Miraculous Movements.*
Nashville: Thomas Nelson Publishers, 2012.

Wommack, Andrew. *God Wants You Well,*
What the Bible Really Says about Walking in Divine Health.
Tulsa: Harrison House Publishers, 2010.

Wright, Henry W. *A More Excellent Way.*
New Kensington, PA: Whitaker House, 2005.

Made in the USA
Las Vegas, NV
01 December 2024

13060271R00174